The Morality of Pluralism

John Kekes

PRINCETON UNIVERSITY PRESS

PRINCETON, NEW JERSEY

Library of Congress Cataloging-in-Publication Data

Kekes, John.
The morality of pluralism / John Kekes.
p.   cm.
Includes bibliographical references and index.
1. Pluralism.   2. Values.   3. Ethics.   I. Title.
BJ1031.K24   1993   171′.7—dc20   92-40492   CIP

ISBN 0-691-03230-0 (alk. paper)

This book has been composed in Adobe Baskerville

Princeton University Press books are printed on acid-free paper
and meet the guidelines for permanence and durability
of the Committee on Production Guidelines for Book Longevity of
the Council on Library Resources

Printed in the United States of America

10   9   8   7   6   5   4   3   2

For J.Y.K.

Contents

Acknowledgments

THE STRONGEST influences on the views presented in this book are the writings of Isaiah Berlin and Michael Oakeshott. Their influences are present, not so much by way of arguments, but through their manner of thinking, which, it is hoped, informs the thoughts here presented. Since Berlin is a liberal and Oakeshott a conservative, it may be doubted that their influences are compatible. One of the happy consequences of pluralism, however, is that this doubt is misplaced.

Individual chapters of the book were read and most helpfully commented on by Chong Kim Chong, Felmon Davis, Jean Y. Kekes, and Ernest Schlaretzki. Their help is gratefully acknowledged.

A different sort of debt is owed by the author to two people at Princeton University Press: Ann Himmelberger Wald, philosophy editor, who eased the progress of the book from submission, through revision, to acceptance; and to Beth Gianfagna, production editor, who guided its transformation into a proper book—a process that is becoming a custom, since this is the author's fourth book that she helped to make better. It is with pleasure that a further indebtedness is acknowledged to Carol Roberts, copy editor, for acutely finding and tactfully pointing out the numerous inconsistencies, infelicities, and downright errors that the typescript contained.

Six of the chapters include previously published material: chapter 1 makes use of parts of "Is Our Morality Disintegrating?" *Public Affairs Quarterly* 1(1987): 79–94; chapter 6 is a revised version of "Moral Imagination, Freedom, and the Humanities," *American Philosophical Quarterly* 28(1991): 101–11; chapter 7 is a revised version of "Pluralism and the Value of Life," *Social Philosophy and Policy* 10(1994, in press); chapter 8 is a revised version of "Shame and Moral Progress," *Midwest Studies in Philosophy* 13(1988): 282–96; chapter 9 is a revised version of "On There Being Some Limits to Morality," *Social Philosophy and Policy* 8(1991): 63–80; and chapter 11 is a revised version of "The Incompatibility of Liberalism and Pluralism," *American Philosophical Quarterly* 29(1992): 141–51.

A previous version of chapter 1 was discussed at a conference organized by the Institute for Humane Studies; previous versions of chapters 7 and 9 were presented at conferences organized by the Social Philosophy and Policy Center; a previous version of chapter 8 was read at the National University of Singapore, as were previous versions of chapter 9 at Duke University and chapter 11 at Evergreen State College. The comments received on these occasions helped to improve the arguments, and they are hereby acknowledged with pleasure and gratitude.

This book is a companion volume of *Moral Tradition and Individuality* and *Facing Evil*, both published by Princeton University Press, the first in 1989 and the second in 1990. Each of the three books is intended to be independent, but some overlap among them is unavoidable, since they represent different aspects of the same moral point of view. Readers are asked, therefore, to excuse the several references to these other books. The references indicate where fuller arguments may be found; they are not meant as self-advertisements.

The Morality of Pluralism

Introduction: Setting the Stage

> The purpose of the inquiry is not to define a word, but to detect
> the secret of what we enjoy, to recognize what is hostile to it, and
> to discern where and how it might be enjoyed more fully.
> —Michael Oakeshott, "The Political Economy of Freedom"

IS OUR MORALITY DISINTEGRATING?

The morality in question is the Western one. It is an amorphous, complex, constantly changing system of ideals, principles, customs intended to guide our conduct. It is derived from three main sources: ancient Greece and Rome; the Judeo-Christian religious tradition; and the thought and sensibility of the Renaissance, the Enlightenment, and secular humanism. According to a substantial body of considered contemporary opinion, our morality *is* disintegrating.[1]

It is conceded that in the normal course of events many of us, more or less conscientiously, continue to live according to morality, but its hold on us, it is supposed, gets weaker and weaker. When life goes smoothly, old moral habits still prevail, but, increasingly, life does not go smoothly. We are continually challenged both externally by alien moralities and internally by noxious left- and right-wing extremism, cynicism, a spreading failure of nerve, and the terrible simplicities of fundamentalists of various persuasions. In the face of these challenges, we need to be able to justify our moral values if we are to have an acceptable way of living together. It seems, however, that we cannot do so. Neither the religious appeal to God nor the humanistic reassurance about our basic goodness, rationality, and perfectibility carries sufficiently widespread conviction to save the day. As a result, we cling to our morality as to an article of faith.

---

[1] The following are some representative opinions: "In thinking about what has gone wrong, we need to see [that] what . . . has failed at every level—from the society of nations to the local community to the family—is integration." Also, "Our problems today are . . . moral" (Bellah et. al., *Habits of the Heart*, 284 and 295). "The various meanings, values and beliefs operative in a society were ultimately 'held together' in a comprehensive interpretation of reality. . . . Religion . . . makes possible to man to feel 'at home' in the universe. This age old function of religion is seriously threatened. . . . The final consequence of all this [is that] . . . modern man has suffered from a deepening condition of 'homelessness'"

The challenges to our moral convictions, however, force us to question our faith and drive us to doubt that we can offer a better reason for our beliefs than the challengers can for theirs—yet theirs we reject. We are gnawed by the growing suspicion that our adherence to our values reflects centuries of moral conditioning, but it has no rational warrant. Our morality is disintegrating, it is said, because we are unable to assuage this suspicion. We are consequently helpless in the face of challenges. There was a time, we are told, when our morality did provide clear standards of good and evil, generally accepted rules for living together, and it gave meaning and purpose to our lives. It no longer performs these all-important functions; we have nothing to put in its place, and so the disintegration of morality is producing a cultural crisis of the first order.

The disintegration thesis derives from the observation of deep changes affecting our morality and from the interpretation that these changes are so deep as to present a fundamental threat to our morality. What, then, are these deep changes supposed to be? If we observe prevailing moral opinion, we cannot fail to notice that divorce, homosexuality, and extramarital sex, for instance, are subject to much less censure than they were fifty years ago and that we have become morally alive to matters toward which our predecessors were largely indifferent, such as ecology, animal experimentation, and affirmative action. But these changes are insufficient to substantiate the claim that our morality as a whole is undergoing deep changes. For any reasonable morality is bound to be constantly changing, because moral values must be adjusted to fit changing economic, technological, political, demographic, and other circumstances. Such adjustments, however, are not particularly difficult. We used to see homosexuality as harmful, but we are becoming convinced that homosexuals are no better or worse than others, and so

---

(Berger et al., *The Homeless Mind*, 78–82). "[A] mood of pessimism in higher circles . . . spreads through the rest of society as people lose faith. . . . The political crisis of capitalism reflects a general crisis of western culture" (Lasch, *The Culture of Narcissism*, xiii). "If my account of our moral condition is correct . . . the new dark ages . . . are already upon us. . . . This time however the barbarians are not waiting beyond the frontiers; they have already been ruling us for quite some time" (MacIntyre, *After Virtue*, 263). "[P]revailing value systems offer no convincing answers to such questions as why individuals should under some circumstances be prepared to subordinate their particular ends to the common good. . . . [Thus] public confidence in standards of decency and fairness . . . must eventually crumble" (Reichly, *Religion in American Public Life*, 341). "Many spokesmen for our established normative institutions are aware of their failure and yet remain powerless to generate . . . the necessary . . . faith. . . . Our . . . general misery is that, having broken with those institutionalized credibilities from which . . . moral energy derived, new credibilities are not yet operationally effective" (Rieff, *The Triumph of the Therapeutic*, 18–19).

we are changing our minds about the harm it does. This change, however, alters our morality no more significantly than Christian morality was altered by the growing conviction that witches should not be burned. A morality has a hard center and a soft periphery. Changes are natural and expected on the periphery, but they leave the center unaffected. To point to some ways in which the moral values of a period differ from those of the previous one may, therefore, provide evidence for no more than the most routine moral change.

The argument for deep moral change is that the change in our values has spread from the periphery to the center. It is not just that our attitudes toward divorce, homosexuality, and extramarital sex have changed, but also that our changing attitudes reflect our uncertainty about the relations between men and women and about the place and importance of sex in our lives. We are repudiating racism, but that brings us face-to-face with fundamental questions about how much we are willing to sacrifice for equality; how far we are willing to rely on the law to enforce a particular moral point of view; or what, if anything, we owe to the descendants of people victimized by our ancestors. And it is not just sex and racism that force deep questions on us. Civil disobedience, drug abuse, capital punishment, the increasing power of bureaucracy and corporations, the demands of patriotism, starvation and torture in distant foreign places, euthanasia, vivisection, abortion, and so on and on, all contribute to a basic questioning of the values by which we have been living.

The sea of moral conflicts threatens to drown us. There seems to be nothing to which we can appeal without our opponents calling its credentials into question. We are all for equality and we are all for freedom. But what do we do when they conflict? We all recognize the necessity of the law, but what if the law is used to perpetuate injustice? No one is for censorship, but does that mean that we should allow children to copulate with animals in pornographic films? The conflicts are so numerous, so varied, permeate so many different areas of our lives; the arguments about them are so hopelessly inconclusive, carry so little conviction; and the opponents are so deeply imbued with their sharply conflicting moral fervor, that the fact of basic moral change is undeniable.

The question is whether this basic change amounts to disintegration. Why should we suppose that our morality is cracking under the strain? Because, defenders of the disintegration thesis reply, it lacks the resources to resolve moral conflicts. The sign of disintegration is not that there is a lot of immorality around. The rot goes deeper than that. Indeed, the prevalence of immorality *presupposes* the existence of values that the people or actions judged to be immoral violate. Rather, we face disintegration because there is a general confusion about values. The salient fact is not immorality, but moral confusion. Our trouble is that we no longer know how far our morality extends; we have become confused about the distinction between the moral and the nonmoral.

The disagreement between supporters and critics of abortion, euthanasia, suicide, animal experimentation, divorce, homosexuality, or our use of natural resources is not that one side regards the conduct in question as morally good, while the other thinks of it as morally bad. The dispute is whether moral judgments are normally appropriate. Defenders of these practices want to exempt them from moral judgment altogether or regard them as only incidentally subject to reasonable moral concern. Their opponents insist that the practices are central to morality. Suicide, for instance, is said to be morally wrong because the deliberate killing of a human being is wrong. Opposed to this is the claim that moral considerations apply only if the victim is someone else; how people dispose of their lives is, in normal circumstances, entirely up to them. Just as one can argue whether a particular action comes under legal jurisdiction, so one can argue about the relevance of morality to it. We are facing moral disintegration, it is said, because so many of our conflicts are about the appropriateness of moral considerations. Our confusion is not about whether we should praise or blame, but whether praise or blame are fitting responses. And the source of this confusion is that we no longer know what constitutes a moral question.

This confusion is not caused by the shrinking of morality. It is true that our morality is contracting in some ways; extramarital sex, suicide, and divorce, for instance, are beginning to be exempted from moral censure. But in other ways our morality is expanding because animal experimentation, smoking, spreading AIDS, and advertising are becoming moral issues. It would be a mistake, therefore, to diagnose the source of moral confusion as the liberal tendency not to count as moral what conservatives count as such. Liberals are just as morally engaged as conservatives. The difference is that they tend to care about different issues.

Liberals tend to be morally concerned about equality, sexual freedom, capital punishment, and commercialism; conservatives tend to direct moral attention to the family, social order, and the free market. Sometimes the two sides meet and argue because they recognize that the issue is how to balance the competing claims, say, of freedom and equality, or sexual experimentation and family life. But even in these rare cases, when there is sufficient common ground to begin to argue, the argument is bound to end in an impasse, because there is no moral authority, no value, that both sides are willing to accept. If the issue is pressing, there will be a contrived legal or political compromise, but it will leave everyone dissatisfied. What thinking person in our society can be satisfied with the morality of the compromises we have arrived at, after decades of haggling, about pornography, abortion, the hundreds living on death row, the welfare system, or the measures taken to ensure the honesty of politicians?

But the fact is that it rarely happens that opponents can even begin to argue. For what can a right-to-life advocate say that would persuade a militant feminist, a gay liberationist to a moral majoritarian, a champion of law and order to a lawyer specializing in getting criminals acquitted on technicalities, a Mormon to a hippie, a marine to a transcendental meditator, or, for that matter, a philosophy professor to a junkie? The moral sensibilities of these people are so far apart that there is no common ground for one even to explain to the other his or her position. Or so the disintegration thesis goes.

The result is that informed moral debate is disappearing from our society. In its place, we have cynical or despairing indifference or an assertive shrillness masquerading as moral indignation. This is the state of affairs Yeats laments in *The Second Coming*:

> Things fall apart; the center cannot hold;
> Mere anarchy is loosed upon the world,
> The blood-dimmed tide is loosed, and everywhere
> The ceremony of innocence is drowned;
> The best lack all conviction, while the worst
> Are full of passionate intensity.

The disintegration thesis, then, is that "things fall apart; the center cannot hold," because we have lost a rational foundation for our moral convictions. Inevitable moral change turns into moral decay. Our confusion about our values leads to intractable moral conflicts and these, in turn, create a climate of opinion in which everything is questionable and no question has a reasonable answer. "The best lack all conviction, while the worst / are full of passionate intensity."

The disintegration thesis is a powerful challenge to our moral convictions, but it is mistaken. Moral conflicts are indeed prevalent, but they betoken change, not disintegration. We are witnessing the new struggling to be born, not the death throes of the old. Our morality is changing in deep ways, but it is still *our* morality: alongside discontinuity, there is substantial continuity. The disintegration thesis is not mistaken about the facts but about the interpretation of the facts. What defenders of it observe is there, but it is not as they interpret it.

The deep moral changes do indicate that something is disintegrating; it is, however, not our morality but merely a particular conception of it. The reason why the disintegration thesis misinterprets our present moral situation is that it mistakenly identifies our morality with this conception, and it mistakenly supposes that as it becomes untenable, so our morality is itself threatened. The disintegration thesis recognizes only two alternatives—the acceptance or the rejection of a particular conception of morality—and it falsely supposes that our morality itself stands or falls with the fortunes of that conception.

The conception of morality that defenders of the disintegration thesis have in mind is monistic. Monism is the view that there is one and only one reasonable system of values. This system is the same for all human beings, always, everywhere. Human lives are good to the extent to which they conform to this system, and particular values are better or worse depending on their standing in the system. It is acknowledged, of course, that countless people do not conform to it. The reason for this is sought, however, in the deviating people, not in the system of values that the conception embodies. People are supposed to deviate either because they are insufficiently reasonable or because they are handicapped by character defects or adverse circumstances. According to monists, the task of morality is to create institutions, formulate principles, and educate people so as to further their living and acting according to this one reasonable system of values. Since deep moral changes are symptomatic of our radical disagreements about the nature of this system, given the monistic interpretation of morality, it will seem that our morality is disintegrating.

The alternative that monists fear may replace their position is relativism, the view that ultimately all values are conventional. Human life would be inconceivable without values, but what values people accept depends on the context in which they were born, on their genetic inheritance and subsequent experiences, on the political, cultural, economic, and religious influences on them; in short, what they value depends on their subjective attitudes and not on the objective features of values. The implication of relativism is that there cannot be a uniquely reasonable system of values, because when all is said and done no value any conception embodies can be justified on objective grounds.

What defenders of the thesis interpret as the disintegration of morality is the gradual replacement of monism with relativism. They observe our moral conflicts, the deep moral changes, the loss of our old certainties, our growing despair, and our distrust of reason—and they interpret them as monism yielding to relativism. But this interpretation is mistaken, because monism and relativism do not exhaust our moral options and because there is a better interpretation of the observed facts of our moral life. The additional option and the better interpretation are both provided by pluralism.

A PRELIMINARY SKETCH OF PLURALISM

Pluralism is a theory about the nature of the values whose realization would make lives good.[2] The primary concern of pluralism is with the relation in which these values stand to each other; the identity of the values is of interest to pluralists, *qua* pluralists, only in so far as it is relevant to understanding their relations. Pluralism thus is a theory only about one aspect of good lives. Pluralists may disagree with each other and agree with non-pluralists about the identity of the values that warrant our allegiance.

The goodness of a life may be thought to depend either on the personal satisfaction it provides to the agent or on the moral merit it possesses. Discussions about what makes a life good are therefore ambiguous, and clarity requires removing the ambiguity. A life will be called here "good" only if it is both personally satisfying and morally meritorious. Either component alone would not be sufficient to make a life good. For personal satisfaction may be obtained at the cost of causing much evil, and the price of moral merit may be the frequent frustration of reasonable desires, and neither evil nor frustrated lives should be supposed to be good.

The signs of a life's being good, then, are that the agent is satisfied with it, does not look to change it in radical ways, does not regret the major decisions that have shaped the life, does not feel lastingly unfulfilled, and would be content to let the life continue in the direction that has been given it. But it is equally important for the goodness of a life that the balance between the good and the evil that the agent has caused in its course be preponderantly in favor of the good. For its being reasonable to claim that a life is good, the judgment of the agent should concur with the judgment of knowledgeable observers of the life, and both judgments should be grounded on lasting personal satisfaction and overall moral merit being reasonably attributed to the agent.

Thinking of a good life in this way requires understanding the relation between its good-making components.[3] One possibility is that personal satisfaction and moral merit are unrelated aspects of a good life. But this

---

[2] In contemporary philosophy, "pluralism" is used also to denote a metaphysical theory, often referred to as "systematic pluralism." The version of monism that is the subject of this book is a theory only about the nature of values and it makes no metaphysical claims beyond those that concern values. Perhaps the best source of information about systematic pluralism is a collection of essays—Ford, ed., *Systematic Pluralism*. For a survey of some of the different forms pluralism of values may take, see Amelie Rorty, "Varieties of Pluralism in a Polyphonic Society."

[3] For a discussion of this point, see Nagel, *The View from Nowhere*, chapter 10.

is implausible, because it is not morally indifferent what personal satisfactions an agent seeks, because whatever is morally meritorious is often also personally satisfying, and because a good life normally excludes the inconsistency of motives and actions that the existence of unrelated good-making aspects is likely to produce.

Another possibility is that what makes a life good is that the personal satisfaction and the moral merit it yields coincide. In such a life, what the agent finds personally satisfying is the same as what has moral merit. One difficulty with this is that the coincidence of the two good-making aspects can only be partial at best, because reasonable agents often derive personal satisfaction from experiences and activities that are normally morally neutral. Connoisseurship, aesthetic pleasure, peak physical condition, a sense of humor, artistic creativity, the cultivation of style, and so forth, are usually personally satisfying without possessing either moral merit or demerit. We should recognize, therefore, that personal satisfaction may derive from the realization of both moral and nonmoral values, and, consequently, living a good life—whose achievement is the aim of pluralism—is not entirely a question of moral good and evil.

Living a good life, therefore, is not the same as living a moral life, for good lives have both moral and nonmoral components, and personal satisfaction is usually derived from both. Conceptions of a good life are broader, more inclusive than conceptions of a moral life. Yet the relation between the two is not simply that a good life is a moral life with some personal satisfactions derived from nonmoral sources being added to it. For one of the complications to which pluralism gives rise is that the moral and nonmoral components of a good life may conflict, and it may be reasonable, in some circumstances, to resolve the conflict in favor of the nonmoral component. We must postpone consideration of this complication, however, until chapter 9.

Nevertheless, pluralism is an evaluative theory, because it is not an uncommitted analysis of the relations among various types of values involved in good lives but a theory motivated by a concern for human beings actually living good lives. Consequently, pluralism is at once descriptive and evaluative. It offers a description of some conceptual and factual features relevant to good lives, but it also undertakes to evaluate these features on the basis of their contribution to good lives. The result of this evaluation may be to justify the descriptively identified features, or it may be to criticize them. But the evaluation, and thus the justification or the criticism, proceeds from a point of view that is centrally concerned with enhancing the chances of human beings to live good lives.

It may be asked whether pluralism, thus understood, is a moral theory. The answer depends on how broadly we wish to conceive of moral theories. There is ample historical precedent for regarding theories about good lives as moral. Indeed, this is the central concern of the eudaimonistic theories of Plato, Aristotle, the Stoics, and their contemporary followers.[4] In this broad sense, pluralism is a moral theory. But there is also a tendency in moral philosophy to restrict moral theories to the domain of moral values. The Kantian tradition is perhaps the most uncompromising example of this approach.[5] In this narrower sense, pluralism is not a moral theory.

No substantive issue turns on which usage is followed. What matters is that pluralism is a theory about good lives. According to it, good lives depend on both personal satisfaction and moral merit, and personal satisfaction depends on the realization of both moral and nonmoral values. We shall refer to pluralism as a moral theory, interpreted in the broad sense, mainly to stress the connection between morality and good lives, even though good lives admittedly have a nonmoral dimension.

The basic belief that unites pluralists is that good lives require the realization of radically different types of values, both moral and nonmoral, and that many of these values are conflicting and cannot be realized together. Living a good life requires the achievement of a coherent ordering of plural and conflicting values, but coherent orderings are themselves plural and conflicting. Thus, just as there is a plurality of conflicting values, so also is there a plurality of conflicting conceptions of a good life comprising these values. The plurality of good lives, therefore, is a plurality twice over: on account of the values it embodies and on account of the ways in which coherence among the values is achieved.

The key descriptive thesis of pluralism is that central features of good lives, as they are conceived in contemporary Western circumstances, at any rate, are best understood in pluralistic terms. These features are, first, that we are motivated by various moral values, such as the common good, duty, personal ideals, love and friendship, self-development, loyalty, justice, human rights, and so on. Second, that we are also motivated by nonmoral values of different sorts, for instance, beauty, playfulness, physical well-being, career plans, creativity, adventure, style, and the like. Third, that we often encounter conflicts in which we feel the tension between and among moral and nonmoral values, and these values motivate contrary choices and courses of action. Fourth, a sense of loss often accompanies the choices and actions our values require because, although we do what we feel it is, on balance, reasonable to do, we are nevertheless often forced in this process to sacrifice important values. And last, we often experience conflicts, not merely within morality, but

---

[4] A contemporary version of the theory is developed in Kekes, *Moral Tradition and Individuality*.

[5] For the dispute between eudaimonism and Kantianism, see Kekes, *Moral Tradition and Individuality*, chapter 2.

between morality and such other dimensions of life as politics, aesthetics, intimate personal relationships, or a reasonably interpreted conception of self-interest.

The central evaluative claim of pluralism is that although our commitments to various moral and nonmoral values produce conflicts and the resolution of these conflicts unavoidably engenders loss, nevertheless the plurality of values is not a regrettable feature of our life but a positive value. For the plurality of values enriches the possibilities for our living good lives, increases our freedom, motivates us to assert greater control over the direction of our lives, and enlarges the repertoire of conceptions of life that we may recognize as good. The evaluative claim of pluralism, of course, has serious moral, personal, and political implications, which will be discussed in chapters 9, 10, and 11.

Pluralism is a recent moral theory, although there were thinkers before our times whose approach was receptive to pluralism. Aristotle, Montaigne, Hume, John Stuart Mill in *On Liberty*, and William James come readily to mind. Yet not even they were unambiguously pluralists, as the term is understood here, mainly because pluralism was not yet a category of thought with respect to which they were obliged to clarify their positions. It is easier to identify contemporary thinkers who have been struggling in recent years with the more or less systematic development of pluralism: Annette Baier, Isaiah Berlin, Richard Brandt, Stuart Hampshire, Thomas Nagel, David Norton, Martha Nussbaum, Michael Oakeshott, Edmund Pincoffs, John Rawls, Michael Stocker, Peter Strawson, Charles Taylor, and Bernard Williams are some who have published influential books or articles on the topic.[6]

Pluralism, then, is a moral theory, in the broad sense, but there are serious doubts about the possibility and desirability of having any moral theories at all.[7] These doubts derive from the supposition that a successful moral theory would have to provide universal and impartial principles of moral evaluation. If this supposition were correct, "pluralistic moral theory" would be oxymoronic. Pluralists naturally share the doubts about morality requiring exclusively universal and impartial prin-

---

[6] Annette Baier, *Postures of the Mind*; Berlin, *Four Essays on Liberty*; Brandt, *A Theory of the Good and the Right*; Hampshire, *Morality and Conflict* and *Innocence and Experience*; Nagel, "The Fragmentation of Values"; Norton, *Personal Destinies*; Nussbaum, *The Fragility of Goodness*; Oakeshott, *Rationalism in Politics* and *On Human Conduct*; Pincoffs, *Quandaries and Virtues*; Rawls, *A Theory of Justice* and "Justice as Fairness: Political Not Metaphysical"; Stocker, *Plural and Conflicting Values*; Strawson, "Social Morality and Individual Ideal"; Charles Taylor, *Sources of the Self*; and Williams, *Problems of the Self*, *Moral Luck*, and *Ethics and the Limits of Philosophy*.

[7] See the anthology of representative writings by Clarke and Simpson, *Anti-Theory in Ethics and Moral Conservatism*, Edwards, *Ethics without Philosophy*, and Louden, "Virtue Ethics and Anti-Theory" and *Morality and Moral Theory*.

ciples, yet this does not doom the effort to develop a pluralistic moral theory. For theories in morality may aim at thinking systematically about diverse moral phenomena, considering how moral judgments could be reasonably criticized or justified, and arriving at some coherent view of the nature of the values that may make life good. And one can aim to do these without supposing that success would have to yield only universal and impartial principles. It is in this sense, then, that pluralism is a moral theory.[8]

It may be asked whether it is an ethical or a metaethical theory. It is arguable whether this distinction is tenable, but if it is, then the answer is that pluralism is both. For it is concerned both with first-order moral phenomena, such as various values and their relations to each other, and with the second-order analysis, justification, and criticism of the judgments we make about first-order moral phenomena.

Another distinction in terms of which moral theories are currently classified is between cognitive and noncognitive theories. This distinction is neither sharper nor clearer than the previous one. Calling moral theories "cognitive" may mean that the moral judgments that follow from them are open to rational evaluation and can be criticized or justified on objective grounds independent of the theory. In this sense, pluralism is certainly cognitive. But "cognitive" may be used in contrast with "emotive," and it is taken then to mean that the source of moral motivation is reason rather than feeling, imagination, or the will. And in that sense, it is unclear whether pluralism is cognitive. If this sense of "cognitive" commits one to holding that reason is or ought to be the *exclusive* source of moral motivation, then pluralism is noncognitive. But if this second sense of "cognitive" is taken to permit, in addition to reason, also feeling, imagination, and the will as morally acceptable motivating forces, then pluralism is cognitive in the second sense as well. The main point is not the label, but what it signifies. In the present case, that is the claim that the moral judgments that follow from pluralism can be justified or criticized on objective grounds and, furthermore, the conceptions of a good life that pluralists regard as reasonable are sufficiently capacious to leave room for the moral importance of feeling, imagination, and the will, as well as of reason.

In holding this ideal, pluralists partly agree and partly disagree with both monists and relativists. In agreement with monists and in disagreement with relativists, pluralists claim that a conception of a good life must be reasonable if it is actually to yield a good life. And that means that the plurality of values and their comparative rankings that the con-

[8] For a discussion of the issues involved in this approach, see the special issue of *Ethics*, ed. Becker, "Impartiality and Ethical Theory."

ception embodies must be not only subjectively accepted but also objectively justified. In agreement with relativists and in disagreement with monists, however, pluralists deny that there is a uniquely reasonable conception of a good life embodying something like the one true system of values. Good lives are plural because they are constituted of the realization of different valued possibilities as well as differently valued possibilities.

Pluralists stress that good lives embody the conjunction of these two essential elements: the available possibilities and their being valued. The first is often beyond our control, because the possibilities we have depend largely on the political, economic, historical, educational, and genetic influences on us, and these are usually given as facts of life with which we have to contend. By contrast, there is normally a much greater scope for control over the attitudes we form toward our possibilities. And since different people will form different attitudes, this will contribute further to the plurality of good lives.

One source of the appeal of pluralism is that it concentrates on the possibilities whose realization may make lives good, and it thereby wishes for us what we wish for ourselves. In this respect, pluralism is quite unlike monism. For what monists wish for us is that we should overcome the obstacles that prevent us from embracing the one true system of values through which we could achieve a good life. The pluralistic ideal is that we should *make* a good life for themselves. The monistic ideal is that we should *find* the one life that is good for all of us. The pluralistic view of individuality is that it involves constructing a good life out of the available plural possibilities. The monistic view is that individuality involves plurality in the ways of reaching the one life good for all. Both see living a good life as the goal. But for pluralists the goal is to achieve what we individually want to achieve, while for monists the goal is to achieve what all individuals alike ought to want to achieve.

Pluralism involves not only the celebration of human possibilities, but also the necessity of imposing limits. Not all possibilities are reasonable, reasonable possibilities often conflict with each other, and not all ways of trying to realize reasonable and compatible possibilities are acceptable. Limits need to be imposed to exclude unreasonable possibilities and unreasonable ways of pursuing them, as well as to minimize conflicts. If pluralists are right in rejecting the monistic view that there is one and only one reasonable system of values whose realization would lead to *the* good human life, then they must provide some other ground for regarding some limits as reasonable and some other justification for imposing these limits on possibilities that individuals may legitimately pursue.

Relativists deny that this can be done. They concede that any society must impose limits on those living in it, but these limits will be denied to have any objective basis. They will be said to have nothing to do with the intrinsic nature of the possibilities they are intended to curtail; they stem from the need to have order, and, according to relativists, any order is bound to be merely conventional. They will grant that it may be, and it usually is the case, that some limits have become traditional and customary in a society, so much so that they may to seem to be natural to the people living in it. But this will be taken to reveal only the force of habit, not the reasonability, of limits. Pluralists must show, therefore, how reasonable limits could be placed on the pursuit of the plurality of values.

The limits follow from the pluralistic view of the nature of values. Possibilities are valued from the human point of view, anthropocentrically. Possibilities are seen as being good or evil depending on the effects their realization has or would have on us, human beings. And these effects are benefits that we may enjoy or harms we may suffer. Reasonable limits exclude harmful possibilities, help to resolve conflicts among beneficial possibilities, and protect people in their endeavors to make a good life for themselves. But these limits will not extend so far as to allow only one conception of a good life, only one system of values, because the valued possibilities the limits are intended to safeguard, as well as the comparative evaluations attached to them, will vary from person to person.

We may now return to the facts of our moral life that defenders of the disintegration thesis interpret one way and pluralists another. There certainly are deep changes and radical conflicts in our morality. And these changes and conflicts are serious enough to cause the disintegration of monistic morality. But they are not sufficiently serious to force us to embrace the relativistic view that all values are ultimately subjective preferences, and thus to compel us to accept the conclusion that our morality itself is disintegrating. What the changes indicate is that we are passing from a monistic to a pluralistic morality, and some of the changes we are witnessing around and within ourselves are deep because the passage from monism to pluralism is as fundamental as any in the history of our morality. Similarly, the constant conflicts we are encountering are not symptomatic of our weakening moral commitments, presaging moral disintegration, but an inevitable by-product of the plurality of values.

THE PLAN OF THE BOOK

The aim of the book is to present a version of pluralism and to explore some of its implications. For the sake of brevity, this version will be referred to as "pluralism," but the reader should be aware that there are other versions. These will be indicated when appropriate, but they will not be discussed in any detail. It should also be noted that the book is exploratory, and it does not aim at anything like a final account of plural ism. Working out the implications of pluralism will take more than one author and one book. But it is necessary to begin somewhere, and that is what is here intended.

In the next chapter, we shall continue the development of pluralism by introducing six theses that jointly constitute the core of the theory. These theses are the plurality and conditionality of values, the unavoidability of conflicts, the nature of reasonable conflict-resolution, the possibilities of life, the need for limits, and the prospects of moral progress. Chapters 3 through 8 will be devoted to a more detailed consideration of each of the six theses in turn. But the development of pluralism will not be merely an exposition of the six theses; it will also involve showing why pluralism is preferable to monism and relativism. After the theses have been explained and defended in this manner, some of the radical and perhaps surprising moral, personal, and political implications of pluralism will be discussed in chapters 9 through 11.

CHAPTER TWO

The Six Theses of Pluralism

> The delicate and difficult art of life is to find, in each new turn
> of experience, the *via media* between two extremes: . . . to
> have and apply standards, and yet to be on guard against their
> desensitizing and stupefying influence, their tendency to blind
> us to the diversities of concrete situations and to previously
> unrecognized values; to know when to tolerate, when to
> embrace, and when to fight. And in that art, since no fixed and
> comprehensive rule can be laid down for it, we shall doubtless
> never acquire perfection.
>
> —Arthur O. Lovejoy, *The Great Chain of Being*

THE PURPOSE of this chapter is to introduce six central theses of pluralism and some of the key terms in which the discussion about them will be
conducted. The theses are interdependent, and that is why it is important to have an overview of them before we proceed to discuss questions
of detail.

THE PLURALITY AND CONDITIONALITY OF VALUES

Whether the world is one or many is among the oldest questions of philosophy. Is there an underlying unity behind the multiplicity of ways in
which the world appears to human observers, or is the world really as
varied as appearances suggest? The axiological question of whether values are one or many is one component of the larger and more complex
metaphysical question. Whatever may the answer be to the larger question, pluralists believe that in the case of values at least, appearances do
not deceive. The reason why it seems to us that there are many values
worth pursuing is that there *are* many values worth pursuing.

The discussion of values will be restricted throughout the book to benefits and harms affecting human beings. This restriction excludes many
different kinds of values, but it serves to focus the discussion and keep it
within manageable proportions. Given this restriction, then, we may illustrate the plurality of values by drawing a number of distinctions regarding the benefits and harms that normally affect human beings.

To begin with, some benefits and harms are due largely to nonhuman causes, while others are caused predominantly by human agency. The former will be called "naturally occurring values" and the latter "humanly caused values." Health and disease are often naturally occurring, while kindness and cruelty are humanly caused. We can put this distinction immediately to use to explain the distinction between moral and nonmoral values, which we have already employed in the previous chapter, although without explanation. Humanly caused values are constituted of benefits and harms that chiefly affect either ourselves or others. We may identify moral values, then, as humanly caused values in which the benefits and harms affect primarily others. By contrast, nonmoral values will be either naturally caused values (benefits and harms stemming largely from nonhuman sources) or humanly caused values in which both the causes and the recipients are primarily ourselves.

The plurality of values is due not merely to the different sources and recipients of the associated benefits and harms but also to the different reasons there are for seeking or avoiding them. Some benefits and harms are normally regarded as such by all reasonable human beings. Circumstances would have to be exceptional not to count as benefits to satisfy our basic physiological needs, to be loved, or to live in a society in which our endeavors are respected. It would require similarly extraordinary events for being tortured, humiliated, or exploited not to be regarded as harms. It seems reasonable to suppose that some benefits and harms are, under normal circumstances, universally human. Let us call the resulting values "primary." We should note that there is a plurality even among primary values themselves, since the associated benefits and harms are various, such as physiological (e.g., food and torture), psychological (e.g., love and humiliation), and social (e.g., respect and exploitation).

In addition to primary values, there are also values that we shall call "secondary." Secondary values vary with persons, societies, traditions, and historical periods. Their variability is due to two reasons. One is that what is regarded as beneficial or harmful often depends on conceptions of a good life that reason allows but does not require us to hold. These conceptions incorporate a very extensive range of values deriving from the social roles we have (e.g., being a parent, spouse, colleague, lover), the way we earn a living (e.g., being a physician, teacher, miner, politician), the personal aspirations we cherish (e.g., being creative, influential, well-liked, knowledgeable, ambitious), the preferences we develop (e.g., for certain kinds of food, aesthetic enjoyment, hobbies, physical exercise, sexual contacts, literature, vacations), and so forth. What is rightly valued in one kind of life may equally rightly be regarded as a matter of indifference or even positively harmful in another. Reasonable

no overriding values. But from this it does not follow that some values may not usually be more important than others, or that in the normal course of events some values should not regularly take precedence over some others. Consequently, one central question to which the first thesis of pluralism gives rise is whether there is some reasonable way of deciding which value should prevail in particular situations when there is a conflict among values.

The Unavoidability of Conflicts

Pluralists are committed then to the view that the conceptions of a good life and the values on whose realization good lives depend are plural and conditional. These conceptions and values, however, are often related in such a way, according to pluralists, that the realization of one excludes the realization of another. Consequently, conflicts among reasonable conceptions of a good life and reasonable values must be recognized as unavoidable features of an adequate understanding of morality and politics. Pluralists believe that living a good life must be essentially concerned with coping with these conflicts, but doing so is formidably difficult because the conflicts are often caused by the incommensurability and incompatibility of the values whose realization is regarded as essential by particular conceptions of a good life.

The incompatibility of values is due to qualities intrinsic to the conflicting values. Because of these qualities, the realization of some values entirely or partly excludes the realization of the other. Having a restful sleep and engaging in an interesting conversation are entirely incompatible, while political activism and solitude are partly so.

The basic idea of incommensurability is that there are some things so unalike as to exclude any reasonable comparison among them. Square roots and insults, smells and canasta, migrating birds and X ray seem to exclude any common yardstick by which we could evaluate their respective merits or demerits. That this is so is not usually troublesome because the need to compare them rarely arises. But it is otherwise with values. It often happens that we want to enjoy incompatible values, and so it becomes important to compare them in order to be able to choose among them in a reasonable manner. If, however, incompatible values are also incommensurable, then reasonable comparisons among them become problematic.

The reasons why pluralists suppose that values are incommensurable are, first, that it does not seem to them that there is a highest value, such as happiness, to which all other values could always be reasonably subordinated and with reference to which all other values could be authoritatively ranked. Second, they are also dubious about there being some medium, such as pleasure, in terms of which all the different values could be expressed, quantified, and compared in a way that reasonable people would generally accept. And third, they are similarly skeptical about claims made on behalf of some one or few canonical principles, such as the categorical imperative, which could be appealed to in resolving conflicts among values to the general satisfaction of reasonable people.

Incommensurability and incompatibility are logically distinct notions. Incommensurable values need not be incompatible, and if they are not, then they could, and often do, coexist in a life. Patriotism and spelunking are incommensurable but not incompatible. If values were merely incommensurable, without being incompatible, it would not be hard to reconcile them, for we should only have to develop sufficiently capacious conceptions of a good life to include all the incommensurable values we want to realize. The reason why this strategy cannot work is that many values are not only incommensurable but also incompatible. They cannot, therefore, all be fully realized in even a most receptively rich conception of a good life. Conflicts of the relevant type occur precisely because we want to realize both incompatible and incommensurable values.

Nor need incompatible values be incommensurable. We often want to realize two readily comparable yet mutually exclusive values. If I want to be alone for a few days, I could go camping or fly to a strange city, but not both; or, if I want to improve my finances, I could spend less money or make shrewd investments, but the more I do of one, the less I could do of the other. Pluralists are committed therefore to the conjunction of two claims: conflicts are frequent, and many of them are due to our wanting to realize incompatible and incommensurable values.

This provides a deeper reason for the plurality of values. Below the surface of the distinctions we have drawn between naturally occurring and humanly caused, moral and nonmoral, primary and secondary values is the fact that many of these values are incompatible and incommensurable. And it is this deeper reason that motivates pluralists to reject the monistic appeal to an overriding value for settling conflicts. For it seems that the claim that any particular value should always override any incompatible and incommensurable value that may conflict with it is bound to be arbitrary. On what grounds could any value be regarded as invariably overriding if the values it is supposed to override are so utterly unlike it as to exclude the possibility of comparison between it and them?

Pluralists do not deny that many conflicts among values can be resolved by appealing to some reasonable ranking of the values in question. Such rankings are acknowledged by pluralists to be both possible and desirable. The point they insist on is that rankings are reasonable only in particular situations because they depend on the variable and individual conceptions of a good life held by the participating agents. And just as there is a plurality of equally reasonable conceptions of a good life and values, so also there is a plurality of equally reasonable rankings of them. According to pluralists, reason does not require commitment to some one highest value or to some medium for comparing values or to some one or few authoritative principles. On the contrary, reason allows people to commit themselves to any one of a plurality of equally reasonable values, ranking schemes, or principles.

Nevertheless, it is just a brute fact about our lives that we cannot realize all the possibilities we reasonably value. Making a good life unavoidably involves losing something valuable. The recipe for a good life, therefore, cannot merely be that we should find out what possibilities it would be reasonable for us to realize and then do what we can, within the appropriate limits, to realize them. For usually there are more possibilities available than we could realize, and the obstacle is not just the shortness of life and insufficient human energy. There are also obstacles in the valued possibilities themselves. We may value love and independence, but the more we love someone, the less we can act independently; we may value equality and prosperity, but if prosperity depends on a free market, then it is inseparable from there being profit and loss, and that is detrimental to equality; we may value justice and friendship, but since the first depends on impartiality, while the second excludes it, our valuing both creates a tension.

This has the consequence that the necessity of resolving conflicts becomes a central problem for pluralism. It is not so for monists, since they deny the conditionality of all values. If conflicts occur, monists resolve them by letting the overriding value prevail. And they explain the occurrence of conflicts by handicaps that prevent us from being sufficiently reasonable to recognize the overridingness of some value. Nor are conflicts problematic for relativists, since they think that values depend on attitudes. In case of conflicts, relativists urge the clarification of the attitudes responsible for the conflicts, and that means, not to put too fine a point on it, finding out which of the conflicting attitudes has a stronger hold on us. But pluralists cannot resort to these expedients, because they think that the conflicting values are conditional and that what it is reasonable to value is not merely a matter of our attitudes. How, then, can pluralists resolve conflicts?

The Approach to Reasonable Conflict-Resolution

The conditionality of values has a formative influence on the manner in which moral and political arguments about the resolution of conflicts should be conducted, provided the participants aim to arrive at some reasonable settlement. In the normal course of events, these arguments occur because there is disagreement over what ought to be done in some practical situation. Should we raise taxes, support affirmative-action programs, legalize marijuana, negotiate with terrorists, and so forth. And then the various sides appeal to some value that, if it prevailed, would favor one course of action over another. The disagreements are difficult because the values appealed to are conflicting. Prosperity conflicts with equality, merit conflicts with compensation for past injustice, freedom conflicts with order, saving lives conflicts with opposition to lawlessness, and so forth. In such disagreements, we each proceed then to champion the value we favor. The dispute is usually terminated either by some compromise that obliges us to violate our values or by the democratic expedient of counting heads, heads predictably turned by the combination of strong passions and moral or political intimidation.

If the implications of the conditionality of values were more widely understood, an additional consideration would enter into our thinking about the merits of the conflicting values. This consideration would redirect our attention and help to make the conflicts more tractable. We would come to see, then, first, that the conflict we are facing is usually not a crisis produced by our adversary's stupidity, wickedness, or perversity but merely another manifestation of the unavoidable conflicts that will continually occur if values are plural, conditional, incommensurable, and incompatible. And we would come to see also that the resolution of any particular conflict involves not merely deciding what ought to be done about the situation at hand but also considering how resolving the conflict by opting for one value, or for the balancing of one value against another in some compromise, would affect the whole system of values of which the conflicting values are merely a part.

It is the second consideration—what things depend on the resolution of a conflict—that is of decisive importance for making ubiquitous conflicts tractable. For what the redirection brings to our attention is that the vast majority of conflicts we encounter occur within particular traditions or within particular people. And the significance of that is that we can normally count on the existence of a system of values in the background in whose maintenance the disputants have a vested interest. In the case of conflicts occurring within people, the system of values is the conception of a good life of the agent who faces the conflict. Conflicts among people who adhere to the same tradition occur against the shared background of the whole system of values that partly constitutes the tradition. If we acted reasonably, either for ourselves or on behalf of our tradition, we would recognize that a large part of the explanation of why we are involved in the conflicts is that we are motivated by our conception of a good life or by the traditional system of values to which we adhere. And this fact about us provides both a common ground on which we, who may be the factions of our divided selves, can agree to stand and a device for resolving our conflicts.

In all but the most extreme situations, the value of our conceptions of a good life or the value of the traditional system of values to which we adhere will be greater than that of either of the two values whose conflict we are facing. By taking the larger view suggested by conceptions of a good life or by traditions, we come to see the conflict at hand in a different light. We shall not merely ask: what should we do here and now? We shall ask instead: what should we do here and now so that we could resolve this conflict in a way that would be best from the point of view of the system of values we, as disputants, share? And if we are reasonable, we shall answer by stepping back from the immediacy of the conflict in which we participate in order to reflect on what would be best not here and now but in the long run, given the values of our tradition or our conception of a good life.

We should be clear about what this approach to conflict-resolution can and cannot do. What it can do is redirect our thinking. The result of that will stand as a systematic reminder to those who have come to think in this pluralistic way that very many conflicts are not as intractable as they seem, because the parties to them are united by more important values than those that divide them. The search for conflict-resolution will take the form of articulating our shared important values and judging the effect on them of various ways of resolving the conflict at hand.

It must not be supposed, however, that this approach will yield a blueprint for conflict-resolution. What it gives is a manner of thinking not conclusions reached by means of it. The approach is not a method but a cast of mind, a tendency to ask certain questions rather than others and to look for answers in a particular direction and not in different ones. And of course reasonable people sharing this cast of mind may disagree with each other. We may interpret differently the effects a particular conflict-resolution has on our tradition or conception of a good life, and these interpretations may also produce conflicts. The new conflicts may then stand in the way of resolving the original conflicts that occasioned the interpretations themselves. But this is neither a logical defect nor an insuperable practical obstacle. For the conflicts among interpretations are amenable to resolution in precisely the same way as other conflicts are. The key question is the same as before: which interpretation is more likely to be the best from the point of view of the system of values the interpreters share?

It may be objected, however, that there will be disagreements about what "the best" is just as often as there will be disagreements about values and about interpretations concerning which of the conflicting values is more important from the point of view of the system of values as a whole. This is clearly true. But these disagreements about "the best" will no longer involve us in a conflict about values. We shall be arguing about means, not about ends. The question to which we shall give different answers is about the course of action that ought to be adopted given that we agree about attributing first importance to the system of values we share and given also that we disagree about which particular value within our shared system of values should guide us in the particular situation we face. The disagreement about "the best" will be about the course of action that will be most likely to lead to our shared goal, namely, the maintenance of our common system of values. The strategy for resolving conflicts will be to transform them from conflicts of values to conflicts about the means of resolving conflicts.

It should be emphasized that the outcome of this approach to conflict-resolution need not be a clear and precise action-guiding prescription. Finding the best means to an agreed upon end is often difficult because there is not enough time, knowledge, skill, money, or energy to find or to do what would be the best. But this, although sad and frustrating, is a fact about practical limitations and not a theoretical objection to this pluralistic approach to conflict-resolution. To repeat the point previously made, the immediate product of the redirected thinking that this approach calls for is a changed mental disposition, leading us to pose different questions and to look for answers to them in a different place. The product need not be immediately available new answers. Translating a manner of thinking, a cast of mind, a mental disposition into practical terms is a skill that has to be developed after the old habits have yielded to new ones.[1]

Nor should it be supposed that if this approach were adopted, then all conflicts could be resolved by means of it. There are two main reasons why some conflicts may fall outside its scope. The first is that conflicts may occur among people who do not share a system of values. It is important to see both that such conflicts could occur and that they are bound to be rare. Even if we are moved by utterly different systems of values, we are still human beings, and hence we are going to prize, if we are reasonable, the primary values, which must be recognized in all systems of values. There will normally be some commonly shared values that may be appealed to in settling at least some conflicts.

But what if the people we face are unreasonable? Well, that can happen too, and if it does, then we finally arrive at conflicts where there is no prospect of a reasonable resolution. Yet, although this can happen, the

[1] An incomparable account of the thinking here described is Oakeshott's "Political Education."

conflicts are unlikely to persist for long. For if a tradition or an individual systematically ignores the primary values, it will soon have no opportunity to participate in conflicts. What is much more likely is that while the primary values will be normally protected, there will be some religious or political ideology that dupes people into sacrificing themselves by foregoing the realization of primary values. As we know, such ideologies can endure, and if they do and if we come into serious conflict with their champions, then there is no alternative but to use force.

The second reason why some conflicts may persist is that although the value of a traditional system of values or of a conception of a good life is normally greater than that of any particular value, this is not always so. It should be remembered that values are not only means to good lives, but also constituents of them. And some values may be indispensable constituents. We may reasonably judge that if our system of values permitted the violation of such an indispensable value, then the system would become unworthy of our allegiance. That there may be conflicts of this intractable sort is not a surprising consequence of the pluralistic thesis that all values are conditional. For, in that case, not even the value of whole traditions or of our reasonably adopted conception of a good life may be exempt from being overridden. That this can happen to any value or any combination of values is entailed by pluralism.

These two reasons, however, derive from conflicts that occur only in exceptional circumstances, when civilized life breaks down and barbarism takes its place. It is the very function of our system of values to make this possibility remote. And the best way of doing so is to make the system sufficiently agile, flexible, and hospitable to a plurality of values so that on the other side of inevitable conflicts there would not loom the threat of barbarism.

THE POSSIBILITIES OF LIFE

Pluralism focuses on values as constituents of good lives. They are made good by the personal satisfaction and the moral merit they possess. These good-making components depend on the realization of possibilities we may reasonably value. As we have seen, however, the possibilities whose realization may make lives good are many, rather than one. And the reason for thinking that there is no unity behind the apparent plurality of valued possibilities is that very many of them are incommensurable and incompatible.

It follows from this that good lives cannot consist in the realization of all reasonably valued possibilities because, being incommensurable and incompatible, they cannot all be realized together. Good lives, therefore, must involve the selection of some among the available possibili-

ties, and this requires us to find some way of reasonably comparing, ranking, or balancing the claims of the plural and conflicting possibilities we
value. But finding such a way, although essential for living a good life, is
possible only if certain conditions are met. These conditions depend
partly on ourselves and partly on the tradition of the society in which we
live.

One such condition is that the tradition must make available a sufficiently rich supply of possibilities from which we may select some as
choiceworthy. These will be available only if we can reasonably regard
them as possibilities that we ourselves may endeavor to realize. This requires that we should have an adequate notion of what it would be like
for us, given our characters and circumstances, to realize these possibilities. We need, therefore, as a second condition, a sufficiently developed
imagination to enable us to form an adequate notion of the nature of
our possibilities. Providing the possibilities is largely a function of the
tradition, while coming to a reasonable view of what their realization
would entail for us personally is mainly up to us.

The conjunction of the possibilities our tradition provides and the
imaginative grasp of them as values that may become constituents of our
conceptions of a good life supplies a third condition: the enlargement of
our freedom. For the more numerous are the available possibilities and
the better we appreciate the nature of these possibilities as possibilities
we may try to realize, the greater will be our freedom to make for ourselves what seem to us like good lives.

The enlargement of the area within which we are free to construct a
good life is certainly a direct benefit to us, so, in so far as we are reasonable, we should wish to have as much freedom as possible. Beyond this,
however, freedom is also an indirect benefit to others. This indirect benefit is derivable from our acquaintance with what Mill so aptly called
"experiments in living." For what we make of the possibilities we have
adds to the stock of experiments in living that our tradition has. Our
freedom is thereby increased through the enrichment of our possibilities and through the provision of new possibilities for our imaginative
appraisal. This remains true even of failed experiments in living, of lives
that have been ruined by the exploration of wrong possibilities or by the
wrong exploration of otherwise valuable possibilities. Imagination may
bring home to us not only valuable but also base, corrupt, and ignoble
possibilities, and we can benefit from them too. The joint forces of the
available possibilities, the imaginative exploration of them, and the utili-
zation of the moral space we call freedom therefore provide some of the
conditions we require for making a good life.

We may think of this thesis as expressing the positive vision of pluralism. It holds out the promise of a tradition in which having a plurality of

possibilities is recognized as intrinsically valuable. It is a tradition in which that possibility is the ideal. The ideal of course is conditional, not overriding. For particular ways of realizing it are open to criticism, and some of the ways may be justifiably excluded. The next thesis we shall discuss is concerned with what limits are reasonable.

Within these limits, however, the greater the plurality of valued possibilities is, the better it is for us and thus also for traditions, since the value of traditions derives from their contribution to good lives we may live by adhering to them. But this plurality should not be thought of as valuable merely on account of making available the largest number of means to the achievement of a common end. Living a good life *is* the end, but it is not a *common* end. For the plurality of valued possibilities entails the plurality of good lives in a double sense. Different lives may be made good by the realization of different possibilities, and even if the possibilities are the same in some lives, the value attributed to them may differ from one good life to another. The plurality of possibilities is important for good lives, therefore, not merely because the possibilities are means to good lives but also because they are constituents of them.

The pluralistic vision of the human aspiration to live a good life must not be interpreted on the model of there being a common destination that we may reach in different ways. The notion of a common destination is itself deeply at odds with pluralism. If a metaphor is wanted, artistic creation is perhaps less unsatisfactory than others, but as all metaphors, this too must be treated with caution.[2] We make our lives the way artists make works of art. We and artists start from some context, some tradition, some educational influences on us; we are limited by what we bring to it by way of talents, imagination, and skill, as well as by the available possibilities and by the demands and expectations of other people in our context; and then we do what we can, and we succeed, fail, or banally fall somewhere in between. But the product, the life or the work of art, is going to be different in each case, because the contributions made to it by the tradition, by our individuality, and by the mixture we concoct of the two are also different. People aiming to live a good life are no more aiming at the same goal than artists aiming to create a work of art are aiming at the same goal.

If there is a plurality of incommensurable and incompatible values and if we have available to us a rich stock of possibilities, the capacity to exercise our imagination, and a sufficient degree of freedom, then conflicts among values will be an unavoidable feature of our attempts to make a good life. It is thus the conjunction of a fact about valued possibilities, namely, their incommensurability and incompatibility, and a fact

---

[2] See Berlin, "The Apotheosis of the Romantic Will," 236–37, for its sinister aspect.

about us, namely, that we possess possibilities, imagination, and adequate freedom, that are jointly responsible for the unavoidability of conflicts.

From the human point of view, both of these facts are to be welcomed. It is easy to see why it is good that the possibilities of life should be many, that we should have a capacity for imaginatively entertaining them, and that our freedom should be sufficient for choosing among them, so we need waste no words on explaining the obvious. But it is less obvious why the joint incommensurability and incompatibility of valued possibilities is to be counted among our benefits rather than among the adverse conditions of life with which we have to cope.

That our pursuits are plural is worthy of celebration because it makes life interesting, rich, full of possibilities, and provides one of the strongest motives why we should be interested in each other. It is also of great evolutionary value, for in the struggle for survival we do not, as it were, place all our eggs in one basket. The more various our lives are, the better are our chances of being able to cope with a variety of circumstances. Even if it were true that in some historical circumstances there was only one conception of a good life according to which it was the best to live, historical circumstances change, and unless other conceptions were available, adjustment would be, if not impossible, at the very least much harder. From the point of view of both the species and individual members of it, the plurality of conceptions of a good life is a benefit rather than an obstacle.

The plurality of conceptions of a good life, however, is made possible by the incommensurability and incompatibility of valued possibilities. If good lives did not embody such values, they would not be genuinely plural in nature. The incommensurability and incompatibility of values therefore is not an obstacle to good lives but rather that dynamic feature of them which propels us toward conducting our own experiments in living. And so, to return to conflicts, conflicts are the necessary by-products of the incommensurability and incompatibility of valued possibilities. Given the desirable complexity of human nature and the opportunity for us to exercise the capacities that constitute our complex nature, we encounter incommensurable and incompatible possibilities as conflicting. The plurality of good lives would not be possible unless such conflicts occurred, and, as we have seen, unless it was possible also to resolve them in a reasonable manner.

The ever-present conflicts in our lives appear to us as constant adversity we have to face, yet a deeper view would enable us to see them as an indispensable aspect of the process whereby we endeavor to make a good life for ourselves. From that point of view, conflicts will not seem to be necessary evils but welcome signs that we are on the right track in grappling with the possibilities from among which we must choose some to realize.

THE NEED FOR LIMITS

Understanding pluralism is essentially connected with understanding how it differs from monism on the one hand and relativism on the other. Up to now, we have been mostly concerned with distinguishing between pluralism and monism. The distinction required setting a limit on the importance that may be attributed to any one kind of value or combination of values, and the limit was drawn by separating conditional from overriding values. On the pluralistic side, the limit was set by regarding all values as conditional, while on the monistic side of the limit we found the insistence on some values being overriding. Pluralists recognize that some values are more important than others, indeed that some values are extremely important. At the same time, they deny that any value can be important enough always to override the claims of any other value that may conflict with it.

Relativists agree with pluralists in their denial, and they may even agree about regarding some values as more important and others as less so. Nevertheless, relativists and pluralists disagree in their answers to the question of whether judgments of importance can be justified on context-independent grounds. Relativists deny this possibility, pluralists affirm it. And so we encounter the need for another kind of limit. This one is needed to arrest the argument that if there are no overriding values, then any distinction between values based on their respective importance is ultimately relative to the context in which it is made. Pluralists need to show, this time against relativists, that the importance they attribute to some values over others can be defended on context-independent grounds, and this is the motivation behind the thesis we are presently considering.

In order to show this, pluralists appeal to the distinction between deep and variable conventions. Deep conventions protect the minimum requirements of all good lives, however they are conceived. Variable conventions also protect the requirements of good lives, but these requirements vary with traditions and conceptions of a good life. The pluralistic claim is that the values protected by deep conventions have a context-independent justification, while the values protected by variable conventions may legitimately be prized in some contexts but not in others. In opposition to this, relativists may accept the distinction between deep and variable conventions, but they will deny that the distinction has an objective basis that would have to be acknowledged by reasonable people who view the context as uncommitted observers rather than as participants. Consequently, just as monists and pluralists are divided over the question of whether all values are conditional, so relativists and pluralists are divided over the question of whether deep conventions have a context-independent justification.

It would be a relatively simple matter to resolve this dispute in favor of pluralism if pluralism were not committed to a broad rather than a narrow view of deep conventions. If deep conventions were interpreted merely as having the purpose of protecting individuals in their pursuit of primary values, then the argument against relativism would need to point out merely that these values derive from aspects of human nature that all normal members of our species share. There is, therefore, a context-independent reason for recognizing primary values as normally having the greatest importance in all traditions; and the reason is that their protection is a minimum requirement of all good lives, quite independently of how such lives are conceived by individuals or by traditions. Pluralists could reasonably claim then that all traditions and all individuals ought to observe the deep conventions that set limits to interference with the realization of primary values.

The issue between relativism and pluralism, however, is more complex than this. Primary values represent only a very thin layer of context-independent requirements for all good lives, and it is something of a letdown to have a theory tell us only that starvation, humiliation, exploitation, and the like, will harm everyone. It is true that some relativists deny even this much, but it is perhaps only they and some other theorists, like the present author, who take their denials seriously. The issue is more complicated, because pluralists include among the values deep conventions ought to aim to protect not only primary ones but some secondary values as well. Pluralists claim that these secondary values can also be justified on objective grounds, although the objectivity of these grounds does not involve the same kind of context-independence as the objectivity of primary values does. And the relativistic denial of this broader pluralistic claim has considerably more plausibility than their doubts about the narrow claim restricted to the universal importance of primary values.

What, then, are the secondary values in question? They have at least the following characteristics: they will be among the minimum requirements of good lives as conceived in the context of a particular tradition; they will be likely to vary from tradition to tradition; and reasonable people who stand outside of the tradition in which they are held would regard as objectively justified the claim made on behalf of these values that it is indeed reasonable to count them among the minimum requirements of good lives as conceived in that tradition. The problem for pluralists is to show how it could be consistently maintained both that it is objectively justified to regard these secondary values as part of the minimum requirements of good lives and that whether they are so regarded depends on conceptions of a good life, which vary from tradition to tradition. Objective justification, after all, is context-independent, and yet it has just been conceded that the justification is relative to conceptions of a good life, which vary with the contexts of traditions. The plausibility of a form of relativism that concedes the objectivity of primary values but denies it of secondary values derives from the seriousness of this problem for pluralists.

Yet the problem has a solution. The key to it is that, while the primary values are the same in all contexts because they derive from the universal aspect of human nature, the ways in which the primary values are realized may and do differ from context to context. The satisfaction of basic physiological and psychological needs and the existence of a stable social order are universal requirements of all good lives. But how basic physiological and psychological needs are satisfied and how a stable social order is understood and maintained vary from context to context. We might say that primary values are the content, while secondary values give form to them; or that primary values are satisfactions of brute, blind, uninterpreted needs, while secondary values provide their interpretations, which take into account the surrounding facts; or that primary values are derived from primitive urges, while secondary values are derived from the necessary attempt to civilize them. And of course these forms, interpretations, attempts at the civilization of our raw drives— choose the metaphor that pleases—these secondary values, that is, will be different in different contexts.

The point, however, is that they will be different forms of the same content, different interpretations of the same universal human facts, different attempts at civilizing the same primitive urges. This is why reasonable outside observers can look at some of the secondary values of a tradition, see that they are different from those that are held in their own contexts, and yet recognize that it is reasonable to attribute to them great importance in that tradition. And such observers can also see that although these secondary values may be alien, strange, and perhaps even repulsive to them, they are nevertheless merely different ways of trying to satisfy basic human needs shared by all normal members of our species. Moreover, they can go on to make perfectly legitimate judgments about how reasonable it is to hold any particular secondary value of this sort. For they can compare the way in which the secondary value in question facilitates the realization of the primary value to which it gives form with how some other secondary value in some other tradition accomplishes the same purpose. It is on the basis of such judgments that it is reasonable to regard as immoral slavery, child prostitution, female circumcision, vendettas, trials by torture, and similar noxious practices.

The pluralistic claim on behalf of the objectivity of some secondary values is that these secondary values are context-independent in the sense that they represent ways of satisfying needs that all human beings have independently of the context in which they live. In this respect, some secondary values are as objective as primary values are. But these secondary values are not context-independent in the sense that the particular ways in which they satisfy universal needs would have to be accepted by all reasonable people in all traditions. And in this respect, these secondary values are unlike primary values. The case for relativism is based on the difference that holds in the second respect, and the case fails because it overlooks the similarity that holds in the first respect.

This pluralistic argument is intended to apply only to secondary values that do indeed give appropriate forms to primary values. In traditions and in conceptions of a good life, there are many secondary values other than these. And this latter type of secondary value has nothing to do with the universal aspect of human nature; it is derived rather from our individuality, from that aspect of our nature which distinguishes us from one another. Part of the reason why so many people find relativism appealing is that they think of this aspect of human beings when they are considering the relativistic case. But if they were to think also of the other aspect, they would find relativism implausible. This is why it is a useful corrective of those enamored of relativism to ask whether their opposition to racism, torture, concentration camps, or nuclear, biological, or chemical warfare is confined only to their own tradition and whether their opposition is meant to appeal only to variable conventions in respect to which different traditions may reasonably hold different views.

The pluralistic view is that in a morally acceptable tradition there must be some deep conventions. What makes them deep is that they protect the minimum requirements of all good lives. Their protection is couched in terms of primary and secondary values, and it is the pursuit and realization of these values that deep conventions are intended to protect. The protection is provided by setting limits that are the most basic and serious limits recognized in that tradition.

THE PROSPECTS FOR MORAL PROGRESS

One of the strengths of monism is that it can give a clear account of what the moral progress of humanity would consist in: it would be the general and widespread realization of whatever the overriding value is. Monism would also permit reasonable judgments about the comparative moral standing of various traditions and conceptions of a good life on the basis of their contribution to the realization of the overriding value. This strength of monism dissipates of course as the existence of overriding values is called into question.

By contrast, one of the weaknesses of relativism is that it cannot draw reasonable moral comparisons among different traditions and conceptions of a good life, because it admits of no context-independent grounds for making such comparisons. As a result, it can perhaps recognize moral progress within traditions and conceptions of a good life, but it cannot answer such questions as, for instance, whether the contemporary Western tradition is morally better or worse than China under Mao, the Soviet Union under Stalin, or Turkey under Ataturk. Or whether the Islamic conception of the good life for women, the Roman one for slaves, or the Nazi one for Untermenschen are better or worse than the ones championed by moderate feminists, civil libertarians, or defenders of human rights.

The question we have to consider now is this: If pluralists reject overriding values, how can they then escape the relativistic incapacity to take account of the obvious fact that some traditions and conceptions of a good life are better than others because they represent moral progress toward a closer approximation of valued possibilities not just from one particular point of view but for humanity as a whole?

The motivation for asking this question is not a whiggish impatience to measure the distance we have traveled toward perfection but to face a serious problem for pluralism. If we give up the idea of overriding values and if we regard all values as conditional, then what ideal could we share that would permit us to say that the lot of humanity has improved or deteriorated compared to what it has been at some other time? And we are not asking this in order to strengthen or weaken some preexisting optimistic or pessimistic opinion. The point is to have some ideal with reference to which we could formulate social or personal policies to make things better or to prevent them from becoming worse.

Pluralists have an answer both on the level of traditions and on the level of individual lives. On the level of traditions, the answer is not couched in terms of some ideal that is supposed to appeal to all reasonable people; that would be a reversion to monism. Rather, the ideal is of a tradition that is as receptive to a plurality of conceptions of a good life as is consistent with the limits needed to maintain the tradition. The ideal is of a framework that fosters the realization of plural, conditional, incompatible, and incommensurable values; it is not the advocacy of some specific value. At the same time, the ideal is incompatible with relativism, because some of the limits the tradition is thought to need to place on the values that may be legitimately pursued under its aegis will be objective and context-independent.

On the level of individual lives, the ideal is to construct for ourselves a reasonable hierarchy of the possibilities we value. The possibilities would normally be derived from our tradition. Our own contribution would be to select some of these possibilities and rank them according to their importance to the kind of life we aspire to living. The ranking of these valued possibilities would be indicated by the strength of the commitments we make to them, ranging from basic commitments to the most important ones, through conditional commitments, to loose commitments to the least strongly held ones. If life were going well for us, we would act according to our commitments; resolve conflicts among values we hold by giving precedence to the more important one, or, if they were equally important, then to the one that was more important as a means to living according to the conception of the good life in the background; and our commitments would be to reasonably valued possibilities, that is, to possibilities within the limits set by deep conventions, suitable to our characters and circumstances, and, taken together, representing a range that was neither impractically wide nor impoverishingly narrow.

If some people lived in this manner for an appropriate period of time—measured in years, not in months or decades—then it is likely that they would have put behind them the agony, the soul searching, the turmoil, the strife within themselves, and the need for constant self-examination involved in trying to decide how they should live. They have decided, they have been living according to their decision, living that way is reasonable, and the life they have imagined as good has indeed turned out to be good. For such people, their conception of a good life has become a second nature. They have identified themselves so completely with their hierarchy of values that what earlier would have seemed to them to be wrenching conflicts now appear to be trifling questions having obvious answers. They can afford to act spontaneously, because the cognitive, emotive, imaginative, and volitional aspects of their character coexist in a state of harmony. Few of us achieve this ideal. But those few who do demonstrate that the ideal is attainable, that, while moral progress toward it involves us in constant conflicts, nevertheless conflicts are not unremovable obstacles to it.

Just as pluralists can make sense of the notion of moral progress on the level of tradition, so they can also do so on the level of individuals. In both cases, the progress is toward an ideal, but the ideal is not a specific value, not even a combination of specific values. The ideal is of a form of life in which the widest possible range of specific values may be pursued.

CONCLUSION

This completes the initial account of the six theses of pluralism. These theses are interdependent and mutually reinforcing, and that is why they had to presented first together, even if only briefly and in outline, before a more detailed account could be given of each. The next step is to give such accounts, by devoting a chapter to each thesis. The step after that is to explore some of the implications of pluralism, understood as the conjunction of these theses.

CHAPTER THREE

The Plurality and Conditionality of Values

> [G]ood is not a general term corresponding to a single Idea.
> —Aristotle, *Nicomachean Ethics*

THIS CHAPTER concentrates on the first thesis of pluralism. It focuses on the distinction between primary and secondary, moral and nonmoral, and overriding and conditional values. By appealing to these distinctions, it also distinguishes among different versions of relativism and shows how one of them is untenable.

PRIMARY AND SECONDARY VALUES

Let us now be more precise about the nature of the values whose plurality and conditionality is one thesis of pluralism. Values in general are understood as benefits whose possession would make a life better than it would be without them and whose lack would make a life worse than it would otherwise be. We may regard something as a value and be mistaken because having it would not improve our lives, nor would its lack affect us adversely. There is a difference, therefore, between something's being a value and something's being valued. The essential point about values, as they are understood here, is that they are connected with benefits and harms. And the reason why we may be mistaken in valuing something is that we may be mistaken about what we regard as beneficial or harmful. The key to understanding values is to understand the benefits and harms with which they are connected as well as the nature of their connections.

To this end, we have distinguished between *primary* and *secondary* values. Primary values are connected with benefits and harms that count as such for all conceptions of a good life, while secondary values have to do with benefits and harms that vary with conceptions of a good life. The idea behind primary values is that human nature dictates that some things will normally benefit all human beings and, similarly, that some things will normally harm everyone. We have referred to these universally human benefits and harms as "primary goods" and "primary evils." Correspondingly, "secondary goods" and "secondary evils" have been taken to refer to benefits and harms that derive their status not from the universal requirements of human nature but from historically, socially, and culturally conditioned conceptions of a good life.

The distinction between primary and secondary values is drawn by appealing to human nature, and we must now clarify what that appeal involves. We are human beings, and thus we are members of the same species. Consequently, there are bound to be many similarities among us, including many things that would be beneficial or harmful for any human being in the normal course of events. Circumstances would have to be exceptional for it not to be harmful for us to be tortured, maimed, or deprived of our legitimate livelihood, and it requires similarly unusual events for physical security, the availability of opportunities, or being justly appreciated not to be beneficial. This is not to say that we can be adequately described in terms of the characteristics we share with others. Individual, social, cultural, and historical differences patently exist among us. But these are differences among human beings, and what makes us human is that in some fundamental ways we are alike. The existence of these ways allows us to speak of human nature.[1]

The description of human nature we are about to give merely repeats what everybody knows anyway. But the repetition has a point because the moral significance of the commonplaces we shall recite tends to be overlooked. Human nature, then, is composed of universally human, culturally invariant, and historically constant characteristics. The obvious place to start looking for them is the human body. Our physiology imposes requirements on all of us: we need to eat, drink, and breathe to survive, and we need protection from the elements; rest and motion, maturing and aging, pleasure and pain, consumption and elimination, and sleep and wakefulness form the rhythm of all human lives; if uninjured, we perceive the world in the same sense modalities, and, within a narrow range, we are capable of the same motor responses. It is part of human nature that all healthy members of our species have many of the same physiological needs and capacities. Can we go beyond these truisms?

We can by noticing that there are also psychological similarities shared by all human beings. The fact is that we want not merely to satisfy our physiological needs by employing our capacities but to do so in particular ways. These ways differ, of course, from person to person, culture to culture, age to age. But there is no difference in the psychological aspiration to go beyond necessity and enjoy the luxury of satisfying our needs in whatever ways happen to count as civilized. We all know the difference between a state of nature characterized by doing what is necessary for

---

[1] Those who like to have evidence for the obvious may find it supplied by Kluckhohn, "Universal Categories of Culture," and by George R. Murdoch, "The Common Denominators of Culture."

survival and a civilized state in which we have leisure, choices, and the security to go beyond necessity. And we all prefer the civilized state to the primitive one. We are also alike in our capacity to learn from the past and plan for the future; we have a view, perhaps never clearly articulated, about what we want to make of our lives. We have desires and aversions, and we try to satisfy the former and avoid the latter. We have the capacity to think, remember, imagine; to have feelings, emotions, moods, motivations; to make efforts, go after what we want, restrain ourselves.

These physiological and psychological needs and capacities will be referred to as "the facts of the self." These facts, however, concern only human agents themselves. We can go still further in describing human nature, because contact with others is also an inevitable feature of human lives. These contacts may be more or less personal; let us begin with more personal ones.

We are born into small human groups, usually families, and we depend on them for the first few years of our lives. We live in a network of close relationships with our parents or guardians, other children, and later with our sexual partners; and we extend our relationships when we enter the larger community of which the small one is a part. We acquire friends and enemies, we cooperate and compete with, look up to, patronize, teach, learn from, imitate, admire, fear, envy, and get angry at people we come to know. We share the griefs and joys of those close to us; we have various positions in life that others recognize; we love and hate others; and we are made happy and sad by them. These are also parts of human nature, and they will be called "the facts of intimacy."

Beyond these are "the facts of social order." Human vulnerability, scarce resources, and limited strength, intelligence, energy, and skill force cooperation on us. Social life exists because only within it can we satisfy our physiological and psychological needs in the ways we want and establish close relationships. The form social life takes is the establishment of some authority, the emergence of institutions and conventional practices, and the slow development and deliberate formulation of rules; all these demand conformity from members of a society. This imposes restrictions on what we can do and provides forms for doing what we want and society allows. Different societies have different authorities, institutions, conventions, and rules. But no society can do without them, and we cannot do without some participation in social life, provided we seek the satisfaction of our physiological and psychological needs.

We have now reached the end of this list of truisms. They allow us to conclude that there is a universal and unchanging human nature. It is composed of the facts of the self, intimacy, and social order. We can now go on and ask what bearing human nature, thus understood, has on good lives. Since morality, in the broad sense, is centrally concerned with living good lives, it is not surprising that understanding human nature is morally important, for it helps us to understand at least some of the things that count as beneficial or harmful for all good lives. And since human nature is composed of some universal characteristics, the understanding we can derive from human nature of the benefits and harms will apply to all human beings. If we have reached the right conclusions about human nature, conclusions sketched in the list of truisms, then we may identify many benefits and harms that will be such for everyone, always, everywhere, in normal circumstances. These are the primary values, including primary goods and primary evils.[2]

The primary goods are the satisfactions of the needs by exercising the capacities included in the description of the facts of human nature. They are universally good, because it is good for all human beings to have the capacity to satisfy and actually to satisfy the physiological and psychological needs just enumerated. For ease of reference, these will be called "the goods of the self." It is also good for everyone to be able to and actually to establish close personal relationships with some other people and thereby enjoy "the goods of intimacy." And it is similarly good for all of us to live in the kind of society in which the enjoyment of these goods is not only possible but welcome, thus to have "the goods of social order." It seems obviously and clearly true that any human life is better if it possesses the goods of the self, intimacy, and social order, and worse if it does not. Since morality aims to foster good lives, it must be committed to fostering conditions in which people can have these primary goods and prohibiting conditions in which people are hindered from having them. We can say, therefore, that the primary goods of the self, intimacy, and social order define the minimum requirements of all conceptions of a good life. They are necessary for good lives, however such lives are conceived, because they are required for the satisfaction of needs that all human beings have due to our shared nature. Primary evils, then, are the frustration of those needs whose satisfaction human nature requires.

Yet, although we can go some way toward understanding the nature of values by understanding human nature, we cannot go very far. For while we can derive from human nature the primary values that constitute one minimum requirement of all conceptions of a good life, not all values are primary. The primary goods and evils of the self, intimacy, and social order do not exhaust the values there are. Various traditions and conceptions of a good life aim at the realization of values that are the products of the particular historical, cultural, and psychological conditions that prevail in those contexts. Furthermore, while human nature makes

---

[2] For similar discussions, see Gewirth, *Reason and Morality*, 2.3, and Rawls, *A Theory of Justice*, chapter 2, par. 15.

it a universal and unchanging truth that it is reasonable to seek the goods of the self, intimacy, and social order and avoid the accompanying evils, these primary values may take different forms in different contexts. There certainly are obvious cultural variations in these matters.

On the other hand, there are no cultural variations in stressing the desirability that people should obtain the primary goods and avoid the primary evils. This is the universal element present in all cultures. Cultural variations concern the conventionally recognized *forms* of primary values. But the variations among these forms, great as they are, do not extend so far as to call into question the truism that one minimum requirement of all good lives is set by primary values. Indeed, the aim of these variable conventional forms is to safeguard that minimum requirement.

For instance, murder, social ostracism, and anarchy are recognized in all traditional contexts as violations of primary values. The variations concern the question of what sort of killing counts as murder, what kind of exclusion constitutes ostracism, and what sort of tearing of the social fabric qualifies as anarchy. The existence of such traditional differences, however, is symptomatic of deeper similarities. For the differences merely betoken different ways of interpreting the same primary values. If the primary values of the self, intimacy, and social order were not appropriately recognized in these different contexts, then there would be no need to interpret them, and hence there would be no scope for differences in their interpretations.

We must acknowledge therefore that in addition to universal primary values, which constitute the minimum requirement of good lives and are derivable from the facts of human nature, there are also secondary values, whose identity depends on variable social and personal circumstances. Good lives depend on both primary and secondary values. Calling them "primary" and "secondary" is not intended to imply that the latter are dispensable. The implication is, first, that secondary values are contingent on the primary ones, and, second, that primary values are the same for everyone, while secondary values vary with traditions and conceptions of a good life.

Let us now consider these implications. One way in which secondary values may be said to be contingent on primary ones is that some secondary values are the particular forms in which primary values are interpreted in some context. For instance, the primary value of the self requires an interpretation that specifies the acceptable forms that pleasure, the satisfaction of physiological needs, and the employment of our capacities may take; the primary value of intimacy must similarly involve the specification of the kinds of sexual practices, child-rearing arrangements, and friendship that are regarded as appropriate; and so also the primary value of social order must be spelled out in terms of concrete institutions, rules, and practices that are customary in particular contexts.

Another way secondary values depend on primary ones is that some secondary values are genuinely new goods, which enrich life by introducing possibilities beyond the minimum requirements of good lives set by primary values. Such secondary values are, for instance, desirable professions, prized talents, the acceptable balance between political involvement and private life, work and leisure, competition and solidarity, independence, creativity, honor, comfort, success, privacy, and so on. These secondary values are also contingent on primary values because their realization is possible only if the minimum requirements of good lives are first satisfied. If people are hunted or starving; if they are deprived of companionship, affection, or the concern and appreciation of others; if they live in a lawless anarchic society, then they must concentrate on survival and on escaping lasting damage, and they will have little time or energy left to seek the enjoyments derivable from leisure, privacy, or the creative participation in art or science. Although the realization of secondary values is contingent on the realization of primary values, this is not to say that good lives are possible without secondary values. For, as we have just seen, secondary values make concrete the primary values and give us possibilities of life beyond the level where only our most elementary needs are satisfied.

This brings us to the second implication of the dependency of secondary values on primary ones: the two kinds of values play different roles in morality in general, in particular traditions, and in individual conceptions of a good life. Morality is found in all societies. One of its chief aims is to define a framework within which individuals may seek to live in accordance with primary and secondary values. Particular traditions go beyond general moral requirements by developing and maintaining a particular framework safeguarding the primary values as well as the particular secondary values recognized in that context. Morality normally appears to us through the mediation of our particular tradition. A tradition contains a much richer inventory of secondary values than any of us can reasonably pursue in a lifetime. We must, therefore, construct for ourselves some conception of a good life out of the primary and secondary values our tradition supplies. This conception will aim to combine in a coherent framework the primary values with such secondary values as we ourselves favor. These secondary values will translate into personal terms some of the secondary values our tradition makes available: the way we earn our living, our political allegiances, our aesthetic sensibility, and our attitudes to sex, having children, social life, and so on. Such a coherent individually constructed framework is a conception of a good life.

As we go from the generalities embodied in morality to the concrete values of individual conceptions of a good life, so the emphasis shifts from universal primary values to traditional and individual secondary values. The former define a grid within which beings like us must endeavor to make a good life for ourselves, while the latter provide the ways in which we individually fill in the grid. Both are necessary for living a good life, but the first must be in place before the second could be.

Moral and Nonmoral Values

Another distinction we have previously introduced is between moral and nonmoral values. The distinction is based on the different sources values have and on who is experiencing the associated benefits and harms. Moral values are humanly caused benefits that human beings provide to others. Nonmoral values are either humanly caused benefits that we secure for ourselves or naturally occurring benefits that we receive or derive from nonhuman sources.

Both moral and nonmoral values allow for harms as well as benefits. This makes it convenient, although awkward, to speak of positive and negative values, or, more naturally, of good and evil. Accordingly, there will be moral goods and evils, as well as nonmoral goods and evils. In both cases, evils are harms inflicted on human beings, but moral evils are harms inflicted by human beings on other human beings, while nonmoral evils are either harms inflicted by us on ourselves or harms produced by nonhuman causes. A full account of moral and nonmoral goods and evils would have to take into account benefits and harms to animals, plants, and perhaps inanimate things, as well as to possible extraterrestrial beings not presently known, but these complications will be ignored here.

By way of illustration, we may say that love and justice are moral goods, and exploitation and torture are moral evils because they involve either benefits or harms we cause to others. Knowledge and the choice of a suitable career for ourselves are nonmoral goods, and self-indulgence and insensitivity to beauty are nonmoral evils, since they are benefits or harms we produce for ourselves. A perfect pitch and well-proportioned bone structure are also nonmoral goods, and genetic defects and crippling diseases are also nonmoral evils, but they are benefits or harms whose sources are not human but naturally occurring.

The distinction between moral and nonmoral values is not intended as a denial of the obvious, and the less obvious, connections between the two kinds of values. Moral values often presuppose nonmoral values, as for instance acting generously presupposes possession of the required resources. Nonmoral values, such as one's choice of profession, often have beneficial and harmful consequences for others. And being lucky or unlucky in our natural circumstances often exerts considerable influence on both the moral and nonmoral values we are capable of enjoying. Also, as with most distinctions, there are inevitable mixed and borderline cases, as well as clear ones. We shall tackle these complications as they arise in the course of the coming discussion.

The distinction between moral and nonmoral values cuts across the distinction between primary and secondary values. Primary and secondary values may each be either moral or nonmoral; likewise, moral and nonmoral values may each be primary or secondary. What makes some moral values primary is that they are benefits and harms human beings cause one another and their status as benefits and harms derives from the universal facts of human nature not from the context of particular traditions or conceptions of a good life. Secondary moral values, then, are still benefits and harms we bestow or inflict on others, but they count as benefits or harms only because a tradition or a conception of a good life makes them so. By contrast, the distinction between primary and secondary nonmoral values rests on benefits and harms that either we provide for ourselves or stem from natural sources, but the primary ones are or ought to be universally recognized as benefits and harms, while the secondary ones are context-dependent.

The following scheme describes these relations graphically:

Values

	Primary	*Secondary*
Moral	universal requirements of all good lives humanly caused and affect others	vary with traditions and good lives humanly caused and affect others
Nonmoral	universal requirements of all good lives humanly caused and affect the agent or naturally occurring	vary with traditions and good lives humanly caused and affect the agent or naturally occurring

None of these four types of values is dispensable for living a good life. The contributions that stem from sources external to the agent are as important as our own efforts are. And enjoying universally human benefits and avoiding harms that are injurious for all human beings are no less necessary than possessing variable benefits and escaping from variable harms.

The substance of the pluralistic claim about the plurality of values is provided, first, by the distinctions between primary and secondary, moral and nonmoral, and naturally occurring and humanly caused values; second, by the diversity of benefits and harms within these different types of values; and third, by the multiplicity of traditions and conceptions of a good life in whose contexts we endeavor to realize these values.

OVERRIDING AND CONDITIONAL VALUES

The plurality of values is a central pluralistic claim, but it is not by any means uniquely pluralistic. Relativists are just as committed to it as pluralists are. What distinguishes them is that relativists conclude that the plurality of values excludes the possibility of the objective justification and criticism of values, while pluralists believe otherwise. Nor need monists reject the plurality of values. They could easily accommodate it, provided they could show that it is possible to impose some authoritative ranking on the plural values we encounter. Such a ranking would have to be objective, in the sense that it would have to be accepted by all reasonable people who were in possession of the relevant information. The possibility of the authoritative ranking of plural values depends on there being some highest value, which we have called in the previous chapter "overriding." Pluralists differ with monists because pluralists deny that any value can be overriding, and they assert, by implication, that all values are conditional. Let us now consider this disagreement in order to arrive at a more precise understanding of the first thesis of pluralism.

A value is overriding if and only if it is

1. the highest, i.e., in conflict with any other value it ought to take precedence over the conflicting value; and
2. universal, i.e., its precedence over any other conflicting value ought to hold for all normal human beings; and
3. permanent, i.e., its precedence over any other conflicting value ought to hold at all times; and
4. invariable, i.e., its precedence over any other conflicting value ought to hold in all contexts; and
5. either absolute, i.e., it ought not to be violated under any circumstances, or prima facie, i.e., it holds normally but may be justifiably violated if and only if the violation is required by the value in general.

If a value is not overriding, then it is conditional. It is in this sense, then, that monists claim that there is at least one overriding value, while pluralists regard all values as conditional.

This account of a value's being overriding is sufficiently broad to include a great variety of conceptions of what the overriding value actually is. It may be the utilitarian ideal of the greatest happiness for the greatest number of people, the Kantian principle of the categorical imperative, the welfare economists' goal of preference satisfaction, the contractarian list of fundamental human rights, a Platonic notion of whatever the Good may be, a Christian commitment to doing the will of God, and so on. Consequently, the overriding value need not be single, for it may actually include some small number of values, it may be some conception of the *summum bonum*, or it may be some principle or procedure by which individual values could be ranked. What matters to a value's being overriding is not so much its identity but its being held to be highest, universal, permanent, invariable, and either absolute or prima facie.

By contrast, if all values were conditional, as pluralists claim, then the commitment to establishing some hierarchical order of precedence among values that would command the allegiance of all reasonable and adequately informed people, regardless of time, place, and context, would have to be abandoned. In that case, there would be no authoritative way of settling conflicts among values, for the status of whatever was being appealed to in settling the conflict would itself be subject to argument. Yet, according to pluralists, this does not lead to the disintegration of morality, because both the conflicts about values and the conflicts about ways of settling conflicts about values could be resolved reasonably. It is just that these reasonable resolutions will not appeal to an overriding value but to historically conditioned traditions and conceptions of a good life that the opposing protagonists share.

This distinction between overriding and conditional values does not, of course, show what needs to be shown, namely, that there are no overriding values. That will be done as the argument progresses. But the direction of the argument should be clear from the overview provided in the previous chapter. The reason for thinking that all values are conditional is that there is a plurality of values, these values conflict, the conflicts are often produced by the incompatibility and incommensurability of values, and it is this kind of conflict that rules out the possibility of there being overriding values. If this line of thought proves successful, it will provide arguments for pluralism and against monism. The dispute between pluralism and monism, however, is left open. Pluralists may go so far in opposing monism as to succumb to relativism. But we are already in a position to show that pluralism is to be preferred over at least one version of relativism.

PLURALISM VERSUS RELATIVISM

We may now put the distinctions we have drawn to use by considering the dispute between pluralists and relativists. Based on the distinction between morality, tradition, and individual conceptions of a good life, we can distinguish between three versions of relativism. In each version, relativists contend that values are context-dependent, but they differ about what the relevant context is. *Radical relativists* take the context to be morality as a whole, and they think that all moral judgments are relative to the particular conception of morality that has emerged in a specific historically, culturally, and socially conditioned setting. *Conventionalists* concede what radical relativists deny, namely, that all reasonable conceptions of morality must recognize that some values are primary and that these values depend on human nature, which sets the minimum requirements for all conceptions of a good life, and not on the beliefs and practices that vary with particular contexts. Conventionalists claim that only secondary values are relative, and they are relative to the conventions of particular traditions. Since some of these conventions prescribe the acceptable interpretations of primary values, conventionalists can recognize the necessity of primary values and still allow for context-dependent variations in their interpretations. *Perspectivism* is an even more moderate version of relativism. It accepts that human nature and traditions require the recognition of both primary and some secondary values, but it holds that what other values are regarded as secondary is relative to the conception of a good life of the agent.

In a summary form, we may say then that radical relativists regard all values as context-dependent; conventionalists accept the universality and objectivity of primary values and regard only secondary values as relative to the context of traditions; and perspectivists go beyond conventionalists in accepting also the objectivity of some secondary values, while regarding only some secondary values as relative to the context of individual conceptions of a good life.

We are now in a better position to appreciate how pluralists can agree with relativists that values are plural and conditional and that there are no overriding values, and yet disagree about the alleged impossibility of reasonably settling conflicts at least about some values. One central contention of pluralists is that although there is no way of specifying in advance what a good reason would be for defeating the claim of any particular value, this most emphatically does *not* mean that there are no ways of deciding whether putative reasons are good. In the first place, it is possible to specify in advance what *type* of reason would be good, even if it is impossible to say in advance what the particular reason of that type would be in a specific situation. One type of good reason for defeating the claim of a particular value is that it is a secondary value whose realization would conflict with the realization of some primary value that is more important than it for all conceptions of a good life. If this is correct, then radical relativism is mistaken, since it denies that there are any values whose importance could be established on context-independent grounds. As we have seen, however, it is implausible to deny this in the case of primary values.

Conventionalists and perspectivists may concede this but go on to argue that the way we decide which value is actually more important depends on the conception we happen to have of a good life. Rorty, for instance, argues, "To say that convictions are only 'relatively valid' might seem to mean that they can only be justified to people who hold certain other beliefs—not to anyone and everyone. But if this were what was meant, the term would have no contrastive force, for there would be no interesting statements which were *absolutely* valid. Absolute validity would be confined to everyday platitudes, elementary mathematical truths, and the like: the sort of beliefs nobody wants to argue about."[3]

The trouble with this argument is that it misses the significance of the "everyday platitudes . . . the sort of beliefs nobody wants to argue about." Such platitudes and beliefs have primary values among their objects, and, as we have seen, primary values constitute one minimum requirement of all conceptions of a good life. For all reasonable conceptions of a good life must recognize the universal human need for the realization of primary values. This being so, we can argue that the goods of the self, intimacy, and social order are normally more important than any of the secondary values, which may indeed vary with traditions and conceptions of a good life. For instance, we can be conventionalists about the forms of killing we recognize as murder or the forms of child rearing we regard as acceptable, but we cannot reasonably deny, as radical relativists mistakenly do, that it is a minimum requirement of all conceptions of a good life that lives must be protected from undeserved destruction or that someone must take responsibility for the raising of children.

This is just the point Walzer, another relativist, fails to recognize: "There is no single set of primary or basic goods conceivable across all moral and material worlds—or, any such set would have to be conceived in terms so abstract that they would be of little use. . . . A single necessary good, and one that is always necessary—food, for example—carries different meanings in different places. Bread is the staff of life, the body of Christ, the symbol of Sabbath, the means of hospitality, and so on. Conceivably, there is a limited sense in which the first of these is primary . . . and even there, we can't be sure. If the religious uses of bread were to

---

[3] Richard Rorty, *Contingency, Irony, and Solidarity*, 47.

conflict with its nutritional uses . . . it is by no means clear which should be primary."[4]

The point rests on the confusion between primary and secondary values. Nutrition is a primary value, while religion is secondary. For nutrition is, and religion is not, among the minimum requirements of all conceptions of a good life. This is compatible with recognizing that there may be occasions on which the claim of some particular form of nutrition, like bread, is defeated by the claim of some particular form of religious observance, like fasting. But the second could defeat the first only in a context where the minimum requirements of the prevailing conceptions of a good life are generally met. For if the claims of nutrition were not generally satisfied, there would be no one left to fast.

Generally speaking, it should be recognized that it could happen in the case of each and every particular primary value that its claim is defeated by appeal to some consideration that would normally be regarded as less important than it. A case can be made for letting some children die (e.g., those suffering from fatal and extremely painful diseases). But the reason why appeal to such cases is misleading is that they are disguised appeals to the same minimum requirements of all conceptions of a good life that the cases were intended to call into question. Letting suffering children die without heroic measures to save them may be reasonable precisely because these unfortunate children cannot have the minimum requirements of all conceptions of a good life.

The argument against radical relativism, therefore, is that there is a type of reason for resolving conflicts between primary and secondary values in favor of the former. For the fact that the claim of a primary value may be reasonably defeated in exceptional cases does not weaken but actually strengthens the reason for it. This is so because both the reason for it and the reason for defeating it appeal to the same consideration, namely, to the respective importance of the conflicting values to conceptions of a good life: those children may be allowed to die who are doomed to live a short life without many of the minimum requirements of a good life. So radical relativists cannot consistently deny that the primary goods of the self, intimacy, and social order are minimum requirements of all good lives by appealing to exceptional cases where the reason for them is defeated.

Moreover, the argument can be carried further to count against conventionalism and perspectivism. For it is not merely possible to specify in advance the primary values that all reasonable traditions and conceptions of a good life must acknowledge to have a reason for protecting; it

[4] Walzer, *Spheres of Justice*, 8.

is also possible for there to be good reasons for attributing to some values a higher status than to others even if the reasons cannot be given in advance. The possibility that should be recognized is that even though there are some reasons that arise only in some particular context, their status as reasons may still be independent of that context. This possibility is that of criticizing or justifying specific traditions and conceptions of a good life not on the ground that they violate or protect the minimum requirements of all conceptions of a good life but on the ground that they are faulty or successful in fostering good lives beyond the minimum level. Such reasons are context-dependent in the sense that they support or call into question secondary values recognized only in some particular contexts, but they are not context-dependent in the sense that they can be acknowledged as reasons only by those who are already committed to the relevant secondary values.

For instance, we can evaluate the comparative merits of two traditions each of which is committed to the primary value of having an institution for adjudicating disputes among its members. If the corresponding secondary value in one tradition is that of reading the entrails of freshly slaughtered cattle, while in the other it is something like the common law, then we can say that in this respect the second tradition is better than the first. And the reason we can give for that judgment is that decisions based on common law are much more likely to take account of the intrinsic merits of the cases presented by the disputing parties than decisions reached by examining the entrails of dead animals. Having a common-law system is certainly not a minimum requirement of all conceptions of a good life, and we do not criticize the entrail-reading system for violating that requirement. The criticism is that one secondary value is actually better than the other for adjudicating disputes. If conventionalism were correct, and our moral judgments necessarily reflected our tradition, then we could not recognize the force of the reason just presented. But, of course, we do recognize it. And we can recognize it because we may not be committed to either procedure for adjudicating conflicts or because we are already committed to the procedure we now judge adversely and self-interest dictates that we improve our tradition if we can.

It may be objected that this is too simplistic a case to make the point that conflicts even about secondary values may be settled reasonably. And it should be acknowledged that many conflicts are much more difficult to approach reasonably than the one just mentioned. But the point of the case was to establish a possibility, not the frequency with which the possibility is realized. The reason for emphasizing the possibility is to show that conventionalism is mistaken in so far as it is committed to denying the possibility.

We found two initial reasons for pluralism and one each against radical relativism and conventionalism. The first is that since radical relativists cannot, and pluralists can, recognize that some conflicts among values can be reasonably resolved by appealing to the context-independent ground provided by the minimum requirements of all conceptions of a good life, pluralism is to be preferred. The second is that even conflicts among secondary values may be open to reasonable resolution, because different traditions often prize some of the same values and one tradition may be better at achieving a shared value than the other. To the extent that conventionalists deny this possibility while pluralists acknowledge it, pluralism has the stronger case.

It has to be emphasized, however, that these are only initial arguments against radical relativism and conventionalism. That all reasonable traditions must recognize the primary values whose realization constitutes the minimum requirements of all good lives does tell against radical relativism, which regards all values as based on context-dependent judgments. But conventionalism, which grants the universality of primary values and insists only on the relativity of secondary values, is untouched by this objection. The second objection is directed against conventionalism, but it remains inconclusive until the possibility of the reasonable resolution of conflicts among traditions is translated into actuality.

This still leaves perspectivism, the version of relativism that is closest to pluralism. Perspectivists and pluralists agree about the context-independence of primary values and about the possibility of there being reasonable resolution of conflicts between secondary values that play pivotal roles in competing moral traditions. They disagree about the prospects of reasonable conflict-resolution regarding secondary values that occur in the context of different conceptions of a good life. Perspectivists deny that these kinds of conflicts can be resolved on rational grounds, while pluralists claim that some of these conflicts can be so resolved. The discussion of this disagreement must be postponed, however, until chapter 8, by which point the ground will have been laid for it.

In the meantime, two conclusions follow. First, radical relativism is mistaken. Second, if relativism takes the form of conventionalism or perspectivism and claims only that different traditions and conceptions of a good life may involve commitments to secondary values, then there may be no substantive disagreement between pluralists, on the one hand, and conventionalists and perspectivists, on the other. Whether or not there is such a disagreement depends on whether or not defenders of these versions of relativism agree with pluralists about the possibility that the conflicting evaluations can be justified or criticized by reasons whose force does not depend on the evaluations themselves.

CHAPTER FOUR

The Unavoidability of Conflicts

> [T]he optimistic view . . . that all good things must be compatible, and that therefore freedom, order, knowledge, happiness . . . must be at least compatible, and perhaps even entail one another in a systematic fashion . . . is perhaps one of the least plausible beliefs ever entertained by profound and influential thinkers.
>
> —Isaiah Berlin, "From Hope and Fear Set Free"

ONE OF THE AIMS of the previous chapter was to make more precise the first thesis of pluralism about the plurality and conditionality of values. We have seen that values may be naturally occurring and humanly caused, moral and nonmoral, primary and secondary. We have also seen that there is a context-independent reason why primary values should normally take precedence over secondary values if they come into conflict with each other. The reason is that the realization of secondary values is contingent on the realization of primary values. As a result, we could show that radical relativism was mistaken, because it denied that there were context-independent grounds for resolving conflicts between any values.

The resolution of conflicts between primary and secondary values, however, does not resolve all conflicts between values. For conflicts may occur between different types of primary values as well as between different types of secondary values. One purpose of this chapter is to consider these remaining conflicts as well as the second rival of pluralism: monism. Monism is the view that *all* moral conflicts can be resolved on the basis of an overriding value whose authority all reasonable people should recognize. According to pluralists, however, there are no overriding values, so we must also discuss here this disagreement between monism and pluralism.

THE INCOMPATIBILITY AND INCOMMENSURABILITY OF VALUES

Let us begin by noting how very often we encounter conflicts in our everyday experience. It is a common occurrence that we want to enjoy two different things we regard as good, but we must choose between them, because if we have one we cannot have the other. We cannot live an independent, unencumbered, self-reliant life in which we are accountable only to ourselves and have a large family and a close marriage. Being ambitious, striving for success, and having committed oneself to some discipline, profession, or institution cannot coexist with maintaining the bemused, distant, uninvolved perspective of an observer. Life in politics does not go with a life of contemplation and privacy. A risk-taking adventurous life excludes the peace of mind that derives from cautiously cherishing what one has. Breadth and depth, freedom and equality, solitude and public spiritedness, good judgment and passionate involvement, love of comfort and love of achievement, ambition and humility coexist in a state of tension, and the more we have of one, the less we can have of the other.

These conflicts are not due to unfortunate circumstances pitting normally composable values against each other. It is not as if we had to choose between our money and our life at the behest of an armed robber. For there is no reason inherent to life and money that would prevent one from having both. But conflicts among many other values are intrinsic to the conflicting values themselves, and so we simply have to choose between many values. The choice need not be all-or-none; we can compromise and try to strike a balance. Whatever we do, however, it remains a fact of human life that as we seek one of two conflicting values, so we must put up with missing out on the other.

The sense of loss, therefore, is a frequent experience in our lives. It need not be due to having made a choice that we come to regret. For we can feel that we have lost something important even if we are convinced that we have made the right choice and that we would make it again if we had to. If the loss is accompanied by regret, the regret is about life's being such as to exclude the realization of all the values we prize.[1] But the ubiquitous conflicts we experience are not only on account of goods, for evils also conflict. It frequently happens that we are confronted with having to choose between courses of action that morality prohibits. Overall commitment to a good life often requires us to choose the lesser of two evils. Nevertheless, the choice is still between evils. We can hide the incompetence of an unfortunate colleague, or we can worsen his misfortune; we can hypocritically defend our friend's inexcusable conduct, or we can cause her downfall; we can sacrifice innocent people for the common good, or we can worsen the conditions on which depends

---

[1] Conflict and consequent loss is a constant theme in the writings of pluralists. For some examples, see Hampshire, *Morality and Conflict*, chapters 6 and 7, and Stocker, *Plural and Conflicting Values*, chapters 4, 6, and 8.

the welfare of people we are committed to protecting; we can lower the standards by which performance is judged and thereby betray our responsibility, or we can uphold the standards but endanger the context in which the standards may prevail; we can collaborate with unsavory people in power, or we can withdraw and thereby remove yet another curb on their power.[2]

In each of these situations, choice forces on us a normally immoral course of action. We may claim that what we have done was the best under the wretched circumstances, yet the burden of having violated our moral convictions has still to be borne, although it may be lightened somewhat by the context in which the violation has occurred. We would think ill of people who did not have scruples about doing the normally immoral thing they resolved they had to do. We may understand why Truman decided to drop the bomb on Hiroshima, but we may think that it was either reprehensibly callous not to lose a night's sleep over it, as he is reported to have said, or we shall attribute the claim to braggadocio.

Part of the reason why pluralists are so interested in conflicts is that they think that conflicts are strongly confirmatory evidence for the plurality and conditionality of values. The best explanation of these conflicts is that the conflicting plural and conditional values are incompatible and incommensurable.

The incompatibility of values is partly due to qualities intrinsic to the conflicting values. Because of these qualities, some values are so related as to make living according to one totally or proportionally exclude living according to the other. Habitual gourmandizing and asceticism are totally incompatible, while a lifelong commitment to political activism and solitude are proportionally so. The incompatibility of values, therefore, derives at least in part from the nature of the values, rather than from our attitude toward them. For the favorable attitude of some people toward both of the incompatible values does not make them compatible. Their compatibility depends also on whether or not the intrinsic qualities of the values exclude each other. But the intrinsic qualities of some values are only partly responsible for their incompatibility. Another part is contributed by human nature. It is only for beings like us that the intrinsic qualities of some values are incompatible. If gourman-

---

[2] Much has been written recently about such conflicts under the description of moral dilemmas or situations involving dirty hands, a name derived from Sartre's play of the same name. See the anthology of representative writings and bibliography in Gowans, *Moral Dilemmas*, as well as Sinnott-Armstrong, *Moral Dilemmas*, and Stocker, *Plural and Conflicting Values*, chapters 1 and 2.

dizing did not give us pleasure, it would not be incompatible with asceticism. And if split personalities were normal for us, then we could combine solitude and political activism.

It is worth noting, if only in passing, that the incompatibility of values, created by the conjunction of qualities intrinsic to them and qualities intrinsic to human nature, constitutes a further reason for regarding at least some values as objective. For their incompatibility shows that prizing them is not merely a matter of having a favorable attitude toward them but that we prize them also because our favorable attitudes are toward qualities intrinsic to the values which it is reasonable or unreasonable for beings like us to prize.

The idea expressed by incommensurability is that two or more values are incommensurable if and only if[3]

1. there is not some one type of highest value or combination of values in terms of which all other values can be evaluated by considering how closely they approximate it (for instance, happiness is not such); and
2. there is not some medium in terms of which all the different types of values can be expressed and ranked without any significant aspects left out, thus allowing for the intersubstitutivity of different types of values (for instance, not all values can be expressed and ranked in terms of preference satisfaction); and
3. there is not some one principle or some principles that can provide an order of precedence among all values and be acceptable to all reasonable people (for instance, duties do not always take precedence over the general welfare and *vice versa*).

We may express this by saying that the denial of incommensurability is the denial of (1) a summum bonum, (2) the fungibility of values, and (3) a canonical principle for ranking values. In arguing for incommensurability, pluralists are committed to the conjunction of (1), (2), and (3), while monists must show that (1), (2), or (3) fails to hold.

It is crucial to understand that what incommensurability excludes is the possibility of ranking values which meets two requirements: the ranking must be based on characteristics intrinsic to the values being ranked, and the ranking has to be acceptable to all reasonable people. Meeting the first requirement without the second would lead to question-begging comparisons, for it would assume that a certain ranking of values is the reasonable one, when that is precisely at issue. We may compare the value of telling a painful truth to a friend with the value of our friend's

---

[3] This account is indebted to Williams, "Conflicts of Values," 77–80, on which it draws but from which it also departs.

happiness by asking which would give more pleasure. But of course whether pleasure is an appropriate basis of comparison is an open question.

Similarly, meeting the second requirement without the first would also fail to yield what we need. For even if, unlikely as it is, all reasonable people agreed to a particular ranking of two values, their agreement may merely betoken a universally held human attitude that may be independent of the respective intrinsic merits of the values in question. We may all think that when push comes to shove, justice is more important than mercy, and we may all be mistaken. In asserting the incommensurability of values, pluralists deny that both requirements could be met simultaneously.

What makes this serious from the moral point of view is that it often happens that incommensurable values are also incompatible and conflicting. That is, the values about whose ranking reasonable people disagree may also be values that reasonable people want to realize but cannot because the values totally or proportionally exclude each other. It is thus the coincidence of the incommensurability and incompatibility of conflicting values that creates what pluralists regard as an unavoidable feature of our moral life and that monists refuse to accept as such.

What reasons are there, then, for the pluralistic claim about the incompatibility and incommensurability of values? The first reason derives from the nature of some conflicts among values. If values were not incompatible and incommensurable, then all conflicts among values should have a decisive resolution, because reasonable people would recognize that the higher of the conflicting values is better and should be preferred. But, then, it would be unreasonable to feel a sense of loss or regret on account of having missed out on the lesser value. If, say, we thought that all values derived from whatever they contributed to happiness, then we would simply choose the value that gave more happiness, and we would not regret having foregone lesser happiness, since what we want is greater happiness. Similarly, if there were a medium, such as money, for comparing all values, then by finding ourselves willing to pay more for one than for the other, we should have no qualms about having gotten the one for which we were prepared to pay more. And lastly, if we really believed in some principle for ranking values—for instance, the principle that duty comes first, then honor, and then country—then it would be a sign of infirm conviction to regret that honor requires us to tell some painful truth about our country. It may be sad that there is a painful truth to tell, but we could not reasonably regret telling it if we really thought that honor required it.

But this is not how we respond to the conflicts we encounter. We do not believe that by choosing the better of two conflicting values we are somehow compensated for the loss of the other. The explanation that makes the best sense of our disbelief and of the experience of loss and regret even about some of our most eminently reasonable choices is that values are incompatible and incommensurable. That is why the choice of one value may go hand in hand with our realistic estimate that it is unfortunate that we had to forego the other.

The second reason has to do with the historical failures of the numerous attempts to establish the compatibility and commensurability of values. More will be said about these failed attempts later in this chapter. But there is a general point that counts against all of them, and we should take notice of it here. This point is that pluralists may reasonably accept theories that advocate ranking values on the basis of how closely they conform to some one type of value, or on the basis of their worth expressed in terms of some medium of exchange, or on the basis of their standing given some canonical principle. What pluralists are committed to denying is that such theories could do justice to all the different types of values there are. We can decide to resolve conflicts by accepting the authority of some principle embodied in a theory. Such decisions however are themselves evaluative because they exclude or demote values that fail to conform to the accepted authority. Theories of this sort are moral not simply in the sense that they have good lives as their subject matter but in the further sense that they represent attempts to promote one conception of a good life over others. There need be nothing wrong with this, for it may be reasonable to accept such a theory. Whatever can be said for a theory of this sort, however, it cannot be used as an argument against pluralism. For what such a theory does is to recommend a particular ranking of incompatible, incommensurable, and conflicting values as a way of resolving their conflicts. Consequently, the theory cannot possibly supply a reason for thinking that there are no incompatible, incommensurable, and conflicting values. Indeed, if there were no values of this sort, values whose conflicts were recalcitrant, one main reason for needing moral theories would disappear.

The third reason is suggested by the facts of moral life sketched earlier. We can adduce these facts more systematically here by remembering that there are different types of primary values—of the self, intimacy, and social order—as well as different types of secondary values. We have seen that reason dictates that conflicts between primary and secondary values should normally be resolved in favor of the former. But there are also conflicts between different types of primary values and different types of secondary values. And more: there are different types of values *within* these types of primary and secondary values, and they may also conflict.

Let us take conflicts among primary values first. It is one of the commonest experiences in each of our lives that the values of the self conflict with the values of social order. The desire to have much of what we like and little of what we dislike—a value of the self—often clashes with the desire for a stable and secure political system—a value of social order. The love we feel for some other person—a value of intimacy—is frequently at odds with the realization of the values of the self that self-interest dictates. Following the rules of institutions—a value of social order—on many occasions requires us to act contrary to the interests of some person to whom we are intimately tied and whose welfare is for us among the values of intimacy. Duty, sacrifice, self-denial, discipline, restraint, punishment, guilt, shame, and remorse are familiar moral experiences caused on countless occasions by finding ourselves in the position of having to choose among conflicting values. Because the choice is hard, we need to steel ourselves to making it, and we blame ourselves if we make it badly.

The situation is similar with secondary values. The different types of values that are peculiar to various traditions and conceptions of a good life routinely conflict. The local interpretations of the demands of criminal and civil law, taxation, prosperity, distributive justice, foreign policy, and public health continually interfere with each other and force us to alter our sexual inclinations, financial status, personal relationships, career choices, and religious practices.

Furthermore, conflicts occur not only among different types of values but also among values of the same type. The feelings of love we have toward sexual partners, parents, children, siblings, and friends do not always coexist in a happy state of equilibrium. We feel jealous, we have a limited capacity for love, the concentration on a person love demands of us becomes less intense the more people we love, so often not all the claims of all of our loves can be simultaneously satisfied. Or take pleasure as another example. It is certainly one of the values we all prize. But the pleasure of sex is not the pleasure of chamber music, the pleasure of being given one's due is different from the pleasure of solving a difficult chess problem, and the pleasure of anticipation is quite unlike the pleasure taken in natural beauty. And, of course, we continually have to choose between these and other kinds of pleasure. Conflicts indicate, therefore, not merely that there may not be a common measure uniting various types of primary and secondary values but also that the same types of values may be incompatible.

CONFLICTS

There is general agreement among pluralists that conflicts between incompatible and incommensurable values are unavoidable features of moral life.[4] But there is no general agreement about what we can do to resolve them. Some pluralists write as if they believe that many conflicts are unresolvable;[5] others, while insisting on the unavoidability of conflicts, think that most conflicts are resolvable.[6] The present account is of this latter kind. For the sake of clarity, therefore, let us separate two considerations: the nature of the conflicts whose occurrence is common ground among pluralists and the resolvability of conflicts about which pluralists differ. The first will be discussed now; the second in the next chapter.

We may begin then with the following formal characterization of the relevant type of conflicts: two values, V_1 and V_2, conflict if there is a person, P, and

1. V_1 and V_2 are incompatible; and
2. V_1 and V_2 are incommensurable; and
3. P wants V_1; and
4. P wants V_2.

To make the formal account concrete, let V_1 be a life in politics and V_2 be solitude, or V_1 be a skeptical disposition and V_2 be a passionate commitment to a cause. This account of the relevant type of conflicts must be understood in the light of several clarifications.

To keep the discussion simple, it is assumed that the conflicts hold between only two values. More complicated forms of conflict may occur among three or more values. Furthermore, the conflicts are relativized

---

[4] For example, "[H]uman goals are many, not all of them commensurable, and in perpetual rivalry with one another" (Berlin, "Two Concepts of Liberty," 131). "Our everyday and raw experience is conflict between contrary moral requirements at every stage of almost everyone's life" (Hampshire, "Morality and Conflict," 142). "Human beings are subject to moral . . . claims of very different kinds. . . . Conflicts between [them] . . . cannot . . . be resolved by subsuming either point of view under the other, or both under a third. Nor can we simply abandon any of them" (Nagel, "The Fragmentation of Values," 134). "[I]t is unrealistic to suppose that all our differences are rooted in ignorance and perversity, or else in the rivalries that result from scarcity. . . . [D]eep and unresolvable differences on matters of fundamental importance . . . [are] a permanent condition of human life" (Rawls, "Kantian Constructivism in Moral Theory," 542). "[V]alue-conflict is . . . something necessarily involved in human values, and to be taken as central by any adequate understanding of them" (Williams, "Conflicts of Values," 72).

[5] Berlin, *Four Essays on Liberty*, Hampshire, *Morality and Conflict*, and Williams, "Conflicts of Values," represent this tendency.

[6] Brandt, *A Theory of the Good and the Right*, Oakeshott, *Rationalism in Politics* and *On Human Conduct*, and Stocker, *Plural and Conflicting Values*, are accounts of this sort.

to persons but not to any particular person. Conflicts are conflicts *for* persons. If there were no persons, or perhaps no beings sufficiently like persons, then conflicts would not occur. The source of conflicts, therefore, is not merely the incommensurability and incompatibility of the values but that beings like us try to realize the values together.

The recognition that conflicts occur partly because the conflicting values are valued by some person should be accompanied by the acknowledgment that we undoubtedly make mistakes in what we value, and some conflicts may be resolved by correcting such mistakes. But the conflicts that are of central interest to pluralists concern truly valuable and rightly wanted values, and yet conflicts show that we cannot have them together. The difficulty is not in the values nor in our having a misguided attitude toward them but in the conjunction of the right attitude directed toward the right value and the human situation.

The formal characterization offered above is not intended as an account of all types of conflicts. Duties, rules, principles, and pleasures may and do conflict with each other, but many of their conflicts are irrelevant to the present discussion. Such conflicts are often resolvable by simply determining which of the conflicting items has the stronger claim on one. And the determination involves no theoretical problems if the conflict occurs among commensurable values of the same kind. The duty to save a life is normally stronger than the duty to tell the truth; the rule to drive safely may be broken in an emergency; the pleasure of a young Burgundy is obviously less preferable than the pleasure of a properly aged one; and blood may rightly count for more than water. It is essential to understanding the kinds of conflicts that concern pluralists that the conflicting values are both incompatible and incommensurable. They are related in being both valued, in its being totally or proportionally impossible to realize them together, and in there being no basis on which their intrinsic merits could be compared.

There are further conflicts to which the formal characterization is not meant to apply. Conflicts often occur between two people who want something they value but which only one of them can have, such as a job; or who disagree about some moral issue, like abortion; or who rank differently the same value, for instance, prosperity. Such conflicts turn into the kind that concerns us only if they involve not one value but two or more, and they are incommensurable and incompatible. Nor is it of interest to pluralists *qua* pluralists that people often experience conflicts between what they recognize as their obligation and some tempting alternative to it. If they are conscientious, they will honor their obligation; if they are morally committed but weak, they will succumb and come to feel guilt or shame; or they may not care much about morality, and then they will ignore their obligation. But these conflicts need not show that there are incommensurable and incompatible values in the background; they are caused by insufficiently strong commitment to what ought to be valued.

Another type of conflict that is irrelevant to pluralism is between various means that may be adopted for realizing a value. Some means may be morally or otherwise better than others, or it may be unclear how to evaluate them. Yet, if the choice of method does not hinge on incommensurable and incompatible values, such conflicts have no theoretical import for pluralism. Conflicts may also occur between individuals and institutions. Individuals may think that some institution is committed to mistaken values, or institutions may evaluate individuals adversely. These conflicts, however, need not involve incommensurable and incompatible values; and while they are often deeply serious, they do not affect the issue that separates pluralists from both monists and relativists.

Yet, even after we exclude as irrelevant these types of conflicts, a good many remain. The values that may conflict in the required manner may be different types of secondary values; different types of primary values; and both may involve both moral and nonmoral values. (But the conflict between primary and secondary values is normally not like this, for primary values are presupposed by secondary ones, and thus they normally take precedence over them.) Moreover, the conflicts may occur not only among these different types of values but also among values of the same type. Once we distinguish between different types of values, it becomes obvious how great is the scope for conflicts among them.

These manifold conflicts are primarily conflicts experienced by individual moral agents. And the conflicts confront us in concrete terms. If I want to have a lucrative job and the freedom to dispose of my time but cannot have them both, what should I do? If the institution to which I feel allegiance is corrupted and undermines its own standards, should I opt for the standards or for the institution? If my friend champions an unjust cause, is it friendship or justice that should prevail? In such conflicts, we, as individuals, must choose between two incommensurable and incompatible values both of which we prize.

These concrete and individual conflicts often occur because of an unlucky combination of circumstances, character, and commitments. The conflicts are conflicts for a particular person in a particular situation, while other people in the same situation would face no conflict. This is not because the others are remiss, but because they attach different importance to those same values. But not all conflicts are like this. It also happens quite frequently that in a particular tradition certain types of conflicts are routine. If the conventions of a tradition favor incommensurable and incompatible values, like law-abidingness and the authority of private conscience, then people living in that tradition will regularly encounter conflicts between the conventionally favored values. These conflicts, however, will be due to individuals' having committed themselves to the conventions of their tradition. And since these conventions favor conflicting *types* of values, individuals living in that tradition will encounter concrete conflicts among particular instances of these conflicting types of values.

Conflicts on the personal level, therefore, are typically concrete and particular; while conflicts on the social level are usually more abstract and concern types of values. On the individual level, the resolution of conflicts depends on ordering one's commitments. On the social level, conflict-resolution requires ordering the prevailing conventions. An ordered set of commitments is a conception of a good life, while an ordered set of conventions is a tradition. A conception of a good life aims at living according to one's commitments. A tradition aims at creating a framework of conventionally defined possibilities and limits within which individuals can attempt to live according to their commitments.

THE FIRST VERSION OF MONISM: A SUMMUM BONUM

We shall consider three versions of monism. Each denies the incompatibility and incommensurability of conflicting values, but each denies it for a different reason. For each version, however, the strongest reply monists can make to the pluralistic argument is to concede the facts the arguments are based on and deny that their significance is as pluralists suppose. Monists can accept, therefore, that moral conflicts often occur, that moral theories cannot consistently deny conflicts and propose ways of resolving them, and that moral agents routinely feel loss and regret even about the best choices they have made in various conflict situations. What monists need to go on to do is to offer a better explanation of these facts than pluralists can. If the conflicts are not due to incompatible and incommensurable values then what is responsible for them?

Perhaps the historically most-favored monistic explanation is to attribute conflicts to human imperfections and not to the incompatibility and incommensurability of values. Let us refer to this as the *Platonic explanation*, in recognition of its first systematic defender. According to this version of monism, there exists a summum bonum, which Plato called the "Form" or the "Idea of the Good." The aim of morality, its *telos*, is to approximate as closely as possible the Form of the Good. Virtues are character traits that make it possible for moral agents to engage in its pursuit, and particular values are valuable to the extent to which they partake in the Form of the Good.[7] The Form of the Good sets the standard with reference to which the claims of all particular values must be evaluated.[8]

"The point of having such a theory is not at all hard to see. It is one way of trying to avoid the possibility of conflict in practical reasoning. As we know, conflicts arise if we recognize the claims on us of irreducibly different notions of goodness. . . . But Plato tries . . . to show how we can resolve real or apparent conflicts between seemingly different types of goodness . . . by understanding what the Good is. . . . [A]s Plato views the matter, the proper activity of reason is to be explained as its correct apprehension of the Good and the use of this apprehension . . . when we wish to understand fully how to live and act."[9]

The Platonic explanation can thus acknowledge the occurrence of conflicts and our sense of loss and regret without having to admit the incompatibility and incommensurability of values. For conflicts and many of our reactions to them betoken human imperfections rather than tell against there being a summum bonum. If we were more reasonable in our efforts to try to understand the summum bonum or in our attempts to put our understanding into practice, then conflicts would not occur or would occur much less frequently, and we would not have to accommodate our reactions to them.

The strategy behind this monistic argument is to look at how the world appears to human observers and then argue that appearances are deceptive. Beyond the apparent disorder we experience, there is a moral order. The task of reason is to discern it, and, although it is unclear how far we can go in this direction, we can clearly do better than we commonly do. And the better we do, the fewer conflicts we shall have to face. Thus the Platonic explanation presupposes a metaphysical theory about the nature of reality as it exists beyond how it appears to human observers. Whether the moral order is an intrinsic property of reality, as Plato and his Greek followers thought, or was created by God, as Christian neo-Platonists supposed, makes no difference to the general point that there is a summum bonum, and when we fail to apprehend it because we

---

[7] Plato, *Republic*, 504–9. See also Ross's comment on this passage in his *Plato's Theory of Ideas*, 39–44.

[8] "It is reasonable to offer a teleological explanation of some or all of the facts of nature if we believe either in a benevolent Governor of the universe or in a nisus in natural objects towards the good. But a teleological explanation of the world of Ideas is in a different position. Ideas are not changeable things, plastic to the will of a Governor; they are standards to which a Governor of the universe must conform" (Ross, *Plato's Theory of Ideas*, 40–41).

[9] Nicholas White, *Plato's Republic*, 46–47.

are misled by appearances, or when we fail to act according to it because the nonrational part of our makeup leads us astray, then we are at fault. Hence the Platonic answer to pluralists is that the incompatibility and incommensurability of values is only apparent, while the summum bonum is real.

The pluralistic rejoinder is to call into question the metaphysical theory presupposed by the Platonic explanation. The objection to it is the familiar Kantian argument against all transcendental metaphysical theories. We have reason to believe only those factual statements for which we can have evidence, and the only kind evidence we can have must ultimately rest on observation. Observation may be by the unaided senses or by sophisticated scientific instruments, but unless a factual belief ultimately has an actual or possible observational basis, it cannot be reasonably held. What makes some metaphysical theories transcendental is precisely their claim to have gone beyond the sorts of factual beliefs for which it is possible to have observational evidence. They are theories about facts that are supposed to exist beyond the world to which sense experience and scientific investigation could give us access. And an unanswerable question confronts all such attempts at transcending observational evidence: What reason could there be for accepting factual statements that in principle cannot be supported by any actual or possible observational evidence? Since we are human, we are necessarily confined to the only world we can know, the world that the Platonic explanation regards as the world of appearances. Even if there were a world beyond it, we could not possibly know anything about it, not even that it exists, so the Platonic explanation, having presupposed a transcendental metaphysical theory, has given no good reason for believing that there is a summum bonum.

Suppose, however, that we attempt to hold the Platonic explanation by jettisoning its indefensible metaphysical commitment. We may, then, claim that there is a summum bonum in the world we know, and it is the insufficiency of our reasoning ability that prevents us from recognizing and acting according to it.

The trouble with this line of defense is that it is vitiated by the recalcitrance of the moral conflicts we encounter. It may be that these conflicts are not due to the incompatibility and incommensurability of values, but why should we think that? What reason is there for distrusting appearances in this case? Why should we reject the thoughtful testimony of millions of apparently reasonable people, including ourselves, that they, and we, often want to realize two values but the nature of these values is such that they cannot be realized together? Why should we doubt this evidence that comes from the contexts of radically different societies separated by vast historical, cultural, environmental, and psychological differences? There does not appear to be a convincing answer.

Before we leave behind this version of monism for less indefensible ones, we should consider a contemporary defense of a closely allied position.[10] It rests on a distinction, derived from Aquinas, between primary and secondary moral conflicts. Primary conflicts arise if some moral theory has among its fundamental principles any two that prescribe actions aiming simultaneously at incompatible and incommensurable values. Since such actions cannot be performed, a moral theory that requires performing them is inconsistent, and it should be rejected. But moral theories can consistently allow for secondary conflicts. Such conflicts occur not because the principles prescribe the pursuit of incompatible and incommensurable values but because the context in which we have to act is immoral. A context of immorality is, tautologically, characterized by the breakdown of morality, so it is not surprising that under such conditions conflicts arise to which moral principles suggest no morally acceptable resolution. A monistic theory, therefore, can defend the existence of a summum bonum and allow for secondary conflicts, which are attributable to our immorality much the same way as the Platonic explanation attributed conflicts to our unreasonability.

However, there are two previously considered reasons for rejecting this ingenious defense. The first is that it assumes the already discredited claim that contrary to common experience values do not conflict with each other or that they would not conflict with each other were it not for human imperfections. In this respect, the present defense fails for the same reason as the Platonic one, of which it is, in any case, but a variant. The second reason against it is that it perpetuates the confusion between the incompatibility and incommensurability of values on the one hand, and the supposed irresolvability of conflicts, on the other. Moral theories can propose principles for resolving conflicts and even be successful in doing so, while values can still be incompatible and incommensurable. In fact, proposing such principles is one main task of moral theories. The resolvability of conflicts, however, leaves unaffected the question of whether the conflicts were due to incompatible and incommensurable values. For the resolution of conflicts may involve merely shaping our attitudes to the conflicts without taking account of the values whose nature causes the conflicts. So even if this argument were correct, it would still not show that pluralists are wrong in attributing many conflicts to the presence of incompatible and incommensurable values.

---

[10] See Donagan, "Consistency in Rationalist Moral Systems."

THE SECOND VERSION OF MONISM: THE FUNGIBILITY
OF VALUES

This version of monism rejects the claim that there is no medium in terms of which different types of values could be compared. According to monists of this persuasion, values are not incompatible and incommensurable, because they can be ranked by substituting for them equivalent units of some medium. The number of units provides a common measure, and conflicts can be resolved by counting the units. The intuitive notion behind this claim is that as commercial value is expressible in terms of money, so moral values are also expressible in terms of an analogous medium. The question is: What is that medium?

One historical answer was provided by the hedonistic utilitarianism of Bentham. According to it, the medium is pleasure, and the notorious hedonistic calculus was supposed to allow us to figure out how much pleasure is provided by various values. The more pleasure a value yields, the better it is, and the comparison between any two values is simply a matter of calculating their comparative pleasure quotients. Thus "quantity of pleasure being equal, pushpin is as good as poetry."

The crudeness of this view is obvious. It fails to recognize that pleasures differ not only in quantity but also in quality: the amount of pleasure we derive from some value is indeed relevant to how much we value it, but a small amount of pleasure of one kind may outweigh a great amount of pleasure of another kind; whether we have a sufficient variety of different kinds of pleasure also affects how valuable we think a particular pleasure is; we enjoy pleasures, which are not worth valuing; and there are many things other than pleasure, which we regard as having value. We cannot therefore reasonably compare conflicting values merely on the basis of the quantity of pleasures derivable from them. Nevertheless, it is instructive to begin our examination of this version of monism with Bentham's view, because its defects force monists in a particular, and, as we shall see, ultimately indefensible, direction.

John Stuart Mill improved on Bentham's position by recognizing that pleasures differ also in quality. He insisted that there are higher and lower pleasures, and thus he was committed to denying that there could be the sort of moral arithmetic that Bentham aimed at establishing by his hedonistic calculus. This is a familiar story, and there is no need to belabor it. It is somewhat less familiar, however, that Mill's position required him to provide an alternative to Bentham's way of comparing pleasures. Whatever were the faults of Bentham's way, it had the great virtue of aiming to be an objective, impersonal system of comparison. But, as a result of Mill's alternative—the recognition of higher and lower pleasures—the stress on objectivity and impersonality is greatly weakened. For, as Mill saw, there were individual differences about what pleasures were higher and lower and about when a higher pleasure counted for more than a lower one. As a way of resolving these differences, he suggested that we should rely on the judgments of those who have experienced both pleasures. He was thus forced to move away from Bentham's objective and impersonal comparisons toward comparisons based on the more subjective and personal judgments of individuals in possession of certain kinds of experiences.

Mill did not go far enough, in offering this proposal, to consider how disagreements among the appropriately qualified people could be resolved; when the judgments of these people were based on experiences of adequate length, frequency, and prior education to make them reliable; or how differences in taste, inclination, and capacity for intellectual, emotional, and imaginative appreciation could be eliminated from their judgments. Consequently, while Mill may have provided a way in which some people could reasonably resolve conflicts among values in their own cases, he has not shown why other people should regard those conflict-resolutions as reasonable for themselves.

It is important to see that Mill's point would not be appreciably strengthened even by the unlikely event that the properly qualified people were always unanimous in their judgments about which values gave more of the higher pleasures. For their unanimity could simply be due to talents and education that the qualified people shared and others lacked. And if so, it would be false to say that those who lacked the wherewithal to enjoy some higher pleasures would be better off if they accepted the unanimous judgments of the talented and the educated. We may still wish to say that they ought to accept such judgments, but the reason for that cannot be that it would enable those who lack the requisite talents and education to enjoy more of the higher pleasures, since, lacking those talents, they cannot do so.

Moreover, these difficulties in the way of Mill's attempt to provide a medium for ranking qualitatively different values are compounded by the further difficulty that there are many values in addition to those involved in a balanced mixture of higher and lower pleasures. Doing one's unpleasant duty at great cost to oneself, refusing pleasures on principled grounds, telling the disillusioning truth and thereby diminishing people's happiness, not acquiescing in some pleasure-increasing course of action on account of its reprehensibility may all, on occasion, be of value, even though they decrease rather than increase the net pleasure for everyone. Even if pleasure did provide a medium of fungibility for many values, it would not do so for all values.

To generalize from the cases of Bentham and Mill, the search for a medium for ranking values encounters two kinds of obstacles. First, the more impersonal, and thus objective, the medium is, the less likely it is to allow for the accurate translation into its terms of the many different kinds of personal, and thus subjective, rankings of various values that we routinely make. As the medium is interpreted more personally to accommodate these individual variations, however, so it moves *away* from being an objective medium for the unbiased ranking of all values and *toward* being a system of evaluation favoring a particular type of value. Objectivity works against the medium's capacity to allow for individual differences, while subjectivity, which gives ample scope to personal variations, works against the medium's neutrality toward the values that should be ranked in its terms without prior commitment to their respective values. Although the medium we discussed was pleasure, the same obstacle would hold for other candidates, such as the common good, or duty, or rights, or cost-effectiveness, or the will of God, and so on.

The second obstacle was that the search for the medium was taken to be a search for some specific type of thing, like pleasure, that could serve as a unit in terms of which all types of values could be ranked. Yet as the medium was specified, so it became less able to accommodate without serious loss all the many types of values that should be translatable into its terms. The objection to any specific medium will be that there are some types of values so utterly different from it as to make their translation into the terms of the specific medium grotesquely inappropriate.

It is to overcome these obstacles that the most promising candidate for a medium has been proposed recently. Its proposal is an important and elegant contemporary development of this version of monism. It has not been possible before, because it draws on the formidable resources of game theory, which have become available only recently. The proposal is to make the medium at once completely subjective and completely general. By making it subjective, individual differences in the evaluation of values are given ample scope, and by making it general, the bias in favor of any specific type of value is removed.

The proposal is to regard the preferences of individuals as the medium in terms of which all types of values could be compared. The subjectivity of preferences derives from the claim that the only reasonable constraints on preferences are considerations that weigh with the individuals whose preferences they are, while the generality of preferences consists in the weight of preferences' being entirely dependent on the individuals' having them and not at all on the content of preferences. The first obstacle is thus removed, because through preferences, interpreted in this way, we can conjoin impersonality, neutrality, and the widest variations among individuals; and the second obstacle is also removed, because the individual evaluations of all types of values can be expressed without bias in terms of the preferences individuals have. Morality is then seen as a bargaining process whose aim it is to achieve a condition in which most individuals could realize most of their preferences. Hence the title of the book that is perhaps the most sustained attempt to work out this version of monism, David Gauthier's *Morals by Agreement*.[11]

The first hurdle any such view must face is that it cannot be good to satisfy all preferences because some of them are destructive, stupid, trivial, and inconsistent. A preference is allowed to have value only if it is coherent and considered.[12] The coherence of any set of preferences is a function of their utility, which, in turn, is expressible as the result of game theoretical calculations into whose intricacies we need not enter here.[13] Preferences are considered "if and only if there is no conflict between their behavioural and attitudinal dimensions and they are stable under experience and reflection."[14] The attitudinal dimension is revealed by what agents express about their preferences; the behavioral one by what they do; and stability under experience and reflection depends on the persistence of the preference through changing circumstances, times, and self-critical scrutiny. If preferences are considered and coherent, then they have value, and practical rationality consists in maximizing value: "[U]tility, as a measure of preference, is to be identified with value, and the maximization of utility with rationality."[15]

This view of the nature of value is avowedly subjectivist: "Value, then, we take to be a measure of individual preference—subjective because it is a measure of preference. . . . What is good is good ultimately because it is preferred, and it is good from the standpoint of those and only those who prefer it."[16] Moreover, "[t]here is no restriction on the nature of those states of affairs that may be objects of preference, and so that may be valued,"[17] provided only that our values "are registers of our fully considered attitudes to these states of affairs."[18] If people's preferences are coherent and considered, they have value.

---

[11] Gauthier, *Morals by Agreement*. For an anthology of critical articles and Gauthier's reply to them, see Paul, *Gauthier's New Social Contract*.

[12] Gauthier, *Morals by Agreement*, 24.

[13] Ibid., 23–25 and 38–46.

[14] Ibid., 32–33.

[15] Ibid., 23.

[16] Ibid., 59.

[17] Ibid., 47.

[18] Ibid., 48.

It is important to realize the full extent of the subjectivism of this view. According to it, the only constraint on what preferences it may be reasonable to hold is that they should be coherent and considered. They are considered if there is no discrepancy between what people say and do about them and if they endure through the experiences of the people who have them. And they are coherent if their joint satisfaction is not impossible. The value of preferences is therefore an entirely internal matter and it in no way depends on the suitability of the objects of preferences to being preferred.

The obvious objection to this view is that it has not overcome the hurdle noted above. People can have perverse, trivial, foolish, and self-destructive preferences. And the realization that this is the case may escape the people who have them because they are stupid, or they deceive themselves, or they are ruled by lasting and misguided passions, or they regard as sufficient the very small amount of reflection they have devoted to the subject.

The subjectivist answer to this is that if people themselves see their coherent and considered preferences in a favorable light, then the preferences are valuable. For "[w]hat is good is good ultimately because it is preferred, and it is good from the standpoint of those and only those who prefer it."[19] The subjectivist view is that the content of whatever is said to be valuable is wholly constituted of what is preferred. There is no possibility that coherent and considered preferences could fail to conform to some objective standard of value that exists outside of them, for there is no such value. It is true that the way we talk, the concepts we employ, and the beliefs we commonly hold do often imply the existence of objective standards, but this is just a mistake.

A subjectivist account of value must account for such mistakes, and so it must include an error theory.[20] This would need to explain how it is that both our language and beliefs are mistakenly committed to objectivity. The explanation is that "persons objectify their preferences, and so come to consider their subjective attitudes and affections as properties characterizing the objects of their preferences."[21] Objectivist philosophical theories construct their accounts of value by relying on language and beliefs that are permeated with this error: "If we were to suppose that the correct conception of value could be discovered by an analysis of ordinary language, we should no doubt be led to an objective conception. . . . But if instead we suppose that the correct explanation of value

[19] Ibid., 59.
[20] See Mackie, *Ethics*, 35.
[21] Gauthier, *Morals by Agreement*, 58.

can be discovered only by an appeal to the best explanation of what value is supposed to affect, then we uncover the error present in ordinary views, and establish a subjective conception."[22] In this manner, the objection referred to above as "obvious," is defused by using the error theory to call into question the assumptions on which the objection rests.

If one wishes to argue against subjectivism, it must be done on different grounds. One such ground emerges if we press a little further than was done before the question of how the coherence of preferences could be reasonably ascertained. It will be remembered that coherence was one necessary condition of preferences' having value. If the establishment of coherence involves consideration of the objects of preference, then we must reject the subjectivist position that precludes going beyond the mere having of preferences. Let us, therefore, ask: How could incoherence occur among preferences?

One way is to have inconsistent psychological attitudes. I desire worldly success, but I am also contemptuous of it; I value belonging to a large closely knit family, but I also hate the lack of privacy that involves; I feel obliged to make my voice heard in political deliberations, but I am repulsed by the compromises, waste of time, and insignificant gains such participation entails. My psychological attitudes are ambivalent, and so I have incoherent preferences. The remedy is to find out what I really want, unscramble my mixed motives, and then my preferences will become coherent.

But not all incoherence is like that. My psychological attitudes could be crystal clear and perfectly compatible in themselves, yet my preferences could still be incoherent. I may have a passion for collecting vintage cars and feel a strong obligation to support my aging parents, but since I do not have enough money, I cannot do both; I want to live a life of adventure, derring-do, pushing physical limits and to be a grandmaster of chess, but, of course, I cannot do both because my energies are limited; I love my friend and I love justice, but I cannot love both because my friend is unjust. In each of these cases, the preferences are incoherent because the world makes them so. It is not the ambivalence of my psychological attitudes but the objects toward which my preferences are directed that are responsible for their incoherence. Lack of money, limited energy, injustice, and innumerable similar considerations frequently pit against each other preferences that, in themselves, are quite compatible.

We should recognize as a corrective that preferences have two components: the psychological attitudes of the agents and the objects of these psychological attitudes. Incoherence may be introduced either by hav-

---

[22] Ibid., 58.

ing incompatible attitudes or by seeking incompatible objects. The trouble with subjectivism is that by concentrating exclusively on attitudes and ignoring their objects altogether, it cannot account for one frequent source of incoherence. But it ought to be able to do so, because subjectivism attributes value only to the satisfaction of preferences, and so it ought to eliminate all sources of incoherence. Yet, the further subjectivism goes in recognizing the importance that the suitability of objects of preference has for their coherence, the more it is obliged to abandon the view that "[w]hat is good is good ultimately because it is preferred."[23]

What subjectivism misses is that "psychological states and their objects [are] . . . equal and reciprocal partners. . . . [I]t can be true both that we desire x because we think x good, and that x is good because we desire x. . . . [T]he quality by which the thing qualifies as good and the desire for the thing are equals—are 'made for one another' so to speak."[24] Unless a moral theory recognizes the truism that human beings live in the world and, consequently, their conception of value must take account of the nature of the world, it cannot give an adequate answer to the question of what lives are good.

Perhaps the simplest way of making concrete this general point against subjectivism is to appeal to the notion of primary values. These values are primary because the facts of the self, intimacy, and social order establish some minimum requirements of all good lives. We can say, then, that no set of preferences can be coherent unless it recognizes the importance of primary values for living a good life. If some agents put higher value on preferences that run contrary to primary values than on the primary values themselves, then they are normally mistaken. For whatever conception of a good life they have, it cannot be reasonable if it fails to recognize the requirements presupposed by all conceptions of good life. And some of these requirements are set by the facts of the world, including the facts of human nature, and not by the preferences people happen to have.

We may, then, draw the following conclusion regarding the second version of monism. The attempt to deny the incompatibility and incommensurability of values by finding a medium in terms of which all the different types of values could be ranked without arbitrariness fails. The failure is due to an irresolvable tension at the core of this attempt. The medium must include a subjective component, because it must recognize the vast individual differences among the things regarded as valuable; but it must also include an objective component, because it must have some basis for comparing different types of values. Yet these two

---

[23] Ibid., 59 .
[24] Wiggins, "Truth, Invention, and the Meaning of Life," 106–7.

components are inconsistent, for stressing the objective component leads to ignoring differences among values, and stressing the subjective component involves abandoning the neutrality about different types of values. And the heroic attempt—to combine complete subjectivism regarding preferences with complete objectivism by attending only to the formal properties of preferences and ignoring their content—fails because values depend partly on what the facts are and not merely on our attitudes.

The Third Version of Monism:
Canonical Principle for Ranking Values

Our discussion of this version of monism can be quite brief. For, depending on how it is interpreted, it may or may not be inconsistent with pluralism. We have seen that pluralists and monists need not disagree about the occurrence, or even the frequency, of moral conflicts. Their dispute is about the causes of conflicts. Pluralists think that incompatible and incommensurable values are responsible for many conflicts, while monists deny it. But pluralists and monists can also agree about the importance of settling conflicts, whatever may be their source. The third version of monism may be interpreted in a weak sense as proposing merely a way of resolving conflicts, or in a strong sense as both a proposal for conflict-resolution and an explanation of why the proposal works.

In the strong sense, the claim is that there is a canonical principle for ranking all types of values, and, in case of conflicts, the higher-ranked values should take precedence over the lower-ranked ones. The question about the strong claim is: What makes this principle canonical?

One possible answer is that it is something in the nature of the values. The thought is that just as primary values normally take precedence over secondary values, in case they conflict, so we can establish a ranking among all types of values, and the principle expresses this order. But then, of course, we would want to know what it is in the nature of values that supports the principle. And the supposition must be that it is either the extent to which the values possess some characteristic or the ranking they have on some objective scale that determines their standing. The former alternative assimilates this version of monism to the first version we discussed, for the characteristic that allows for the ranking of values is none other than their approximation of the summum bonum. The latter alternative, on the other hand, reduces this version of monism to the second version considered previously, since it constitutes an appeal to some medium in terms of which all values can be expressed and ranked. As we have seen, however, neither the first nor the second version of monism could meet the criticisms directed against it, so we must conclude that the third version of monism, interpreted in the strong sense, fails as well.

We are still left, however, with the interpretation in the weak sense. This interpretation insists, as does the strong one, on the need for a ranking of different types of values, for unless it was available, there would be no principled way of resolving conflicts among values. But, unlike the strong interpretation, the present one does not suppose that the ranking is, or must be, based exclusively on characteristics intrinsic to values. The weak interpretation is therefore consistent with the pluralistic view that the conflicting values are incompatible and incommensurable. Given that the incompatibility and incommensurability of values is acknowledged or, at least, not denied, the third version of monism, interpreted in the weak sense, and pluralism can be held together. The common concern, then, of pluralists and this kind of monist is with the resolution of conflicts among values. And they agree that the best hope of success is to establish some sort of principled ranking of them. The ranking, however, will not be based merely on the values but also on our attitude toward them. In this way, the sought for ranking would unite subjective and objective considerations about both primary and secondary values. The description and justification of this scheme of conflict-resolution is one main task of the next chapter.

CHAPTER FIVE

The Nature of Reasonable Conflict-Resolution

> Where ultimate values are irreconcilable, clear solutions cannot,
> in principle, be found. To decide rationally in such situations is
> to decide in the light of . . . the over-all pattern of life pursued by
> a man or a group or a society.
> —Isaiah Berlin, *Four Essays on Liberty*

IF PLURAL and conditional values unavoidably conflict because they are
incompatible and incommensurable, then pluralists must answer the
question of how these conflicts can be resolved in a reasonable manner.
The answer that will be developed in this chapter is that reasonable conflict-resolution is made possible by the traditions and conceptions of a
good life to which people who face the conflicts adhere.

A Pluralistic Approach to Conflict-Resolution

In discussing the third version of monism, we distinguished between a
strong and a weak interpretation of the idea that the reasonable resolution of conflicts among values depends on ranking them. The strong
one, which is inconsistent with pluralism, held that the ranking depends
exclusively on the nature of the values. But if many values are incommensurable and incompatible, then this interpretation is untenable,
since the reasonable ranking of values would require what is impossible,
namely, comparisons among incommensurable values. Yet, according to
monists, unless such comparisons were possible, the ranking would be
arbitrary.

The weak interpretation remains committed to ranking values as a
means to resolving conflicts among them, but it does not suppose that
the ranking must be based exclusively on the nature of the values. The
weak interpretation, therefore, may be adopted by pluralists, but we
need an explanation of its basis for the ranking of values if that basis is
not merely the nature of the values but something else as well. What is
that something else?

It is our attitude toward them. The ranking of values is based neither
exclusively on the nature of values, as monists suppose, nor exclusively
on our attitude toward the values, as relativists hold, but on a combination of the two: "[I]t can be true both that we desire *x* because we think

x good, and that *x* is good because we desire *x*. . . . [T]he quality *by* which the thing qualifies as good and the desire *for* the thing are equals—are 'made for one another' so to speak."[1] According to this view, values exist in the world, and they have the qualities they have independently of our attitudes toward them. But we do value them, and we do so on the basis of some quality we suppose they possess. If the values have that quality and if that quality is valuable, then the value and our valuing it are "made for one another." The ranking of values is thus based on our attitude toward them, but since this attitude is directed toward some quality the value is supposed by us to have, its rank is determined by a combination of our attitude and the nature of the value. How reasonable an evaluation is depends on how good our grounds are for regarding some quality of some value as beneficial or harmful. The ranking as a whole, then, will be as reasonable as the evaluations are that constitute it.

Yet we must not lose sight of the fact that these rankings still require comparisons among incommensurable and incompatible values. The comparisons, however, are no longer supposed to depend on the impossible task of overcoming the incommensurability and incompatibility of the values but on judging their respective importance. Some of these judgments will be relative to traditions and conceptions of a good life, but some others will not be.

The importance of primary values must be recognized by all traditions and conceptions of a good life, because secondary values normally presuppose that the minimum requirements of all good lives are satisfied. And that means that the primary values are generally recognized by the people whose tradition or conception of a good life establishes the point of view from which the judgment is made. Consequently we can say that each and every reasonable ranking of values will judge primary values to have normally a greater importance than secondary values.

Of course, different primary values may themselves be incommensurable and incompatible, and consequently they may conflict with each other. So the ranking of primary values themselves remains an open question. And even if primary values normally take precedence over secondary values, the ranking of secondary values also remains similarly open. Many of the judgments regarding the respective importance of these values will vary with the tradition and the conceptions of a good life from whose point of view they are made. But this need not make the judgments arbitrary. For these judgments can still be grounded, and they can be criticized or justified relative to the grounds on which they rest. What then could their ground be?

The grounds on which such judgments rest are the conceptions of a good life regarded as acceptable in the surrounding tradition. What

---

[1] Wiggins, "Truth, Invention, and the Meaning of Life," 106–7.

such judgments express is the respective importance of particular values to some one of the acceptable conceptions of a good life. This makes the judgments relative but not arbitrary.

It is not merely that they are not arbitrary because they can be criticized or justified on the basis of the conceptions of a good life from which they are derived. For conceptions of a good life are themselves open to criticism and justification at least on one ground; namely, on how they compare with respect to the realization of primary values. But, as we shall see, there are other grounds as well. So even though judgments of importance are relative, and correspondingly the ranking of values is also partly relative, we can still distinguish between reasonable and unreasonable judgments.

The fact remains, however, that "human nature, conceived in terms of common human needs and capacities, always underdetermines a way of life, and underdetermines an order of priority among virtues, and therefore underdetermines the moral prohibitions and injunctions that support a way of life."[2] What emerges from the fact of the systematic underdetermination of conceptions of a good life by the context-independent requirements of all good lives is that there is going to be a plurality of reasonable conceptions of a good life. And while some of the limits and possibilities each of the reasonable plural conceptions recognizes will vary, others will not, because although human nature underdetermines a way of life, it also determines it to some extent.

In order to make this claim more perspicuous, we need to clarify further what appeal to reasonability does and does not involve. To say that something is reasonable may mean either that reason requires it or that reason allows it.[3] If something is required by reason, then the choice of any alternative in its place is unreasonable; only the required actions, belief, or judgment accords with reason. If something is allowed by reason, then it is a justified action, belief, or judgment, although the choice of some alternatives to it may also be reasonable. If one wants to live, then nourishment is required by reason, whereas eating cheese as part of nourishment is allowed by reason. Alternatives to what reason requires are forbidden by reason, while alternatives to what reason allows may or may not be forbidden. Both being required and allowed by reason exclude certain alternative actions, beliefs, or judgments. But being required by reason excludes all alternatives, while being allowed by reason excludes only some of them. For instance, nourishment is normally required by reason, so any alternative to taking nourishment is normally forbidden by reason. However, that reason allows eating cheese as a form

[2] Hampshire, *Morality and Conflict*, 155.
[3] See Gert, *Morality*, chapter 2, and its predecessor, *The Moral Rules*.

of nourishment permits beans as a reasonable alternative, but not ping pong balls.

The point about human nature underdetermining reasonable conceptions of a good life thus can be more precisely expressed as follows. Reason requires that any conception of a good life should recognize the importance of primary values, while reason allows considerable variation with respect to the secondary values regarded as important to particular conceptions. The justification for this claim is that reason requires primary values, because, given human nature, they are minimum requirements for all good lives, while reason allows a variety of secondary values, because they are constitutive of conceptions of a good life, which, given human nature, can vary historically, culturally, and personally.

Pluralism thus differs from versions of monism that insist on evaluating all conceptions of a good life on the basis of their conformity to some possibilities and limits each of which is required by reason. According to pluralists, some, but not all, possibilities and limits are required by reason for all conceptions of a good life. Similarly, pluralism differs from versions of relativism that suppose that no possibilities and limits are required by reason because all are relative to historically, culturally, and personally conditioned conceptions of a good life. For, while this is true of possibilities and limits that reason allows, it is not true of those that involve primary values, since primary values are required by reason.

So we have this pluralistic approach to conflict-resolution. Many values conflict because they are incommensurable and incompatible and yet we want to realize them. The resolution of such conflicts depends on shaping our attitudes toward the conflicting values. This is done by ranking the values. Their comparative ranks depend on their importance within the conception of good life of the person who faces the conflict. And although there is a plurality of reasonable conceptions and rankings, it is still possible to criticize and to justify them.

The emerging picture is of people who make reasonable choices among incommensurable and incompatible values by judging their respective importance to the kind of life they want to make for themselves. These choices need not be all-or-none, because the incompatibility among the values may be proportional, not total. Choices among proportionally incompatible values often involve balancing more and less important values by aiming at a life that embodies a mixture of them. But such conflict-resolutions are not always possible, because the incompatibility among the values may be total. Regardless of the sharpness of the conflict, however, its resolution is always, at least in principle, possible, because the respective importance of the conflicting values to the life one wants to live can be judged.

What is not always possible is to eliminate the sense of loss caused by the judgment to subordinate some recognized value to another. But this sense of loss, while it may often be reasonable, need not be serious. For there is a readily available consolation in the form of living the life whose attraction made one incur the loss in the first place. It may also happen, however, that the life for whose sake the loss has been sustained fails to be good, either because the agent was mistaken in valuing that kind of life or because circumstances prevented its achievement. And then the loss is exacerbated by the larger failure. We must acknowledge that lives can be, deservedly or otherwise, ruined. This consequence of pluralism, while sad, is a further reason in its favor. For it takes note of a plain fact we can all observe as we survey the lives with which we are familiar.

We should recognize yet another way in which lives can fail to be good. It has been argued that the realization of primary values is presupposed by the realization of secondary values, and thus the former were said to be normally more important than the latter. It could happen, however, that primary values have been realized while some secondary ones have not been, and the people to whom this happens may still reasonably judge their lives not worth living. For instance, if a resistance fighter secures the primary values for himself by betraying his comrades, he may well think that since his life lacks the secondary value of honor it cannot be good. Or a concert violinist with great talent and a promising career, who has realized all the primary values and many of the secondary ones, may reasonably think that her life still would not be worth living if she were to go deaf. The point of these examples is to remind ourselves that while primary values are more important than secondary ones, this does not mean that some secondary values may not be as indispensable to a particular conception of a good life as primary values are. One value's being more important than the other is compatible with both being necessary.

This approach to conflict-resolution is a program, not a solution. How good the program is depends on how extensive we can make the case for the reasonability of the limits and possibilities that particular conceptions of a good life embody. And that requires an examination of the conventions of traditions and the commitments of individuals that are the particular embodiments of these limits and possibilities. We shall look at conventions first and at commitments next.

CONVENTIONS AND TRADITIONS

The conventions we shall discuss here are moral: their aim is to provide possibilities and set limits regarding the pursuit of values in a particular context.[4] The values whose pursuit conventions regulate may be

---

[4] For a more detailed discussion of conventions and traditions, see Kekes, *Moral Tradition and Individuality*, chapters 1–5.

primary or secondary. Correspondingly, we need to distinguish between deep and variable conventions. As a first approximation, shortly to be refined, we may say that deep conventions guide conduct regarding the pursuit of primary values, while variable conventions prescribe acceptable ways of pursuing secondary values.

As we have seen, the importance of primary values is that they are minimum requirements of all good lives. All reasonable people, therefore, would want to protect primary values. They would certainly want to do so for themselves and for those whose welfare is their concern. But if they are reasonable, they would also want to extend the protection to everybody living in their context, since they would recognize that their own and other people's interests are common, overlapping, and interdependent. If a tradition is committed to protecting the conditions in which people living in its context could make good lives for themselves, then among its deep conventions there will be those that protect the primary values of the self, intimacy, and social order. But the content of deep conventions is not exhausted by the protection of primary values, for two reasons.

First, as we have seen, primary values are much too general and indeterminate, so they must be rendered concrete and specific. For instance, life is certainly a primary value, and in all traditions there is a strong reason for protecting it. But this leaves it an open question how far the protection extends. Does it end at the borders of the society, or does it include members of other societies, strangers, and enemies? And how inclusive is it in the society itself? Does it apply to unwanted members, like radical critics, the decrepit old, defective babies, the insane, or criminals? And against what is the protection provided? Is it only against violence, or does it include dangerous occupations, illness, or self-destructive conduct? And how is the protection provided? By law, custom, or religion? And who provides the protection? The police, the elders, or some political or religious authority, or does everybody take a hand? And how are disputes about suspected violations settled? What are the permissible forms of violations? What is the status of suicide, capital punishment, war, euthanasia, family quarrels, infanticide, and the like? What are the circumstances in which the strong reason for the protection of life is justifiably defeated? All traditions must confront these and similar questions, and they must do so not only about the primary value of life, but also about each and every specific value included among the primary values of the self, intimacy, and social order.

A tradition answers such questions by developing a set of secondary values. Among these values will be the concrete and specific forms in which the primary values are interpreted in that context. So, while the primary values are the same in all reasonable traditions, the secondary values are likely to vary, since a wide array of reasonable answers can be given to the kinds of questions listed above. Although the reasonable answers may vary, once a tradition has arrived at some set of answers and the answers have become widely accepted, customary, and handed down from generation to generation, they become embodied in conventions. And, in a healthy tradition, these conventions will also be deep because they will represent the necessary specifications of the concrete forms primary values unavoidably take. Deep conventions protecting primary values are, therefore, inevitably extended to include the protection of those secondary values that are the context-dependent interpretations of the primary values.

Yet no matter how entrenched are these secondary values and the deep conventions protecting them, they are not beyond reasonable challenge. They can be contested and criticized on the grounds that some other interpretation of the primary values would provide better protection of some particular requirement of good lives. It is, of course, on just such grounds that reasonable debates are conducted about the circumstances in which the strong reason for protecting a primary value may be defeated. And it is important to note, against radical relativism and conventionalism, that the debates need not occur exclusively in terms of the particular tradition whose convention is being challenged. For the criticism of a deep convention accepted in one's tradition may well consist in pointing at an analogous deep convention of another tradition and finding that it provides better protection of the same primary values than one's own. Traditions thus need not be doomed to the perpetuation of orthodoxy.

The second reason why the content of deep conventions includes more than the protection of primary values has to do with yet another function of secondary values. Among the primary values, the values of social order form one type. These values, it will be remembered, consist in the customs, rules, institutions, authorities, and the like, that regulate the interactions of people living together in the context of a particular society. Now, just as some secondary values, let us call them "substantive," make concrete some of the primary values, so some other secondary values, we shall refer to them as "procedural," give concrete expression to some of the acceptable modes of interaction among people. These secondary procedural values define both the limits beyond which it is morally impermissible to go in our treatment of others and the possibilities that form the many ways in which people are allowed and encouraged to relate to each other in a particular context. Some secondary procedural values thus are not intrinsically valuable but valuable because they make it possible to pursue and to realize intrinsically valuable values. The legal system, political institutions; and conventions marking the distinctions among what is encouraged, allowed, tolerated, forbidden, disgusting, shameful, dishonorable, beyond the pale, forgivable, and so on, are some examples of this type of secondary procedural value.

These secondary procedural values typically vary from context to context, and they vary also in the seriousness with which they are held. Traditions differ partly because they regard different things as appropriate matters of honor, shame, disgust, tolerance, and so on, and partly because they attribute different importance to these conventional evaluations. But there is yet another respect in which healthy traditions must be alike, namely, in regarding some matters as having great importance, others as being negligible, and yet others whose importance lies somewhere between. The violation of some specific limits is a taboo, while the violation of others is regarded as a mere peccadillo. A tradition partly defines itself by drawing this distinction and by drawing it at some specific points and not at others. Part of the importance of this self-definition is that it forms a significant portion of the identity of the people whose allegiance lies with that tradition. Their shared identity makes it possible for them to regulate their own conduct, to have reasonable expectations about the conduct of others, to draw the distinctions between various groupings of "us" and "them," and thus to feel secure on one fundamental level of their moral outlook. Consequently, the conventions that protect these secondary procedural values are also among the deep conventions of a tradition.

In addition to the deep conventions of a tradition, there will also be a large array of variable conventions. We might say that conformity to the possibilities and limits defined by its deep conventions is required by a tradition, while conformity to variable conventions is merely recommended. Violations of deep conventions are forbidden; violations of variable conventions are tolerated. But this is not quite right. It is certainly true that in a healthy tradition there will be room left for individuals to experiment with, flaunt, reject, or try to combine various possibilities, as well as to introduce new ones or reform and reinterpret old ones. All this is, or ought to be, within the limits of tolerance. Yet if we take the variable conventions of a tradition, not individually but as a class, then, once again, wholesale rejection of them will be a violation of a deep convention. For although it is a tautology that no individual variable convention is a deep convention, it must also be recognized that the totality of possibilities and limits defined by variable conventions is protected by a deep convention, because it represents an absolutely indispensable element of a tradition's view about the acceptable conceptions of a good life. And since one chief aim of a tradition is to provide the conditions in which individuals adhering to it could make good lives for themselves, it is reasonable to protect the totality of the possibilities and limits with the seriousness that attaches to deep conventions. What is tolerable, therefore, is the rejection of individual variable conventions but not the rejection of all variable conventions. One acceptable form of moral criticism and one way to moral progress lies in criticizing some variable conventions of one's tradition from the point of view of some other variable conventions of the same tradition. Reason consequently requires conformity not merely to deep conventions but also to some set of variable conventions, although reason allows considerable leeway about what particular variable conventions the set contains.

But this is not the only form of moral criticism and the only avenue of moral progress. We can see this if we take care not to mistake deep conventions for strongly held ones and variable conventions for those that are weakly held in some context. Deep conventions are deep because they protect the minimum requirements of all good lives, while variable conventions define possibilities and limits that go beyond the minimum requirements and represent options that are important within some conceptions of a good life but not within others. How strongly or weakly particular conventions are held is a historical-cum-sociological fact about a tradition. One morally significant question about this is whether deep conventions are strongly held and weakly held conventions are variable.

Part of the reason why this is a significant question is that it helps to explain what is meant by the hitherto unexplained reference to traditions as "healthy." What makes a tradition healthy is if its deep conventions are strongly held and its variable conventions are weakly held. Deep conventions protect the minimum requirements of all good lives, and that is why they should be strongly held. Since the violation of particular variable conventions is far less damaging from the moral point of view, it is sufficient to hold them weakly.

Accordingly, traditions can go wrong in two corresponding ways. If some deep conventions are weakly held, then some minimum requirements of good lives are insufficiently protected. If some variable conventions are strongly held, then some particular conceptions of a good life are elevated to the status of orthodoxy and become coercive. When this happens, the tradition is impoverished by repressing possibilities of good lives other than the orthodox ones. In either case, the tradition errs in failing to do what it can to promote its end, good lives for its adherents. Pointing this out is justified moral criticism, and remedying it is a step in moral progress.

Another part of the significance of the distinction between deep and variable conventions, on the one hand, and strongly and weakly held ones, on the other, is that it provides yet a further argument for pluralism and against both relativism and monism. It counts against radical relativism and conventionalism, because relativists deny that traditions can be reasonably criticized from an external point of view. But we can compare two traditions and recognize that one is better than another in that it offers better protection of some minimum requirements of good lives or richer possibilities of good lives than its rival. And such comparisons can be made from the point of view of either of the two traditions or from that of a third.

The distinction is significant also because it provides additional reasons for rejecting monism. For monists are committed to regarding a tradition as mistaken if it has merely weakly held variable conventions. Some variable conventions, according to monists, ought to be strongly held within all traditions because they represent the true conception of a good life. But, as philosophical argument and historical experience amply show, no such conception ever has or should have commanded the assent of all the reasonable people familiar with it. Moreover, the attempt to hold them strongly and thus to force them on unwilling recipients has been responsible, to put it mildly, for much evil and little good.[5]

To sum up, the importance of conventions from the pluralistic point of view is that they are one of the most effective means of resolving conflicts within a tradition. For conventions institutionalize prevailing conceptions of a good life and the permissible ways of trying to achieve them. When individuals encounter conflicts among values, they can turn to the conventions of their tradition for deciding which value should prevail. In general, the decisions will be made by determining the respective importance of the values to the prevailing conceptions of a good life.

These decisions must be seen as relative to particular contexts in two ways. First, through the particular conventions and conceptions of a good life that prevail in the context and, second, through the individuals who are committed to these conventions and conceptions and who, because of their commitments, encounter conflicts among the values they want to realize. But it should be clear by now that this relativity need not be inconsistent with reasonable decisions, because the prevailing conventions and conceptions of a good life can be evaluated on the context-independent ground of how they compare with the conventions and conceptions of other actual or possible traditions.

COMMITMENTS AND CONCEPTIONS OF A GOOD LIFE

As the tradition of a society is characterized by a structure of conventions, so conceptions of a good life are characterized by a structure of commitments. The relationship between these two structures is intimate. "Society," "tradition," and "conventions" are elliptical expressions. Soci-

---

[5] "One belief, more than any other, is responsible for the slaughter of individuals on the altars of the great historical ideals. . . . This is the belief that somewhere, in the past, or in

ety is a collection of individuals, their relations, and the institutions they have developed; tradition is partly composed of the approved possibilities and limits of the conduct of individuals that stretch continuously from the past to the present; and conventions are patterns implicit in what individuals do or not do in various situations. Society is abstract; individuals are concrete. When we say that a tradition forbids or permits this or that, what we mean is that individuals living together in some context agree in forbidding or permitting this or that. And similarly for conventions; conventions are accepted or rejected, observed or violated by individuals. When individuals habitually adhere to some conventions, we can say that they have committed themselves to them. Without the commitment of individuals, conventions could survive only as historical relics. We might say, therefore, that conventions are created by patterns of commitments that individuals make.

As individuals are initiated into their tradition, they are taught to conduct themselves according to conventions, and this translates into being taught, in the first instance, to imitate the conduct of others. When imitation is replaced by intelligent action, individuals have learned the rules or customs to which they have hitherto conformed without understanding. From then on, they can respond to new situations, they can afford to be spontaneous, since they have learned the lessons well, and they can ask reflective, analytical, and critical questions about the rules and customs that their conduct exemplifies and perpetuates. If such conduct becomes second nature for them, we can say that they have made a commitment to some convention.[6]

The conventions of a tradition are far more numerous than the commitments particular individuals are likely to make. For the conventions concern the possibilities and limits involved in the pursuit of both primary and secondary values, and there are more of these values than any individual can realize in a lifetime. If a tradition is healthy, then individuals adhering to it will want to commit themselves to its deep conventions, because these conventions protect them in their pursuit of the primary values they need, regardless of the conceptions of a good life they go on to develop. But this will leave very many variable conventions regulating the pursuit of secondary values. And how valuable individuals will regard these secondary values will vary with their conceptions of a good life. The process of forming commitments will therefore go on

---

the future, in divine revelation, or in the mind of an individual thinker, in the pronouncements of history or science, or in the simple heart of an uncorrupted good man, there is a final solution" (Berlin, "Two Concepts of Liberty," 167).

[6] For a matchless description of this process, see Oakeshott's essays collected in *The Voice of Liberal Learning*.

long after the individuals' initiation into their tradition. For the initiation may teach them what their tradition requires and what it allows, but they themselves will have to decide what possibilities among the allowed ones they should try to realize.

We can speak of "fully formed" conceptions of a good life when the individuals whose conceptions they are have made commitments not only to the deep conventions of their tradition but also to that subset of variable conventions that regulates the possibilities and limits involved in the pursuit of the secondary values they want to realize. Given the plurality of primary and secondary values and the consequent plurality of conventions and commitments, there will be a plurality of conceptions of a good life in any healthy tradition. These conceptions will be plural not merely because different conceptions will incorporate commitments to different secondary values but also because one and the same secondary value may occupy positions of differing importance in the ranking of values associated with different conceptions. Commitments thus determine both the values individuals want to realize and the importance they attribute to a particular value in comparison with other values. Fully formed conceptions of a good life consequently involve having an ordered set of commitments, where the order depends on the comparative importance attributed to the values that are the objects of the commitments.

We may distinguish, therefore, between basic, conditional, and loose commitments. Basic commitments are our most fundamental convictions. They are the rock upon which rest our identity, self-esteem, and the reasons we find the weightiest. They establish both the limits whose trespass fills us with horror and the possibilities we really care about. They are the foundation of our conceptions of a good life. Adversity, coercion, misfortune, stupidity, thoughtlessness, self-deception, or weakness may cause us to violate our basic commitments. If that happens, we inflict grave psychological damage on ourselves. For the violation shows that we were wrong about ourselves: we took ourselves to be a certain sort of person and we proved to have been wrong. We discover evil or corruption at the core of our being, and we are shattered by guilt, shame, or remorse.

Not everyone has basic commitments. There are many people who do not take anything that seriously. But such people are more or less adrift, because they have not discovered what the most important things are for them. In the absence of having made that discovery, they cannot have a fully formed conception of a good life. For basic commitments are inseparably connected with knowing what we are about: the absence of one is inevitably the absence of the other. Yet having basic commitments simultaneously renders us vulnerable and makes it possible to be genuinely satisfied with our life. The risk and the achievement go together.

Conditional commitments are to those forms and manifestations of our basic commitments that constitute the stuff of our everyday moral life. They define the day-to-day obligations that attach to our jobs and to our roles as parents, children, spouses, lovers, friends, colleagues, and citizens—they are commitments to the requirements of what Bradley aptly called our station and its duties.[7] As their name suggests, these commitments to the forms and manifestations of our basic commitments are not held as deeply as our basic commitments are. They can be defeated by sufficiently strong countervailing considerations. We may feel justified in their violation on the ground that we have continued to honor the underlying basic commitment, albeit in a different way.

Loose commitments are on the outer fringes of our conceptions of a good life. Hume referred to them as "a kind of lesser morality,"[8] and Jane Austen called them "the civilities, the lesser duties of life."[9] They guide us in such matters as tact, politeness, conviviality, personal style, hospitality, and the like. They concern form more than content. They are the ways in which we are most open to change, for they concern matters in which we can be easily influenced by the examples of others. Loose commitments are close to the surface; they are the most visible, most easily observable aspects of our conceptions of a good life. Much of our contact with other people consists of conduct exemplifying these commitments. And much of the time when we misjudge each other, we do so by mistaking loose commitments for deeper ones. This is an easy error to make, because in the normal course of events conditional commitments are evoked only in serious moral situations, when we are called upon to justify or criticize the conduct of other people or of ourselves. Basic commitments are usually very private, typically expressed, if at all, only to those closest to us; but most often they are altogether unexpressed because we do not articulate them even to ourselves. What commitments are basic, conditional, and loose varies of course with individuals. This variation is a corollary of the plurality of conceptions of a good life.

The reason why we are considering commitments and the conceptions of a good life they form is that they, in addition to conventions and traditions, are the pluralistic means of conflict-resolution. The pluralistic claim is that it is partly through our conceptions of a good life that we decide among the conflicting claims of the incompatible and incommensurable values. These values are mainly secondary, since primary ones are presumably guaranteed by the tradition in the background.

---

[7] Bradley, *Ethical Studies*, essay 5.

[8] Hume, *Enquiry*, 209.

[9] Austen, *Sense and Sensibility*, chapter 46.

Now, as we have seen, through conceptions of a good life we identify not only the values we seek in preference to others but also their respective importance. Basic, conditional, and loose commitments are commitments to ranking values on the basis of their importance to our conceptions of a good life. There is normally a strong reason for honoring our commitments, since they are commitments to what we value. But commitments may conflict with each other, and if they do, loose commitments should be defeated by conditional ones, which, in turn, should themselves be defeated by basic commitments. These are cases of simple conflicts, because the conception of a good life in the background will readily allow us to judge the respective importance of the conflicting values.

But not all conflicts are simple. The respective importance of conflicting values may be equal or unclear because our commitment to both may be loose, conditional, or basic. There are two approaches to resolving such conflicts. One is to opt for the value whose realization would make it more likely to contribute to the possession of other equally or more important values. Another is to try to strike a balance between the values. This is often possible because the values may be proportionally, not totally, incompatible. They exclude each other only in the sense that the more there is of one, the less there can be of the other. Reward and punishment, even if they are responses to different acts, can hardly be given together. But respect and discipline can be mixed in various proportions. Some conflicts therefore can be resolved by achieving a compromise between the conflicting values.[10]

This is as far as we can usefully go at this stage in discussing the pluralistic approach to conflict-resolution in general. Further discussion needs to be made concrete, and that requires looking at actual conflicts in specific contexts. We shall do so in subsequent chapters.

THE PROSPECTS FOR CONFLICT-RESOLUTION

The approach outlined above suggests that most conflicts can be resolved by ordering our commitments on the basis of their importance within our conceptions of a good life. The remaining conflicts can also be resolved either by judging the respective fecundity of the values or by trying to achieve a balanced mixture of them. It would seem, therefore, that at least in principle all conflicts among values could be resolved by making the ordering of our commitments more and more finely grained. There is in principle no limit to how rigorously we may struc-

---

[10] For a study of compromise in the framework of pluralism, see Benjamin, *Splitting the Difference.*

ture our conceptions of a good life, because, theoretically, we can deliberate about, and settle in advance, any conflict we may come to encounter. And if this is true, then we may attribute the conflicts we do experience to too loosely ordered conceptions of a good life. But as logical points tend to do, this does not take us very far: practical considerations prevent the realization of this logical possibility.

To begin with, the logical possibility of the elimination of all conflicts does not rest on the possibility of undoing the incompatibility and the incommensurability of the conflicting values. Rather, it rests on the possibility of shaping our attitude toward the conflicts we encounter. But this requires us to anticipate the conflicts we shall come to confront. One of the practical limits of conflict-resolution is that our capacity for such anticipation is limited. For the anticipation would require us to explore in our imagination all the implications of our conceptions of a good life in all circumstances we may encounter. And that presupposes what is very unlikely, namely, that we possess fully formed conceptions and information about future contingencies.

Most of us do not have a fully formed conception of a good life. We start out, usually in adolescence, with passionate, but quickly changing, enthusiasms; we get a glimpse of some possibility, we hold to it for a while, and then, as it fades, we are engrossed by another. As time goes on, we may begin to be steadier, more realistic, and we may try to find a fit between some conception of a good life, incorporating some possibilities, and our character and circumstances. Yet the resulting conceptions of a good life will still be viewed largely from the outside. We come to see the world from their perspective and act accordingly only gradually. And even after it has become fully ours, we have insufficient self-knowledge to be able to form a just view of our own character; and, in any case, our characters are continually transformed by the conceptions of a good life we are in the process of making our own. Furthermore, the circumstances surrounding us continually change not simply because political, social, economic, and cultural changes are ceaseless but because we ourselves also change, so how we fit into changing circumstances is always shifting. It is vastly unrealistic therefore to suppose that we could have a firm conception of a good life from whose point of view we could systematically work out strategies for resolving the conflicts we are likely to encounter. We cannot do it, because part of the process of living is not to begin with, but to work toward, a fully formed conception of a good life; and as we work toward it, so we transform our character and the relation between ourselves and our circumstances. The reason why conflicts are practically ineliminable from our lives is that we cannot anticipate the conflicts we shall encounter and thus cannot have preformed attitudes toward them. We form our conception of a good life *by* living, just as much as we live by our conceptions of a good life. We often find out what our commitments are by reflecting on how we feel we must respond to conflicts.[11]

This is not to underrate the importance and the necessity of imagination to the moral life. Indeed, in the next chapter we shall see just how crucial a role imagination plays in the morality of pluralism. But we must recognize that its efficacy is limited, and partly because of that, conflicts will continue to play a role in human lives. Realistically conceived, our aim must be to shape our attitudes so as to resolve, rather than to eliminate, the conflicts we encounter.

However, even if we are conspicuously successful in ordering our commitments so as to minimize the conflicts that beset us, we are not thereby in possession of one necessary condition of good lives. For the obverse side of conflict-resolution is the sense of loss that we are bound to experience. Conflicts occur because we *want* to realize two incompatible and incommensurable values, and their resolution consists in subordinating one of our values to the other, in teaching ourselves to do without the less important value. But coming to regard one value as less important than another does not mean that we shall cease to value it and consequently cease to miss having it or having more of it. We shall put up with the loss, but there is a loss with which we have to put up. And the better ordered our commitments are, the more fully we have succeeded in forming our conceptions of a good life, the more loss there will be, for the more possibilities we shall have foreclosed for ourselves.

We must guard however against the temptation to manufacture a paradox out of this state of affairs by supposing that the better formed our conceptions of a good life are, the more impoverished they will be. Or that the more articulated conceptions of a good life are, the fewer possibilities they will leave to the agent to explore. For it must be remembered that the regulative ideal behind the formation and articulation of commitments is a conception of a good life. It is that ideal that makes the inevitable losses bearable. What we forego we forego in order to achieve something that we think is better. We regulate ourselves, and we do so for our own good, and that is what gives us, if we are reasonable, a sense of proportion about the losses we incur.

There are many pluralists, to whom the present version is deeply indebted in numerous *other* respects, who succumb to this temptation. Berlin, for instance, writes, "If, as I believe, the ends of men are many, and

---

[11] "Moral change and moral achievement are slow, we [cannot] . . . suddenly alter what we see and ergo what we desire and are compelled by. In a way, explicit choice seems less important. . . . If I attend properly I will have no choices left and this is the ultimate condition to aim at. . . . The ideal situation . . . is . . . a kind of necessity" (Iris Murdoch, *The Sovereignty of Good*, 39–40).

not all of them in principle compatible with each other, then the possibility of conflict—and of tragedy—can never wholly be eliminated from human life, either personal or social. The necessity of choosing between absolute claims is then an inescapable characteristic of the human condition."[12] Berlin and others see life beset by conflicts as the unavoidable consequence of the plurality of values.[13] At the root of their mistake, there is the confusion between the true claim that many values are incompatible and incommensurable and the false claim that we cannot resolve conflicts among them. We can and we continually do resolve such conflicts, and the price we pay is very much less than grievous loss. Life is often hard, but rarely tragic.

The mirror image of this confusion is one to which all versions of monism are prone. They see clearly that some of us are successful at resolving conflicts, and so they mistakenly suppose that the conflicting values could not have been incompatible and incommensurable. But they miss the possibility, as do their pluralist counterparts, that conflict-resolution is possible and that it often succeeds, even though values are incompatible and incommensurable.

The three relativistic positions can also be represented vis-à-vis this confusion. Relativists of all persuasions may agree that values are incompatible and incommensurable *and* that it is possible to resolve conflicts among them. What they deny is that conflict-resolutions can be reasonable, if by that we mean justifying or criticizing them on the basis of objective considerations independent of the particular morality, tradition, or conception of a good life in whose context the resolution is achieved. But we have seen that the minimum requirements of good lives, as specified by the primary values, do provide such objective considerations for particular moralities and traditions, and we promised to point at similar considerations relevant to settling conflicts between conceptions of a good life. Hence relativists are also mistaken.

Integrity and Reasonable Commitments

Pluralism may have many virtues, but providing moral inspiration is not usually counted as one of them. How could a theory be inspiring if it denies the overridingness of any value? Spinoza and Kant, Plato and Augustine, Christianity and Marxism may move some people by their moral visions, but the pluralistic subtext calls for calm reflection, a sense of proportion, a judicious balancing of the considerations that influence our conduct. Pluralistic rhetoric is deflationary.

---

[12] Berlin, "Two Concepts of Liberty," 169.
[13] For illustrative citations, see note 5 of chapter 4.

Part of the significance of Berlin's "Two Concepts of Liberty" is that it eloquently expresses the moral vision that moves pluralists. One of the best of many illustrative passages is the famous last paragraph: "Principles are not less sacred because their duration cannot be guaranteed. Indeed, the very desire for guarantees that our values are eternal and secure in some objective heaven is perhaps only a craving for the certainties of childhood or the absolute values of our primitive past. 'To realize the relative validity of one's convictions', said an admirable writer of our time, 'and yet to stand for them unflinchingly, is what distinguishes a civilized man from a barbarian.' To demand more than this is perhaps a deep and incurable metaphysical need; but to allow it to determine one's practice is a symptom of an equally deep, and more dangerous, moral and political immaturity."[14]

Moving as this is, it has not escaped challenge. The one most apposite for our present purposes is Sandel's, who writes, "Although Berlin is not strictly speaking a relativist—he affirms the ideal of freedom of choice—his position comes perilously close to foundering on the relativist predicament. If one's convictions are only relatively valid, why stand for them unflinchingly? In a tragically-configured moral universe, such as Berlin assumes, is the ideal of freedom any *less* subject than competing ideals to the ultimate incommensurability of values?"[15]

There are three issues implicit in this challenge; two have already been disposed of, so we need little time to show how pluralism resolves them; but the third raises the hitherto undiscussed question of integrity, and it needs to be considered in greater detail. It must be admitted, however, that responding to Sandel's challenge requires going beyond Berlin's argument. But we can do that by enlarging Berlin's position without having to reject anything of substance.

The first issue is the difference between pluralism and relativism. Sandel is right in charging that Berlin does not clearly separate his version of pluralism from the various versions of relativism. Consequently he faces the same predicament as all relativists do: given the plurality (or relativity) of values, there can be no reason to favor one's own values when they conflict with the values to which other people are committed.

---

[14] Berlin, "Two Concepts of Liberty," 172. The writer referred to is Joseph Schumpeter. It is interesting to compare this passage with one written about fifteen years before it by Russell: "Uncertainty, in the presence of vivid hopes and fears, is painful, but must be endured if we wish to live without the support of comforting fairy tales. It is not good either to forget the questions that philosophy asks, or to persuade ourselves that we have found indubitable answers to them. To teach how to live without certainty, and yet without being paralyzed by hesitation, is perhaps the chief thing that philosophy, in our age, can still do for those who study it" (Russell, *A History of Western Philosophy*, xiv).

[15] Sandel, *Liberalism and Its Critics*, 8.

Berlin defends negative freedom against perfectionism and self-realizationism. But if negative freedom is indeed among the plural values, as he claims, then what more could the defense of it be than an expression of personal preference couched in fine rhetoric?

As we have seen, however, there is a clear difference between pluralism and all versions of relativism. Pluralists assert and relativists of all stripes deny that there are objective considerations by which conflicts among values could be reasonably settled. These considerations include the minimum requirements of good lives expressed in terms of primary values as well as the necessity of some secondary values to the maintenance of one's tradition. When conflicts occur between these essential primary and secondary values and other values, any reasonable person has a strong reason to opt for the essential values, since they are more important to living a good life. If Berlin's pluralism is enlarged to include the distinction between different kinds of primary and secondary values, then the first issue raised by Sandel's challenge is readily met.

The second one hinges on the same thought as the first, but it is approached through the notion of incommensurability. If values are incommensurable, then how could conflicts among them have a nonarbitrary resolution? The apparent force of the question derives from the failure to distinguish between the causes of conflicts and the means by which we may resolve them. The incommensurability and incompatibility of values are responsible for many conflicts. But the means for resolving them is to settle the respective importance of the conflicting values within the conception of a good life of the person who faces the conflict. The causes of conflicts are facts in the world; the means for resolving conflicts is our response to these facts. Our responses may or may not be reasonable, depending on the tradition and the conception of a good life that form their background, but the facts of incommensurability and incompatibility do not preclude reasonable conflict-resolution. Sandel supposes, not unjustifiably given Berlin's unclarity on this point, that if incommensurability were conceded, then the choice of one value over a conflicting one would be arbitrary. But if we remove the unclarity by sharply distinguishing between the question of *why* conflicts occur and the question of what to *do* about them, as we have endeavored to do, then this challenge can also be met.

But a third issue still remains, and it brings us to the topic of integrity. To have integrity is to remain faithful to our commitments when adversity makes it difficult to do so. If pluralism is correct, then pluralists must see their own conceptions of a good life as merely one among a plurality of equally reasonable options. And they must see that from a disengaged point of view, given that certain minimum requirements are met, the rational credentials of alternative conceptions may be the same. The requirements that all reasonable conceptions of a good life must meet underdetermine their contents. Beyond the minimum level, there are few constraints on what lives may be good. When pluralists realize that this is so, the challenge is: On what basis could they maintain their commitments steadfastly? How could they have strong convictions, if they see all convictions as optional? If I see the religious, political, aesthetic, and moral commitments you and I hold as being equally allowed by reason, and if they are incompatible, then what reasonable grounds could I have for favoring mine over yours? And if I realize that I have no such grounds, is this not bound to weaken the integrity of my commitments? So the challenge is: How can pluralists maintain their integrity?[16] As Sandel says, "If one's convictions are only relatively valid, why stand for them unflinchingly?"

The answer to this challenge is that it begs the question, so it is illegitimate. The assumption that underlies the challenge is that we cannot have reasons for something unless what we have would count as a reason for everybody else. There are many situations in which this assumption obviously holds. If I have a good reason for accepting or rejecting a scientific theory, an equation, a logical proof, a legal decision, or a medical diagnosis, then it would be a reason for anybody else in my position. But there are also many other situations in which the assumption, equally obviously, fails to hold. My reason for getting a divorce, valuing literature over music, refusing to make risky investments, preferring winter to summer vacations, finding incivility incompatible with friendship, wanting charity to be personal rather than impersonal are *my* reasons. And the strength of these reasons in no way depends on whether they would count as reasons, or count as heavily, for anyone else as they count for me. They are *my* reasons because they issue from my conception of a good life. From the point of view of some other conception, they may or may not be reasons or strong enough reasons. But this does not diminish their force for me. They are my reasons because my conception of a good life is constructed out of my character and circumstances, out of what I have adapted of the resources of my tradition, and out of my ranking of the respective importance of such values as I can try to make my own. Many reasons are relative to conceptions of a good life. What this shows, however, is not that such reasons are arbitrary, but that people differ in some of their judgments. How good these reasons are depends in two ways on the conceptions of a good life that form their ground.

[16] The irony of this challenge is that it was with the failure of integrity that Williams, one of the best-known defenders of pluralism, charged utilitarianism in his contribution to Smart and Williams, *Utilitarianism: For and Against*, 108–18. His target, Smart, may be allowed to murmur *tu quoque*.

The first is that our conceptions of a good life give us a good reason for ranking some value over a conflicting one, namely, that the higher-ranked value is more important than the other is to living what we believe would be a good life. This is both a very good reason and one that is relative to one's conception of a good life. To bring out why it is such a good reason, we should recall that conceptions of a good life embody an ordered set of commitments to primary and secondary values. In having a conception of a good life, what we have therefore is our own experiment in living, one that is conducted by adapting the resources of our tradition to our character and circumstances.

Integrity consists in adhering to the commitments that partly compose our conceptions of a good life. If we bear in mind what such conceptions are, it is easy to see why reasonable people would want to maintain their integrity, even in the face of serious challenges to their commitments. For integrity is not a marginal virtue, like grace, sensitivity, or quick-wittedness, but an indispensable part of living according to our conception of a good life. It is so because the extent to which we abandon our commitments when we encounter adversity is the same as the extent to which we abandon our efforts to make a good life for ourselves. No reasonable person would wish to abandon that, so all reasonable agents would want to maintain their integrity quite independently of the specific nature of the conceptions of a good life they are thereby protecting. Failures of integrity do occur of course, but they are brought on by insufficient reflection; by confusion due to stress, fatigue, lack of confidence, unrealistic appraisal of danger; and by similar culpable or understandable deficiencies of the intellect, feeling, or the will.

The bearing this understanding of integrity has on Sandel's criticism that pluralists could have it only in a weakened form is that integrity is independent of the particular conceptions of a good life individuals have. The reason for integrity has nothing to do with the beliefs of agents regarding relativism, monism, or pluralism. Integrity has its source in our wanting to realize *our* conception of a good life, and it is unaffected by whether or not other people share our conception. If I believe that a way of life is good and I want to live that way, then I have an excellent reason to try to live that way and to continue to do so with all the integrity I can muster in the face of difficulties. The reason is *my* reason. No doubt, you also have similar beliefs, and they supply you with reasons of your own. But none of this requires that we should share our beliefs about what way of life is good. The supposition that my reason is a good reason only if it derives from shared beliefs about good lives is question-begging as a criticism of pluralism, because it rests on an assumption that pluralists reject, namely, that there are such shared beliefs.

Discussing the second way in which the reasons we have may be good, even if they are relative to our conceptions of a good life, requires us to distinguish between sound and defective conceptions of a good life. Our conceptions of a good life can give reasons for our ranking one value over a conflicting one, but what if the conceptions are themselves in some way unreasonable? To understand this possibility we need to understand how we can be mistaken in our belief that some particular conception of a good life would indeed be good for us to realize. This is a large question, and an extended discussion of it is irrelevant to the development of pluralism. It will suffice for the present purposes to establish the possibility that reasonable agents may find their own conceptions of a good life defective. A more systematic exploration of this possibility is provided elsewhere.[17]

The most obvious way in which a conception of a good life may be defective is if it fails to rank primary values higher than secondary ones. Such a conception involves the violation of the deep conventions of the tradition on whose resources it depends. The deep conventions protect the minimum requirements of good lives, hence a conception of a good life that fails in this respect is self-defeating.

But conceptions of a good life can be defective even if they conform to deep conventions. This can happen if they are unsuitable for the people who try to live according to them. As we have seen, conceptions of a good life are intended to select those values of the tradition whose possession would best fit the agents' character and circumstances. The selection of the values and finding a fit between them and us depend on a realistic appraisal of our own character and circumstances. We can go wrong in these appraisals through lack of self-knowledge; through self-deception; through allowing fantasy, hopes, fears, or sentimentality to sway our judgments; or through unwillingness to look hard at unpleasant facts or at disagreeable aspects of our character.

Another way conceptions of a good life can be defective is by allowing only a too-narrow or a too-wide range of values. If the range is too narrow, it fails to satisfy normal human aspirations. Good lives should have some scope for the appreciation of beauty, playfulness, and nonutilitarian relationships, as well as for tackling difficult projects that require hard work, discipline, and self-control. Lives involving single-minded concentration on a very narrow range of values will be impoverished. The opposite defect is illustrated by lives that are too scattered. Projects are begun and then discontinued, enthusiasms ebb and flow, the attractions of many possibilities are perceived but too few of them are realized.

[17] See Kekes, *Moral Tradition and Individuality*, chapters 8–12.

In such lives, there are many values, but between their favorable evaluation and realization come the distractions of other values whose realization also recedes for the same reason.

Let us say, then, that a conception of a good life is defective if it is self-defeating, unsuitable, impoverished, or scattered; while it is sound if it does not have these, or similar, defects. Suppose, then, that moral agents claim that a reason for their ranking one of two conflicting values higher than the other is that it is more important to their conception of a good life and their conception is sound. If their reason rests on these grounds, then it is a good reason. And since whether such reasons are good has nothing to do with the number of sound conceptions, pluralists, committed to a there being a plurality of conceptions, could have as good reasons for their evaluations as anyone else. The corollary is that, Sandel's contrary claim notwithstanding, pluralists can maintain their commitments as unflinchingly, with as great an integrity, as anyone else, since their integrity will be motivated by the reasons they have for the evaluations that follow from their own conceptions.

CHAPTER SIX

The Possibilities of Life

> A person . . . explains himself to himself by his history, but by
> the history as accompanied by unrealized possibilities. . . . His
> individual nature, and the quality of his life . . . emerge in the
> possibilities that were real possibilities for him, which he
> considered and rejected for some reason or other. From the
> moral point of view, it is even a significant fact about him . . . that
> a certain possibility, which might have occurred to him as a
> possibility, never actually did occur to him. In self-examination
> one may press these inquiries into possibilities very far, and this
> pressure upon possibility belongs to the essence of moral
> reflection.
>   —Stuart Hampshire, *Innocence and Experience*

IF PLURALISTS are right, our primary moral experience is of many often-
conflicting values, which appear to us as possibilities created by our tradition. As we endeavor to make reasonable commitments to some of these
possibilities, so we form our individual conceptions of a good life. These
conceptions will be shaped both by the possibilities we want to realize
and the limits that impose constraints on our commitments. The concern of this chapter is with two notions that are essential to understanding the process whereby we encounter possibilities and commit ourselves
to some of them: moral imagination and increasing our freedom. Moral
imagination is a psychological process involved in the mental exploration of our possibilities. Increasing our freedom consists in enlarging the
moral space in which this exploration may occur.

MORAL IMAGINATION

Isaiah Berlin remarked that "the deepest convictions of philosophers are
seldom contained in their formal arguments: fundamental beliefs, comprehensive views of life, are like citadels which must be guarded against
the enemy. . . . [A]lthough the reasons they find, and the logic that they
use may be complex, ingenious, and formidable, they are defensive
weapons; the inner fortress itself—the vision of life for the sake of which
the war is being waged—will, as a rule, turn out to be relatively simple

and unsophisticated."[1] One good way to get to the deepest convictions of pluralists is to understand why they regard moral imagination as so very important.

Writing about Mill but reading him as a pluralist, Berlin says that man "is most himself in choosing and not being chosen for; the rider and not the horse; the seeker of ends, and not merely of means, ends that he pursues, each in his own fashion: with the corollary that the more various these fashions, the richer the lives of men become . . . the more numerous the possibilities for altering his own character in some fresh or unexplored direction, the more paths open before each individual, and the wider will be his freedom of action and thought."[2] Moreover, "the plurality of values is itself a good. . . . [O]ne who properly recognizes the plurality of values is one who understands the deep creative role that various values play in human life. . . . [O]ne is prepared to try to build a life around the recognition that these different values do each have a real and intelligible significance, and are not just errors, misdirections or poor expressions of human nature."[3] This is "the vision of life" at the core of the pluralistic defense of moral imagination.

The means by which the pluralistic vision is supposed to permeate moral life is, in Lionel Trilling's words, "[T]he moral imagination . . . which . . . reveals to us the complexity, the difficulty, and the interest of life in society, and best instructs us in our human variety. . . . [I]t is the human activity which takes the fullest and most precise account of variousness, complexity, difficulty—and possibility."[4] And Geertz chimes in, "If Trilling was obsessed with anything it was with the relation of culture and moral imagination; and so am I. He came to it from the side of literature; I come to it from the side of custom."[5] Geertz marshals the formidable resources of his ethnographic experience and reflection in support of the central pluralistic idea that as we increase our possibilities through moral imagination so we increase our freedom of thought and action and thus allow the plurality of values to play their deep creative role in human life. As he says, "[T]he range of signs we manage somehow to interpret is what defines the intellectual, emotional, and moral space within which we live. The greater that is, the greater we can make it become by trying to understand what flat earthers or the Reverend Jim Jones (or Iks or Vandals) are all about, what it is like to be them, the clearer we become to ourselves."[6]

[1] Berlin, "John Stuart Mill and the Ends of Life," 200–210.
[2] Ibid., 178.
[3] Williams, "Introduction" to Berlin's *Concepts and Categories*, xvi–xviii. The order of the quoted passages is rearranged.
[4] Trilling, *The Liberal Imagination*, vii–viii.
[5] Geertz, *Local Knowledge*, 40.
[6] Geertz, "The Uses of Diversity," 263.

Let us now try to understand just what moral imagination is. Imagination in general is responsible for a wide variety of human activities, among which four are particularly important.[7] The first is the formation of images, like the face of an absent friend; the second is resourceful problem solving, exemplified, for instance, by nonlinear thinking; the third is the falsification of some aspect of reality, as when we fantasize that the facts are other than they are; and the fourth is the mental exploration of what it would be like to realize particular possibilities, such as being very rich.[8] Moral imagination belongs to the fourth kind of imaginative activity. It is moral because one central concern of the agents engaged in it is with evaluating the possibilities they envisage as good or evil.

It is an obvious observation about human lives that we are endlessly involved in trying to understand the conduct of particular agents. If we could not do this successfully with much of the conduct of other people as it affects us, our civilized interaction would break down. Social order presupposes some degree of predictability, and in most cases involving social life we can reliably predict only what we at least to some extent understand. The same point holds, although for different reasons, with respect to the necessity that we, as agents, should have some understanding of our own conduct. If we did not know what we wanted, what our goals and interests were, and if we could not reasonably predict that our wants, goals, and interests will persist for some time, we could not plan for the future, and since such planning is necessary for living a good life, however it is conceived, we would be doomed to frustration.

The first step toward achieving this desirable understanding of ourselves and others involves gathering knowledge of what the agents actually have been doing. It is possible to reconstruct the lives of individuals by compiling a list of their more important publicly observable actions. But this cannot be more than a first step, for unless we understand something about the context in which they lived, the reasons for their actions, and what made some of their actions important, we could not be said to understand the actions. We might, then, know what they did, but not the significance of their deeds.

Understanding the context, the reasons behind, and the importance of actions matters because it reveals what the agents' possibilities were and what led them to realize one among their various possibilities. It is the nature of this type of understanding that it should attempt to illuminate the significance of what happened by considering what might have

---

[7] The literature on imagination is vast. It is a central concept in Hume, Kant, romantic thought, and aesthetics. Warnock's *Imagination* is an excellent guide to the subject.

[8] This kind of imagination is a central theme of Hampshire's *Thought and Action* and *Innocence and Experience*. Both works have influenced the argument.

happened. The assumption behind it is that the significance of a particular action emerges only by viewing it against the background of competing possibilities and by identifying the agent's reasons for attempting to realize one of these possibilities.

Moral imagination is an essential element of this understanding because it is the activity by which we attempt to re-create the possibilities particular agents faced. But this attempted re-creation is a complicated matter. It must involve ascertaining both the possibilities that were available to the agents and the possibilities the agents believed themselves to have. Both are needed for understanding the significance of particular actions, but it is necessary to keep them separate, otherwise we could not evaluate the reasons agents give for realizing a particular one among their possibilities.

It is a further complication that not even for thoroughly reasonable agents do these two sets of possibilities coincide, since even they may lack all sorts of information that is generally available in their context. If they had them, their beliefs about their possibilities would change accordingly, but they are not blameworthy for not having them, for their ignorance is not self-inflicted. Of course, few agents, if any, are thoroughly reasonable. The beliefs they form about their possibilities may be mistaken, and often these mistakes could and should have been avoided by them. So it is essential to evaluating the reasons agents give for their actions to form some conception of what beliefs about their possibilities it was reasonable for them to have, given the available possibilities. Understanding the significance of particular actions thus requires the imaginative re-creation of three sets of possibilities: those that were generally available in the agents' context, those that the agents could reasonably have been expected to believe themselves to have, and those that the agents actually believed themselves to have.

This threefold imaginative re-creation of possibilities goes beyond the bare knowledge *that* there were such and such possibilities. To know that much does not require imagination. To understand the significance of particular actions, the attractions, risks, novelty, general regard, emotive connotations, prestige, and so on, associated with the possibilities must be appreciated, and appreciated as they appear to the agents. The understanding of significance, therefore, cannot be merely cognitive, it must also have a large affective component capable of conveying the appeal the relevant possibilities had for the agent. We need a cognitively and affectively informed imagination to re-create the richness of the possibilities whose significance we want to understand. Only against that background does it begin to become understandable why agents realize a particular one among their possibilities.

Yet the imaginative re-creation of the background is still insufficient for understanding the significance of actions. For there is also the question of the evaluation of the reasons agents give for what they do. The most straightforward situation is when the possibilities the agents actually believe themselves to have coincide with the possibilities reasonable agents would have in that context, and the agents give as their reason that the attraction of the possibility they realized outweighed the attraction of its competitors. In such a case, having re-created the agents' possibilities, we come to appreciate how one of them could have been found to possess greater attraction for the agent than others. And then we could rightly claim to have understood the significance of the particular action.

But what if we encounter what is so often the case, namely, that some of the beliefs the agents have about their possibilities are in some way unreasonable? It may be that their possibilities are more or less numerous than they believe, or that they find possibilities attractive or unattractive because they ignore readily available features whose acknowledgment would incline them in another direction, or that they are deceiving themselves, or that their beliefs are misled by anger, fear, fantasy, spite, or envy. In such cases, knowing the reasons the agents give is not enough for understanding the significance of their actions. The search for understanding, then, must go beyond these reasons and explore the question of why there is a discrepancy between what the agents believe about their possibilities and what is reasonable to believe about them. By understanding why the agents are unreasonable, we may come to understand the significance of their actions, even though their significance is hidden from the agents themselves.[9]

This sketch of the workings of moral imagination may make it seem dauntingly difficult. But this appearance is deceptive. The kind of understanding described above is routinely achieved by ethnographers in describing the conduct of agents in other cultures; by historians in describing the situations in which various historical figures have acted; by literary critics who, unswayed by current destructive practices, still aim to enhance readers' appreciation of the predicaments of fictional characters; by all of us in trying to enter sympathetically into the frame of mind of someone we want to know intimately so as to understand the significance of his or her conduct; and by all of us again in the course of the necessary task of trying to make palpable to ourselves what it would be like to realize our possibilities and live according to them so that we may

---

[9] Marxists and Freudians in general, and particular sociologists like Goffman, for instance, in *The Presentation of Self in Everyday Life*, and anthropologists like Geertz in *The Interpretation of Culture* and *Local Knowledge*, suppose this to be the typical condition of humanity, a condition from which only exceptional individuals succeeding at exceptional efforts can free themselves. The position defended here is not committed to such extreme views, which are mistaken, although it is compatible with them.

shape our future, if we are reasonable, in as informed a manner as we can achieve.

The systematic cultivation, practice, and achievement of moral imagination is one traditional task of the humanities. Its interest is not in the causes of human conduct but in its significance. Its aim is not to form law-like generalizations but to concentrate on the reciprocal interaction between particular individuals and their cultural contexts. The explanation it yields is not of how anyone would act in that particular context but of why particular individuals have acted as they did in that context. Its task is partly descriptive, yet what it describes are not the objective possibilities that are open to everyone but the evaluations by individuals of what they take to be the possibilities that confront them as different ways of shaping their own future. It aims to explain what happened not by identifying the causes that made it happen but by identifying the reasons the agents rightly or wrongly believed themselves to have for doing what they did rather than the numerous other things they might have done.[10] Imaginative understanding of course is not restricted to the humanities; travel, films, or television may also provide it. But the humanities seek it, as it were, *ex officio.*

Locating the systematic pursuit of moral imagination in the humanities and stressing its differences from scientific understanding is not meant to suggest that there is anything ontologically odd about it. Everything we do has causes, and the causes also have causes, and there is no reason why a scientific account of all these causes should not be possible. The understanding moral imagination yields does not therefore compete with scientific understanding. They are different modes of understanding, each having its legitimate sphere and importance. One aims to understand human conduct from the outside, from the point of view of observers, objectively, *sub specie aeternitatis;* the other aims to understand the same thing from the inside, from the point of view of the agents, anthropocentrically, *sub specie humanitatis.*[11]

The Exploratory Function of Moral Imagination

Let us now consider this imaginative understanding when it takes on a moral emphasis and concentrates on evaluating relevant possibilities in moral terms. As we have seen, the need for this moral evaluation does

[10] Following Hampshire's "Subjunctive Conditionals," the point may be put by saying that the imaginative understanding central to the humanities is characterized by singular subjunctive conditionals in contrast with scientific understanding, which requires general counterfactual conditionals.

[11] This roughly coincides with the objective and subjective views discussed by Nagel, most recently in *The View From Nowhere.* Santayana shows the workings of this kind of imagination in his splendid collection of essays, *Interpretations of Poetry and Religion.*

not occur in the abstract but with reference to the specific agents living in the specific circumstances whose possibilities are being considered. Given this unavoidable individuation, there are still two importantly different ways the evaluation can be interpreted: the agents may be doing it about themselves, about their own possibilities, or about others, about their possibilities. There is a deep connection between these two ways. We frequently begin to learn about our possibilities by imitating others as they are realizing their possibilities. But understanding their possibilities requires an imaginative effort that at least at the time when we learn to make it involves envisaging their possibilities as if they were ours. Moral education develops the learners' moral point of view by teaching them about the moral points of view of others. Our present concern, however, is not with the education of moral imagination but with its exercise by full-fledged moral agents. And we need to concentrate on its self-directed rather than other-directed exercise, since the second presupposes that agents direct themselves to exercise their moral imagination in a particular way.[12] What, then, is involved in the kind of imaginative understanding through which agents are trying to envisage and evaluate their own possibilities by asking whether it would be morally acceptable to live and act according to them?

Moral imagination has both an exploratory and a corrective function. We shall begin with the exploratory one. Our usual situation is that we are born into a tradition, and as we try more or less consciously, with greater or lesser control, to make our lives good, we find our aspirations and opportunities defined by the conventional possibilities our tradition provides. We have a vague sense of what we value, and we attempt to realize it by seeking some non-Procrustean fit between what we take to be valuable and the possibilities we are aware of having. Part of the exploratory function of moral imagination is to acquaint us with these conventional possibilities.

This process is not that of initiating individuals standing outside the tradition into its ways. We do not begin with a self-generated initial conception of a good life and then develop it along conventionally accredited ways. Our first rudimentary view is already couched in terms we have learned from our tradition, since the identification and conceptualization of what we value already presuppose an evaluative vocabulary that we possess, if at all, only if we have learned it from our tradition. Initiation into the tradition, therefore, consists in becoming articulate about ourselves and our surroundings by learning to view both through the available conventional possibilities. Finding a fit between how we think it would be good to live and how we can live is thus a matter of identify-

---

[12] For a general discussion of how the other-directed moral commitments presuppose self-directed ones, see Falk, "Morality, Self, and Others."

ing those among our conventionally provided possibilities that attract us because we think they allow the development, and perhaps the realization, of what we regard as valuable in ourselves. It would be a mistake to suppose, however, that we cannot free ourselves from the consequences of this unavoidable conditioning. For moral imagination enables us to carry the exploration of our possibilities beyond the confines of our tradition.[13]

The scope of our moral imagination enlarges as we become acquainted with possibilities other than those that exist in our tradition. Through the development of a historical perspective, an understanding of other cultures, and immersion in literature, especially novels, plays, and biographies, we come to appreciate that the conventional possibilities available to us do not exhaust the possibilities of life but merely form that small subset of them to which the contingencies of our upbringing have given us access. As we acquire imaginative understanding of new possibilities, so we grow in breadth. And breadth contributes to our own possibilities in two ways.

The first is simply by increasing the number of possibilities we have. History, ethnography, and literature show us ways of living and acting that we can adapt to our circumstances, and thereby enrich our possibilities. But it often happens that the new possibilities we learn about are so remote from our circumstances as to make it impractical even to attempt to adopt them as our own. Yet they can still enrich us in a second way. The increasing breadth of moral imagination helps us to appreciate our own possibilities by providing a point of view from which we can better evaluate them. Breadth allows us to step outside our tradition and view it from an external vantage point not by committing us to it but by providing a basis for contrast and comparison. On that basis, we can see better the dangers, pitfalls, and losses that we confront by committing ourselves to some among our own possibilities.

We may, then, come to see, for instance, that from the point of view of an aristocratic tradition, which we have no wish to revive, our commitment to equality incurs the heavy cost of discouraging personal excellence, or that from the point of view of a puritanical tradition, which we are happy to consign to history, the sexual revolution tends to undermine the sort of intimacy that exists among exclusive sexual partners. These costs of equality and sexual liberation are not easily seen by those who are immersed in their commitments to them because they have nothing to which they could contrast the way they live. The point, of

[13] On this whole question of getting beyond the confines of our tradition, see the exchange between Geertz, "'From the Native's Point of View': On the Nature of Anthropological Understanding," Trilling, "Why We Read Jane Austen," Geertz, "Found in Translation: On the Social History of the Moral Imagination," and Gunn, *The Culture of Criticism and the Criticism of Culture*, chapter 5.

course, is not that if we appreciate the costs, we shall weaken our commitment to realizing some possibilities; rather, by appreciating the costs we shall be able to work for the realization of the possibilities in a more reasonable way.

The exploratory function of moral imagination contributes to our growth in breadth; breadth enlarges the field of possibilities our tradition initially provides; and the new possibilities, derived from exposure to other traditions—usually through history, ethnography, and literature—and, by acting as a basis for contrast and comparison, enable us to view critically the possibilities with which we start.

The Corrective Function of Moral Imagination

The exploratory function of moral imagination is forward-looking, for it concerns the question of which of our available possibilities we should attempt to realize in the future. This is the usual way of thinking about the direction of moral imagination. Yet it is not the only way, and in discussing the corrective function of moral imagination, we turn to an equally important question but one that directs the moral imagination backward, toward the agents' past.[14] This other question is about how reasonable individual agents have been in their evaluations of the possibilities open to them. Answering it requires us to look backward from the present, for it was in the past that we formed our views about what our present possibilities are. The desirable character trait for exploring our possibilities is, as we have seen, breadth. But there is also another desirable character trait needed for correcting our evaluations of the available possibilities, and that is depth. Depth is needed because we are prone to making mistakes in evaluating our available possibilities.

In discussing imaginative understanding in general, we have seen that it requires the re-creation of three sets of possibilities: those generally available in the agents' context; those agents would believe themselves to have, if they were thoroughly reasonable; and those agents actually believe themselves to have. The corrective function of moral imagination is to overcome the gap between the last two. This task is necessary because of our natural propensity to err in evaluating our possibilities. The sources of this type of error are numerous. For our present purposes, it will be sufficient merely to indicate some of the more obvious ones, before going on to discuss how the corrective function of moral imagination can help us to avoid them.[15]

---

[14] Wollheim's *The Thread of Life* is an extended reflection on a journal entry of Kierkegaard: "It is perfectly true, as philosophers say, that life must be understood backwards. But they forget the other proposition, that it must be lived forwards."

[15] For a systematic discussion, see de Sousa, *The Rationality of Emotion.*

The tacit assumption in the argument so far has been that the exercise of moral imagination is good because it improves our view of our possibilities. But observation of the way we actually conduct ourselves belies this assumption. Keeping our possibilities in the focus of our attention is burdensome. Life, after all, cannot be a permanent revolution. Adventurousness of spirit is fine and good, but life largely consists in performing everyday, routine, unadventurous tasks. Even creative artists, explorers, and other free spirits must shop for groceries, have their cars serviced, balance their bank accounts, pay their bills, have their hair cut, and negotiate with countless people on whom they rely for various services. After the embarrassing stage of adolescent rebelliousness is over, we cannot help conforming to the conventions of our tradition if we want to get on with our lives. And getting on with them means, for the vast majority of us, that we live according to some small subset of conventional possibilities. We settle into them—and we settle for them—and it is nothing but unwelcome irritation to have to form some attitudes toward possibilities that people other than ourselves may conceivably entertain.

Step by innocuous step we are thus led down the path to narrow-mindedness. We learn to live by exclusion, by saying "no" to the examination of possibilities that may make our lives better. We suppress our dissatisfactions with the life we have settled for, and we call this suppression a sign of maturity. In this manner, we deprive ourselves of the chances of improving our lives. This understandable propensity toward laziness of spirit, constricting our own horizons, and willingness to stay with the familiar is one source of the mistakes we tend to make about our possibilities: we ignore many of those we could have if we were more reasonable.

At the beginning of this chapter, in the course of distinguishing between different kinds of imaginative activities, we identified one kind as the falsification of some aspect of reality by fantasizing that the facts are other than they are. Another common source of error involved in forming mistaken beliefs about our possibilities is due to the confusion between fantasizing about our possibilities and exploring them in our imagination.[16] The confusion is understandable, since both fantasy and imaginative exploration concentrate on presently unrealized possibilities. Furthermore, both are emotionally charged, since the possibilities we are envisaging are colored by our hopes and fears. They are envisaged as possibilities for us, about how our lives may go, and it is natural to have strong feelings on that subject.

---

[16] Novitz, in *Knowledge, Fiction and Imagination*, discusses this distinction under the label of "fanciful" and "constructive" imagination; see especially chapter 2. Novitz argues for the great importance of the former. The position defended here is in agreement with Novitz about the importance of imagination, but it is in disagreement with him about the kind of imagination that is important.

Envisaging some possibilities changes from imaginative exploration into fantasy when our feelings become disproportionately strong. They do not merely color the way in which we see the relevant facts but come to alter our beliefs about what the facts are. Our hopes and fears may become so assertive as to force our attention only on the facts that seem salient from their point of view. They lead us to ignore, overlook, or forget about other facts that are just as salient but whose salience is obscured by the feelings we have allowed to rule us. In this way, hope may lead us not to take cognizance of the signs of infidelity in the person we love, or it may cause us to miss the seamy underside of the glamorous life on which we have embarked with great ambition. Similarly, fear may make us see opportunities as threats, it may make us overestimate negligible risks in possible ways of life, or it may cause us to deny our own abilities in order to avoid the prospect of failure. The damaging effect of fantasy is to motivate us to explore unsuitable possibilities or to undermine our motivation to explore suitable ones; and fantasy can have this effect because it derives its force from feelings whose strength is disproportionate to the facts that elicit them. Imaginative exploration is free from this defect, then, if the feelings associated with the envisaged possibilities are appropriate reactions to their objects.

Another source of error in the beliefs we hold about our possibilities is a particular form of self-deception. The fundamental reason for concentrating on our possibilities is to make our lives better. We can do so only by attempting to realize values that, we believe, would improve our lot. This, of course, requires the possession of some standard with reference to which we select the values whose realization we seek. But this standard, whatever it is, will not simply be a principle of some sort. Unless we are also emotionally attached to it, it is unlikely to motivate us with sufficient force to overcome the countervailing motivation to satisfy ourselves in ways that fail to conform to the standard. This may be expressed by saying that in the usual course of events the standard is accompanied by a second-order evaluation whose object is to become the sort of person who seeks to realize only those first-order values that conform to the standard. Thus we have first-order values that motivate us to explore some possibilities, and we have second-order values that regulate our first-order values.[17]

First- and second-order values routinely conflict because our second-order values lead us to frustrate many of our first-order values. This conflict is bound to occur, since selecting a value we seek to realize normally dooms some other values to remain unrealized. We often have more possible values available than we can attempt to realize, because scarcity

---

[17] This distinction, and its implications, are the central topics of Frankfurt's *The Importance of What We Care About.*

of resources, prevailing conventions, unavoidable spatial and temporal restrictions, and our limited energy curtail what we can reasonably seek. Self-deception occurs in the context of this conflict. It is a device by which we disguise from ourselves the reasons against realizing some of our first-order values that conflict with our second-order values. Its mechanism is to underplay the significance of violating the standard built into the second-order value by convincing ourselves of the harmlessness of satisfying a first-order value that is incompatible with the standard. We say that one compromise over principle will not make us faithless, that a little padding of the expense account will not break the treasury, or that one broken promise will not turn us into moral lepers. And we believe what we say because in the forefront of our attention is the satisfaction derived from acting as the aberrant first-order value prompts, and not the realization of the possibility that being guided by the second-order value would produce. We contrive to go against what we ourselves believe are the possibilities we should aim to realize.

Narrow-mindedness, fantasy, and self-deception all involve the falsification of facts relevant to our evaluation of our possibilities. The corrective function of moral imagination is to avoid such falsification and thus to overcome obstacles to a realistic estimate of what we can do to make our lives better. The way to arrive at such an estimate is through the imaginative re-creation of past situations in which we faced the possibilities then available to us. The advantage derivable from such a retrospective view is that the loss of immediacy, the absence of much emotional tension, and the knowledge that there is little we can do about our past conduct remove many of the obstacles that stood in the way of realism when the re-created situation was alive and present. As a result, we may come to a better understanding of why it was that we valued some possibilities sufficiently to act on them. And the context of this understanding is partly constituted of our coming to see in this retrospective way what was responsible in us for the discrepancy between what was *reasonable* to believe about our possibilities and what we *actually* believed about them. Thus we understand why our past evaluations were less than thoroughly reasonable.

This imaginative correction, if it becomes habitual, takes as its object very many of the past situations we have faced. It is not surprising if in the course of its exercise there emerge patterns constituted of the ways in which we tend to evaluate our possibilities. Awareness of these patterns enables us to articulate to ourselves what it is in us that makes us less reasonable than we might be: we are too fearful of risks, we are too much inclined to favor competitive possibilities, we are too sluggish emotionally, and so on. And in possession of these articulated patterns of the unreasonable evaluations to which we are prone, we can guard against their recurrence in situations we presently face.

But the habitual exercise of retroactive moral imagination also enables us to articulate patterns of our preferences for certain kinds of possibilities. These patterns, then, may be seen as representing our more enduring values. If we are conscious of them, we can more reasonably approach, in yet another way, our present dispositions in our present situations by seeing them as continuations of, or deviations from, these enduring patterns. And if we contemplate deviations, then the question naturally occurs: Why would we be inclined to go against our past values in the present case? There may or may not be a good answer, but asking the question, made possible by retroactive moral imagination's having become habitual, acts as a guard against present error.[18]

Knowledge of these two patterns, of our characteristic mistakes and values, is a species of self-knowledge. And it has a necessary moral component, since the kinds of mistakes and values we come to know that we are given to making and holding concern those of our possibilities that are involved in making our lives better. If we have this type of self-knowledge, we have a coherent view of an important part of ourselves, we have reasonable beliefs about the kinds of possibilities whose realization would tend to make our lives better, and we are aware of the mistakes we are prone to making. We gain a more reasonable conception of a good life. It is appropriate to describe people in possession of such a conception as having a kind of depth. This, then, is the sense in which the habitual exercise of the corrective function of moral imagination may nurture depth.

INCREASING FREEDOM

Having offered this outline of an analysis of moral imagination, let us now turn to discussing one implication of the analysis. Part of the importance of moral imagination is that it can increase our freedom. Notice that the claim is not that moral imagination makes us free, but the much more modest one that it can make us freer. There may be influences on us whose coercive force we cannot escape. We shall say as little about that as possible, in order to avoid getting entangled in the complications of the vexing tension between freedom and determinism. What needs to be emphasized is that we can increase our freedom, because we can escape a particular kind of influence on us, namely, the cultural.[19]

Let us begin, then, by noting that there are few people so lucky as to avoid in their lives a crisis brought on by the experience of pointlessness. We come to reflect on our lives and circumstances, because we are natu-

[18] On retroactive moral imagination, see Wollheim, *On Art and the Mind*, essays 2 and 3.

[19] The present position is close to the one developed by Velleman in *Practical Reflection*, especially chapter 5.

rally thoughtful; or because misfortune, failure, or grief befall us; or because we tire of facing the relentless adversity we encounter in many areas of our lives, and we come to ask: Why continue to do it? Why carry on our struggles, endure our losses, and suffer the pains caused by this endless Sisyphean activity? In the course of these melancholic reflections, the thought may occur to us that our values are not of our own making, because they are the products of our education and upbringing. We may go deeper and begin to suspect that the standards by which we evaluate whatever we and others do are themselves contingent products of the conditioning of our tradition. It may seem to us, then, that the reasons we believe we have for our commitments are in fact rationalizations. We shall be haunted by the suspicion that even in our basic commitments we are merely the instruments through which our tradition controls us. And then our despair may get even worse because we might conclude that, although our crisis was brought on by some loss, realizing what we value would be just as pointless. Everything in our lives that we have hitherto regarded as meaningful falls prey to the suspicion that it is contrived and inauthentic. We believe in this state that nothing is worth anything, because our beliefs about values are not within our control, because not even in the innermost recesses of our mental life are we free. We suppose that our tradition permeates us through and through, and all of our values and actions are the products of it and not of ourselves. We come to feel manipulated, and, since the manipulation is taken to be thoroughgoing and inescapable, we are overcome by despair.

Our philosophical tradition offers two general lines of thought intended to overcome this sort of despair.[20] Both diagnose its source as insufficient understanding, and both ultimately fail to overcome it, even after the understanding they recommend has been achieved. The first will be called "Spinozistic," to honor its most persuasive defender, although it has long historical roots going back to the Stoics and perhaps to Plato. Its fundamental idea is that the pointlessness we may feel when we first catch a glimpse of the forces that act on us comes from our incomprehension of these forces. The remedy is to endeavor to understand them better. For as we grow in understanding, so we free ourselves from their necessity. It is not that understanding necessity exempts us from its influence; rather, by understanding it, we come to identify with its dictates. And we would identify with what we understand to be necessary because genuine necessity reflects the order in the scheme of things, and that order is ultimately reasonable and good. In so far as *we* are reasonable and committed to the right values, we shall want to conform to genuine necessity. As we understand that resistance is a sign of

[20] For a more detailed discussion, see Kekes, *The Examined Life*, chapter 6.

unreasonability or immorality, so the sense of pointlessness, produced by our realization that we are subject to this necessity, will begin to dissolve.

The trouble with this answer is that there is no reason to suppose that the necessity is reasonable and good, and even if it were, falling in with it, however advisable, would not make us free. If freedom is to have any meaning, it must involve some control over alternative possibilities, and the Spinozistic view does not allow that. What it does do, however, is to bequeath to us the enormously suggestive idea that our freedom increases as our understanding does.

The second line of thought we can appeal to in trying to overcome our sense of pointlessness is Humean, but it too can be traced back to ancient sources, especially to Aristotle. It has a characteristic deflationary thrust, leading us away from metaphysical bathos toward a better understanding of human psychology. According to it, freedom is the absence of coercion. If we act as we want, without interference from external forces, then we have all the freedom we need and all that we can meaningfully be supposed to have. It is true that some of our values may themselves be coercively formed because we have been indoctrinated. But if we can act without external coercion to satisfy our noncoercively acquired values, those that stem naturally from our character and circumstances, that is simply what is meant by saying that we are free. Those who are assailed by a sense of pointlessness should ask themselves the therapeutic question of who or what forces them when they act according to their values. What more, it should be asked of them, do you want when you lament your lack of freedom than to be able to act so as to realize your values?

The fault of the robust common sense of the Humean view of freedom is its superficiality. It merely pushes the question one step back. For what worries us when we are assailed by the sense of pointlessness is that we have no control over any of our values. We value what we value because our tradition has conditioned us to do so. To believe that we have occasion to celebrate our freedom to the extent to which we are able to realize these values is to connive in the imposition of the necessity to which we are subject. Yet the Humean view also provides a seminal idea, namely, that freedom is connected with acting in accordance with our values.

One important implication of the view we have been developing is that through moral imagination we can increase the control we have over our possibilities, and consequently, we can increase our freedom. To appreciate how this is so, we need to see how moral imagination combines the fruitful ideas we can take over from the Spinozistic and Humean views.

Let us begin with the Humean idea that freedom may be viewed negatively, as the absence of coercion, and positively, as being able to act according to our values. The source of the sense of pointlessness is the suspicion that coercion is never absent, it is only that we are sometimes unaware of being subject to it; or, that even when it seems to us that we are acting as we want, we do not, because we have been conditioned in all of our views about what we should want. Assume, if only for the sake of argument, that both this view of freedom and the suspicions about its illusoriness are correct. The position from which we start, therefore, is one of unfreedom imposed on us by our tradition. The imposition is effected by our tradition's providing the language in which we learn to articulate our values, the possible ways of living and acting in terms of which the values can be realized, and the standards by which we evaluate our possibilities.

Moral imagination can overcome these influences through the exercise of its exploratory function. It can acquaint us with possibilities beyond those our tradition provides. It can enlarge the range of possibilities we value. It can also make it possible to reflect critically on the conventional possibilities by comparing and contrasting them with the possibilities we derive from history, ethnography, and literature. As a result, we need no longer be restricted to the evaluations conventional standards dictate.

Crucial to understanding the way the exploratory function of moral imagination is connected with freedom is to see that it *increases* our freedom, rather than makes us free by somehow exempting us from causal influences. If freedom is the absence of coercion and the ability to act according to our values, then moral imagination increases our freedom by allowing us to go beyond the influences of conventional possibilities and standards for evaluating them.

It may be objected to the description of the process just completed that it is misleading to call it an increase of freedom; it is merely an enlargement of the field of causes that exerts its influence on us. Why should we regard it as an increase of *freedom* that we have added historical, ethnographic, and literary influences to the current conventional influences? The answer is that the sense of pointlessness comes from the suspicion that we lack control over the influences on us. But if we can control what influences us, then this suspicion is misplaced, and moral imagination enables us to control them.

This answer, however, does not remove the objection; it only forces its reformulation. For, it will be said, the sense of pointlessness will not disappear if we understand that we have no control over the extent to which we are able to control the influences on us. The development of breadth, presupposed by the ability to control what influences us, depends on character traits and circumstances over which we have no control. It takes intelligence; sensitivity; a good deal of curiosity about other people; a reasonably secure, orderly, comfortable life; and a liberal education. But the extent to which we have these is not within our control. Whether we can control what influences us is itself an effect of what has influenced us in the past.

It is in reply to this objection that we can appeal to the idea suggested by the Spinozistic view, namely, that freedom increases as our understanding of the influences on us increases. The form of this understanding is the kind of self-knowledge that is involved in the exercise of the corrective function of moral imagination.[21] Its objects are the enduring patterns of values and mistakes that reflection on our past conduct reveals. And the values and mistakes characterize our attitudes to the possibilities that we believe we have for making our lives better. But how does this self-knowledge give us greater control; how does it increase our freedom? Or, how does it help us to meet the objection that it is pointless to try to control the influences of the tradition to which we are subject, since the extent to which we can control them depends on character traits and circumstances over which we have no control?

It goes without saying that self-knowledge cannot increase our control over the political and social circumstances in which we live. Nor can it give us character traits that we do not possess. What it can do is make us aware of some obstacles that prevent us from using such intelligence, sensitivity, and curiosity about other people and ways of life as we have, and using them to form a more reasonable view of the possibilities we have open to us. Self-knowledge helps us to avoid the mistakes we habitually make, mistakes that are responsible for forming wrong views about our possibilities. If we understand that it was narrow-mindedness, fantasy, or self-deception that made us dismiss possibilities that might have made our lives better or pursue unsuitable possibilities and thus make our lives worse, then we shall be motivated to remove these obstructions. And to remove them, of course, is to achieve greater control over our possibilities. Self-knowledge thus increases our freedom by helping us overcome internal obstacles to our endeavors to make our lives better.

This is not to deny that different people have different native endowments, and, consequently, they are capable of increasing their freedom in different degrees. One might express this by saying that people differ in their talents for freedom. They differ in the extent to which they can critically examine the influences of their tradition. As a result, some will live entirely unexamined lives and others will, to the extent of their talents for freedom, enlarge their field of possibilities. This is not a surpris-

---

[21] This line of thought follows Hampshire's "Spinoza and the Freedom of Mind."

ing implication of the present position, since it is a plain fact of life that people are different in these ways. If the despair brought on by the suspicion that one's life is pointless assails people immersed in utterly unexamined lives in which they have very little control over their possibilities, then it may be an appropriate reaction. Some lives *are* pointless, even though the people whose lives they are cannot be blamed for it. For some people lack the talent for freedom, and others who have it live in conditions in which their talents cannot be exercised.

Conclusion

It should be remembered that the point about moral imagination is that it *increases* our freedom not that it makes us free. If increasing freedom is seen as a matter of degree, depending on increasing the control we have over our possibilities, then moral imagination makes an important contribution to increasing our freedom. For through its exploratory and corrective functions it enlarges the field of our possibilities beyond what our tradition provides. Increased freedom, of course, can be put to evil uses. The argument presented here should not therefore be taken as an unqualified celebration of the possibilities of life. There are and ought to be limits on the exploration of our possibilities, and they will be discussed in the next chapter.

The subject of this chapter, however, has been possibilities, not limits. And the argument has been that the proper question to ask about the connection between moral imagination and increasing our freedom is not whether moral imagination can free us from cultural conditioning but whether it can help us gain greater control over our lives by helping us reduce the discrepancy between what it is reasonable to believe about our possibilities and what we actually believe about them. If their connection is seen in this light, then it will be obvious that those who wish to improve their lives will cultivate their moral imagination. And if that leads them to reflect on their lives in the light of history, ethnography, and literature, then they will be following the traditional approach that is one lasting contribution of the humanities to the betterment of the human condition.

Finally, let us be clear about what the pluralistic emphasis on the importance of moral imagination does and does not imply. We distinguished between the exploratory and corrective functions of moral imagination. Through the first, we enlarge our possibilities, increase our freedom, and grow in the breadth of our appreciation of various conceptions of a good life. Through the second, we adapt possibilities to our character and circumstances, develop self-knowledge, and deepen our understanding of ourselves and of the appropriateness of some possibilities to what we take ourselves to be. Both of these activities are necessary for living a good life, for, in their different ways, they make available to us the possibilities whose plurality is the central claim of pluralism. Thus all pluralists will be committed to valuing moral imagination.

This value, however, like all the others acknowledged by pluralists, is not overriding but conditional. If pluralists are consistent, they must recognize that moral imagination may be justifiably limited. Not all possibilities of life are worth exploring, not even in our imagination. The fact is that we do not need moral imagination to recognize that the abominable fantasies of the Marquis de Sade, the fanaticism of Khomeni, the murderous resentment of Charles Manson, the inhuman cruelty of Idi Amin, the torture of political prisoners in numerous right- and left-wing dictatorships, and ideologically, religiously, or racially motivated terrorism are evil. It may be necessary for some people professionally concerned with explaining the causes of these horrors to employ their imagination to understand the stories the agents of these crimes tell themselves and others about why they are causing evil. But the understanding of their stories cannot alter the fact that they are about evil; they can, at best, make comprehensible the twisted motivation of the agents. It is quite enough for us to know that there are certain ways in which all human beings, always, and everywhere are vulnerable to being undeservedly harmed and that it is evil to harm them in these ways. Having an imaginative appreciation of the motives and other sources of such conduct cannot alter, and is not necessary for, our condemnation of it.

Pluralists must recognize therefore that moral imagination, as all conditional values, has its limits. There are exercises of moral imagination that do not enlarge our possibilities, increase our freedom, or contribute to the breadth and depth of our appreciation in a way that could make our lives better. Nor does it always have the negative significance of strengthening our commitment to civilized possibilities by contrasting them with the barbarism of some alternatives. It is not necessary to have an ethnographically, historically, or literarily informed imagination to know that people ought not to be harmed in certain ways. The upshot is that if we recognize that moral imagination must itself have limits, then we cannot agree with the unqualified endorsement of it by many pluralists, such as that "the consciousness of the plurality of values is itself a good" and we shall suspect "the deep creative role"[22] of evil possibilities; we shall not want it to contribute to "the vitality of [our] consciousness"[23] or to the "largeness of [our] minds"[24] by making evil possibilities "a working force in our consciousness."[25]

---

[22] Williams, "Introduction" to Berlin's *Concepts and Categories*, xvi–xviii.
[23] Geertz, *Local Knowledge*, 161.
[24] Ibid., 47.
[25] Ibid., 16.

CHAPTER SEVEN

The Need for Limits

Pluralism run to seed is not an engaging spectacle.
—Michael Oakeshott, "The Authority of the State"

IN THE PREVIOUS chapter, we considered the fourth thesis of pluralism. It focused on the importance of the imaginative exploration of possibilities. We stressed that growth in the breadth and depth of our appreciation of possibilities contributes to living a good life, because the possibilities reveal ways of being and acting that may reasonably attract us. It is a widely shared assumption among pluralists that the more extensive our moral imagination is the better off we are from the moral point of view.

The purpose of this chapter is to develop the fifth thesis of pluralism. This will lead us to stress the need for limits in general and for moral imagination in particular. In doing so, we shall disagree with the prevailing consensus among pluralists. One of the most important implications of pluralism is that no value should be unqualifiedly endorsed, because any value may conflict with some other value, and it is often an open question which value should prevail in such conflicts. This must be true of moral imagination as well. It is undoubtedly a good thing, but it too must have its limits. After all, the possibilities moral imagination reveals may violate our values. Moral imagination may contribute not just to good lives but also to evil ones. It is necessary to discuss, therefore, what limits ought to be imposed on the possibilities moral imagination may reasonably suggest. These limits are set by deep conventions, which protect primary values. According to pluralists, however, even primary values are conditional, hence there must be possible cases in which the limits set by deep conventions may be reasonably violated. We shall consider a concrete case in point that involves the primary value of life. This case will raise the question of whether it is possible to determine on context-independent grounds when the violation of a deep convention may be reasonable. The answer will be in the affirmative, and that will be taken to support pluralism against the second version of relativism: conventionalism. But the stronger are the pluralistic arguments against conventionalism, the closer pluralists move to monism. It is necessary, therefore, to show also that the pluralistic arguments against conventionalism do not commit pluralists to monism.

MORAL IMAGINATION AND DEEP CONVENTIONS

Let us begin by noting the obvious fact that the possibilities moral imagination reveals may be such evil ones as slavery, female circumcision, racism, blood feuds, footbinding, child prostitution, political corruption, torture, arbitrary imprisonment, the mutilation of criminals, and similar notorious and regrettably widespread practices. In informing us of the possibilities of life, historians, ethnographers, novelists, and biographers are of course not confined to the pleasant ones. The question naturally arises, therefore, whether we can reasonably place some possibilities beyond limits.

Pluralists must be committed to there being reasonable limits, and the most obvious ones are set by deep conventions. Such limits appeal to a point of view that is independent of the conception of good and evil advocated by any particular tradition. The point of view is established by primary values and by those substantive and procedural secondary values that represent the concrete forms primary values take. It will be remembered that the deep conventions of a tradition protect people in their pursuit and realization of these primary and secondary values. The reason why the point of view these values create is independent of any particular tradition is that deep conventions protect the minimum requirements of a good life, however it is conceived, and all traditions must either be committed to providing that protection or be liable to the most serious moral criticism. The limits we may reasonably set to the exercise of moral imagination thus concern the exploration of possibilities that violate deep conventions. These are the evil possibilities that ought not to play "a deep creative role,"[1] that ought not to contribute to "the vitality of [our] consciousness"[2] or the "largeness of [our] minds,"[3] and that ought not to become "a working force in our consciousness."[4]

What this comes to, in more concrete terms, is that there are some things that all reasonable human beings would have to regard as good or evil, independently of their moral views on other matters. Murder, torture, dismemberment, and enslavement are evil, unless extraordinary circumstances make them otherwise. Similarly, the protection of life, physical security, and some freedom to do as we please are normally good in all historical and cultural contexts. The qualifications indicated by "extraordinary circumstances" and "normally" are reminders that the claim for the universality of these primary values is conditional not overriding. And that means that while the claim normally holds, it can also be

---

[1] Williams, "Introduction" to Berlin's *Concepts and Categories*, xvi–xviii.

[2] Geertz, *Local Knowledge*, 161.

[3] Ibid., 47.

[4] Ibid., 16.

defeated provided there are good reasons for it. In the usual course of events, murder, torture, dismemberment, and enslavement are harmful, and protection against them is beneficial; that is why circumstances would have to be extraordinary and abnormal for these claims to be reasonably defeated. Yet the claims are still not overriding, for the extraordinary and the abnormal may occur.

The universality of the evil of murder, torture, mutilation, and enslavement is compatible with variations regarding what forms of killing constitute murder; the infliction of what pain in what circumstances is torture; what counts as mutilation rather than, say, marks of initiation or cosmetic improvement; and what forms of subordination amount to enslavement. There certainly are obvious cultural variations about these matters. On the other hand, there are no cultural variations in stressing the desirability of protecting people recognized as *bona fide* members of one's tradition from the undeserved infliction of the kinds of harm that in that tradition would be regarded as murder, torture, mutilation, and enslavement. The universal element present in all reasonable traditions is the recognition that people of their own kind are vulnerable to being harmed by the loss of life, the infliction of pain, being crippled, and having drastic restrictions placed on their opportunities to do what they want, and that they should be protected against the undeserved infliction of these forms of harm. Differences concern the variable not the deep conventions regarding the circumstances in which the infliction of such harms is said to be undeserved. But the differences among these variable conventions do not extend so far as to call into question the truisms embodied in deep conventions that all conceptions of a good life require the protection of life, physical security, and some freedom from undeserved violations. Indeed, the aim of deep conventions is to provide that protection.

The implication of these remarks is that imagination is moral only if it involves evaluating the possibilities it reveals in terms of deep conventions. The moral evaluation of possibilities is barely begun if we appraise them merely in such simple terms, but even this much is sufficient to show that morality requires us to place limits on the exercise of moral imagination. And showing this is to raise serious moral doubts about the unqualified pluralistic claim that consciousness of "the plurality of values is itself a good," that "different values do each have a real and intelligible significance, and are not just errors,"[5] and the aspiration of "making it possible for people inhabiting different worlds to have genuine and reciprocal impact upon one another."[6]

---

[5] Williams, "Introduction" to Berlin's *Concepts and Categories*, xvi–xviii.
[6] Geertz, *Local Knowledge*, 161.

The point against giving free reign to moral imagination is that since morality requires us to opt for possibilities that involve less evil and more good than competing possibilities, there cannot be an unqualified moral requirement to enlarge the number of possibilities we have by increasing our freedom of choice and by striving for a more sympathetic under-standing of alien possibilities. For the new possibilities we acquire in this manner may foster evil at the expense of good. Moral imagination thus must be seen as having moral limits.

Conventionalists might object to this attempt to set limits to moral imagination that it rests on the indefensible assumption that deep con-ventions protect context-independent values. They might agree that deep and variable conventions may be distinguished, but they would nevertheless insist that the distinction is bound to be drawn *within* tra-ditions. Consequently deep conventions cannot be relied on for the evaluations of possibilities suggested by other traditions. In order to eval-uate this objection, we need to consider a concrete value in a concrete situation.

Life as a Primary Value

It will be remembered from chapter 3 that primary values are derived from the minimum requirements of all good lives. These requirements, in turn, depend on universally human, culturally invariable, and histori-cally constant facts of human nature. We have grouped primary values into those of the self, intimacy, and social order. And there can be no serious doubt in anyone's mind that life is one of the most important primary values of the self. For clearly one minimum requirement of good lives is to be alive. That this is so is recognized by all legal systems, traditions, and codified or uncodified constitutions. The claim that life is a primary good if anything is, is not controversial.

What is controversial is what precisely this claim implies.[7] There is much cant about the sanctity of life. Schweitzer, for instance, tells us, "The fundamental principle of ethics . . . is reverence for life. . . . [R]everence for life contains within itself . . . the commandment to love, and it calls for compassion for all creature life."[8] Does this mean that without reverence, love, and compassion for AIDS viruses, bedbugs, and turnips we cannot be ethical? But perhaps Schweitzer should restrict his claim to human lives. The question, then, is whether reverence, love, and compassion for human lives commit one to opposing suicide, just

---

[7] See Glover, *Causing Death and Saving Lives*, Kluge, *The Practice of Death*, Kohl, *The Morality of Killing*, Labby, *Life or Death*, and Steinbock, *Killing and Letting Die*.

[8] Schweitzer, *The Teaching of Reverence for Life*, 26.

wars, capital punishment, abortion, motorcycle racing, sunbathing, over-eating, and rock climbing?

Many people have a basic commitment to life as a primary value with-out thereby committing themselves to the indefensible claim that life is an overriding value. They can thus acknowledge that there are circum-stances in which it is reasonable to violate the deep convention protect-ing life. As a corrective to Schweitzer's syrupy sentiment, we should face facts with Charles Taylor: "In our public debates standards which are unprecedentedly stringent are put forward . . . and are not openly chal-lenged. We are meant to be concerned for the life and well-being of all humans on the face of the earth; we are called on to further global jus-tice between peoples; we subscribe to universal declarations of rights. Of course, these standards are regularly evaded. Of course, we subscribe to them with a great deal of hypocrisy and mental reservation. It remains that they are the publicly accepted standards."[9] To get a grip on the question, we need to ask whether or not the mental reservations of which Taylor speaks can be reasonable.

Clearly, the answer is that some reservations are reasonable and some are not. But even a single reasonable reservation about life is sufficient to establish that its value is not overriding but conditional. For the reser-vation shows that there are circumstances in which it is reasonable to violate the deep convention protecting life. The question is: What are these circumstances?

Posing the question in this way has considerable importance. For we are no longer asking *whether* the deep convention can be reasonably vio-lated; we want to know rather *when* such violation can be reasonable. The first form of the question leaves it open whether there ever could be a reasonable violation, while the second form, in which we are posing it, assumes an affirmative answer and prompts us to ask when a violation may be reasonable.

Let us begin to consider the second form of the question by reflecting on our actual situation. As Taylor notes, what we find is a glaring discrep-ancy between rousing declarations and actual practice. We are all op-posed to murder, and we want to lengthen life expectancy and reduce infant mortality. But we also know perfectly well that many lives would be saved if we lowered the speed limit; destroyed tobacco crops; sent drug addicts to concentration camps; discouraged mining; outlawed para-chute jumping, Himalayan expeditions, and spelunking; and instituted such life-saving measures as forcing fat people to lose weight, over-achievers to slow down, and the sedentary to take exercise. The fact re-mains, however, that we neither act on this knowledge nor advocate that

[9] Charles Taylor, *Sources of the Self*, 515.

others should do so; and if we tried either, a great howl would be heard throughout the land. The appropriate laws would be unenforceable, much as Prohibition was and the 55-mile speed limit is. The reason for this is that although we value life, we also value other things. Freedom, justice, autonomy, prosperity, adventure, privacy, free trade, civic harmony, and countless other values continually come into conflict with the value of life. And as the examples just given show, the claims of other values are routinely judged by a very large number of people to override the claims of life. If genuine moral commitments require action according to them, then very few people indeed hold the commitment they avow to the sanctity of life, or to the right to life, or to life's being inalienable, indefeasible, or imprescriptible.

The source of this discrepancy between avowed commitment and actual practice is not so much hypocrisy as lack of thought. People consult their conscience and grow dewy-eyed in declaring their respect for some thing they regard as good, much as Schweitzer did. There is no reason to doubt the sincerity of many of these declarations. The trouble with them is that in the grip of moralistic fervor people forget that they are also committed to other values and that they cannot have all of them. The claims of values must be balanced against each other. As soon as this is understood, sincere commitment to some value must be supplemented by a reasoned account of how the conflicting claims of it and other values should be balanced. And that realization brings us to pluralism, the moral theory whose concern is with reasonable conflict-resolution among a plurality of values.

It may be objected, however, to the description of our actual moral situation—the description that forms the background against which pluralism acquires plausibility and force—that, while it may be true that this is how things are, the concern of moral theory is with how things ought to be. Our actual moral situation reflects our shortcomings: unreasonability, stupidity, moral weakness, uncontrolled emotions, and the like. These lamentable features of our humanity, however, no more tell against the merits of a moral theory than a prevalent form of sickness tells against the merits of a medical theory that proposes a treatment of it. It may be argued therefore that the immorality, inconsistency, and confusion of our actual practice not only fail as arguments against human life's having an overriding value but actually demonstrate the importance of reaffirming our commitment to it. The reasonable way to balance the conflicting claims of life and other primary values is to recognize the priority of the claim of life. And that means the acceptance of some form of monism as opposed to pluralism.

In reply to this regression to monism, we need only remember that what is reasonable to regard as good is not life itself but life with some duration and enjoyment; one that merits self-respect and some sense of accomplishment. In other words, it is a life that is found good, rather than a burden, by the person living it. All of us can imagine circumstances in which we would not want to go on living. In doing so, we tacitly appeal to some values whose lack would make us lose the motivation to sustain life. And this possibility shows that the value of life is not always overriding. Furthermore, such judgments may reasonably be extended to lives other than our own: lives involving irreversible coma, excruciating pain and terminal illness, gross indignities caused by Alzheimer's disease, and so on.

It is important to add by way of necessary caution that the judgment that in some circumstances one's own or someone else's life would not be worth living does not imply any particular action. What follows may be resignation, pity, self-deception, resentment, religious conversion, or a resolve to soldier on or to encourage soldiering on, or it may be suicide, euthanasia, or murder. The reasonability of the judgment is one thing; the moral credentials of the response to the life reasonably judged not to be worth living is quite another. The pluralistic case appeals to the possibility of the former.

If this is right, then it follows from pluralism that in some contexts life may be reasonably taken or given up. And this begins to look suspiciously like conventionalism. For defenders of that version of relativism may agree that life is a primary value but go on to insist that traditions may reasonably differ about the circumstances in which the case for protecting life may be defeated. Different traditions have different conventions about the appropriate ways of treating the old, infants, criminals, enemies, traitors, and so on. Each tradition may recognize life as a primary value, and yet find acceptable widely different reasons for taking it. In the context of a tradition, the exposure of the old, infanticide, capital punishment, or death by torture or mutilation may be regarded as reasonable. As we move away from a monistic insistence on the overriding value of life, so we slide toward the conventionalistic view that any attitude to life is reasonable in a given context provided only that it is sanctioned by the prevailing tradition.

The problem for pluralists, therefore, is to arrest the slide that begins with the rejection of monism and ends with the acceptance of this version of relativism. Or, to put the point in moral terms, the problem for pluralists is to show that if we give up the view that life has overriding value, we still need not embrace the view that there is no reasonable prohibition that all traditions should recognize against taking or giving up life.

But it is useless to try to grapple with this problem in generalities. We need to examine a concrete case. We shall consider one that occurs in the context of a well-established tradition and involves killing one of their own. The killing impresses our Western sensibility as exceptionally brutal. Yet, as we try to understand the tradition in the background, the case will start to look less straightforwardly barbaric. As a result, we shall find our attitude shift back and forth between monistic moral disapproval and relativistic moral promiscuity. This will motivate us to seek a pluralistic position between them where it is reasonable to rest our judgment.

THE MORALITY OF LIVE BURIAL

We shall consider what used to be a custom of the Dinka, a tribe of about a million people, living in Africa, in the Southern Sudan. The custom no longer exists, because the Sudanese authorities have outlawed it. The account of the custom and its significance for the Dinka comes from Godfrey Lienhardt's *Divinity and Experience: The Religion of the Dinka.*[10] Lienhardt is an ethnographer who lived with the Dinka; his book about them is widely regarded as an outstanding work.

The custom is the burial alive of the most important and respected religious and political leaders the Dinka have, the spear-masters. At the appropriate time, the Dinka dig a deep hole in the ground and, in the midst of various religious ceremonies, place the living spear-master into it. Then the assembled people throw cattle dung on the spear-master until it covers the hole in which he lies, except for a very narrow opening, and the spear-master slowly suffocates in the excrement piled on him.[11] This will strike us as a gruesome form of murder, involving the illegitimate violation of a deep convention. But let us look further.

To begin with, the appropriate time for the live burial is when the spear-master is quite old and feels the proximity of death. Furthermore, when that time comes is usually, although not invariably, announced by the spear-master himself. In most of the cases about which Lienhardt has information, the choice of the time, although never the method, of death was left to the spear-masters. They had known that they were to die in this way ever since they became spear-masters. The attitude of the Dinka to the spear-masters' death is also instructive: "[The] people should not mourn, but rather should be joyful. . . . For the . . . master's people . . . the human symbolic action involved in the 'artificial' burial must be seen to transform the experience of the leader's death into a concentrated public experience of vitality."[12] Lastly, it should be noted

[10] Lienhardt, *Divinity and Experience.*
[11] Ibid., 300–304.
[12] Ibid., 316–17.

that cattle dung is not a repulsive object for the Dinka. Their economy depends on cattle, and they believe that cattle dung has curative and restorative powers. The significance of throwing cattle dung on the spear-master therefore is not that of heaping excrement on a moribund old man.

The heart of the matter, however, is the live burial itself. Why do the Dinka and the spear-masters themselves believe that spear-masters should not die a natural death? Lienhardt says, "'Life', *wei*, is the same word in Dinka as that for breath. . . . *Wei* is something which living creatures have and which is the source of their animation, and more, the source of their vigorous animation. Life is therefore in creatures to a larger or smaller degree."[13] The reason why spear-masters are so important and respected is that they are "thought to have in them more life than is necessary to sustain them only, and thereby sustain the lives of their people and their cattle."[14] The Dinka believe that "[i]t is because the master of the fishing-spear's life is bound up with the vitality of his people that he must not . . . die as other men die, for this would be the diminution of the vitality of all."[15]

The significance of the ceremony of live burial of the spear-master is that "[i]f he 'dies' like ordinary men, the 'life' of his people which is in his keeping goes with him. . . . What they [the Dinka] represent in contriving the death which they give him is the conservation of 'life' which they themselves receive from him."[16] Through the narrow opening left in the cattle dung under which they bury him, the life, or breath—the *wei*—of the spear-master leaves him and passes on to his people so that they can continue with their lives: "In his death, then, the Dinka master of the fishing-spear is made to represent to his people the survival with which masters of the fishing-spear are associated. . . . Notions of individual immortality mean little to non-Christian Dinka, but the assertion of collective immortality means much, and it is this which they make in the funeral ceremonies of their religious leaders."[17]

If we come to appreciate how the Dinka themselves see the live burial of the spear-master, then the moral significance we attribute to this violation of a deep convention will change from the initial uninformed judgment of regarding it as gruesome murder to a more sophisticated response. Live burial is clearly a violation of one minimum requirement of good lives. But the Dinka believe that it is morally justifiable because it is

[13] Ibid., 206.
[14] Ibid., 207.
[15] Ibid., 208.
[16] Ibid., 316.
[17] Ibid., 318–19.

necessary for the transmission of life from the spear-master to his people. Live burial for them is like donating blood or a kidney is for us; except that in the Dinka case one person is the donor for all Dinka, while we proceed on a one-to-one basis. It is true that both blood or kidney donors and spear-masters suffer various degrees of injury, but it is in a good cause, and both the altruistic victims and the beneficiaries see it as such. The live burial of the spear-master should be seen therefore both as a morally commendable sacrifice made by good people and as a possible case where there may be good reasons for violating the deep convention protecting life.

Moreover, if we abstract from the point of view of the participating Dinka and ask from outside their context about the moral credentials of live burial, then the answer still remains that provided the underlying beliefs are true, live burial itself is morally justifiable. For without it the vitality of the Dinka would be sapped, as the vitality of those would be who would have to do without the blood or the kidney they need.

Conventionalists will therefore conclude that what counts as a morally acceptable form of killing partly depends on the beliefs that form the background of the relevant actions. And since the background beliefs vary from context to context, so also must vary reasonable judgments of what counts as permissible killing. The pluralistic attempt to provide reasons for defeating the case for life that would carry weight outside the context cannot therefore succeed, because what counts as an acceptable reason depends on the tradition that prevails in the context.

Relativism Redux?

The conventionalist version of the relativistic argument, however, rests on a failure to distinguish between how background beliefs affect the moral status of particular *actions* and the moral status of the *agents* who perform the actions. If the Dinka's beliefs about the transmission of life from the spear-master to the tribe are false, then, by the actions involved in the live burial, they are violating one minimum requirement of good lives. But since they are not doing so knowingly and intentionally, their moral status as agents is quite different from what it would be if their violations were deliberate. Just exactly what that status is depends on the balance of reasons available to them for the continuation of the practice. The position of the Dinka in this respect is analogous to what our position would be if future medical research were to reveal that blood transfusion and kidney transplants were harmful to the recipients. Since we have no reason to think that now, and we have good reasons to think the opposite, we, as agents, like the Dinka, as agents, should not be blamed if future developments force a shift in the present weight of reasons.

None of this, however, affects the question of whether our actions, or the Dinka's, adversely affect the prospects for good lives. If we distinguish between the question of the extent to which *agents,* whose actions violate deep conventions due to reasonably held yet false beliefs, are blameworthy and the question of whether or not particular *actions* violate deep conventions, then it is the conventionalistic rather than the pluralistic argument that fails. For we can subject various actions to a context-independent moral evaluation by asking how they affect the possibility of living good lives, and we can answer without thereby necessarily committing ourselves to praising or blaming the agents of the relevant actions. We can reasonably claim, from a moral point of view independent of any tradition, that a tradition in which rightly respected leaders are allowed to die a natural death is, in that respect, morally better than one in which they are buried alive under cattle dung. And we can make the claim without prejudice to the moral status of the people who perpetuate either tradition.

Let us, however, go a little deeper. Suppose that a reflective Dinka or an ethnographer responds to doubts about the truth of the Dinka's beliefs about the passing of life from the spear-master to the tribe by saying that what matters is the symbolic, not the literal, truth of their beliefs. The fact is, it may be said, that as a result of the ceremony the tribe *is* revitalized. They reaffirm their identity, the continuity of their tradition, their solidarity, their determination to face adversity together, and that is as good as if *wei* actually passed from the suffocating spear-master to the tribe. The significance of this for the issue between conventionalism and pluralism is that if this claim were acceptable, then there would be a new reason for thinking that what justifies overriding the case for life depends on the context. Live burial would be justified in the Dinka context because it would be a sustaining part of the tradition on which the good lives of the Dinka depend, while in another context, such as ours, live burial would remain morally impermissible. The moral status of live burial depends, therefore, on the tradition in which it plays a part. Given this symbolic interpretation, it is a mistake, it will be said, to attempt to evaluate actions from a perspective external to the larger context in which they occur.

The pluralistic response to this modified conventionalistic claim is that while it is true that the moral evaluation of actions must take into account their context, it is false that reasonable evaluations must appeal to considerations that carry weight only in the tradition that provides the context. Contrary to the conventionalistic claim, the Dinka custom of live burial supports the pluralistic case.

To see why this is so, we need to focus on the nature of the convention-alistic argument.[18] Conventionalists think that the reason why live burial is a justifiable violation of the deep convention protecting life is that for the Dinka it symbolically sustains life. The conventionalistic case thus concedes the fundamental point at issue, namely, that the Dinka think as we do about the value of life. It is precisely because they value life as highly as we do that they celebrate the spear-master for sacrificing his life in order to sustain the life of the tribe. The difference between our tradi-tion and the Dinka's is not that the primary value we assign to life is demoted to a secondary value in theirs. They and we agree about its primacy. What we disagree about is whether what they regard as a reason-able case for violating the deep convention to which we are both commit-ted is indeed reasonable.

Nor is this disagreement closed to reasoned resolution. As the con-ventionalistic argument shows, the Dinka and we also agree about what a good reason would be for taking a life. Such a reason would be that by taking it we protect many lives. If the Dinka were right in believing that the killing of the spear-master was the best way to sustain the life of the tribe, then we would have to agree with them about live burial's being reasonable. The disagreement we have with the Dinka is made possible only by a deeper agreement between them and us that the taking of a life is morally permissible if it is the best way of preventing the loss of even more lives.

Reflection on the Dinka custom of live burial, which on first encoun-tering it strikes us as a barbaric aberration, reveals two deeper levels on which the Dinka and we see eye to eye on moral matters. On the deepest level, the Dinka agree with us about the value of life. For if they did not, they would not kill the spear-masters, since it is by killing them that they aim to protect life. On the next level, the Dinka also agree with us about what reason would be good for taking a life. For if they did not, they would not celebrate the death of their respected leaders. Only on the third, morally much more superficial, level do we have a disagreement with the Dinka. They think, and we do not, that live burial is a reasonable way of protecting life. But we should note, before turning to that dis-agreement, that it would be logically impossible to have it if we did not have the agreement on the two deeper levels, for the disagreement pre-supposes the agreements. And we should note also that such plausibility as conventionalism has derives from concentrating on the more superfi-cial disagreement, while ignoring the deeper agreement about the value of life and about one morally permissible reason for taking it.

---

[18] For an antirelativist argument that in many ways parallels the present one, see Bam-brough, *Moral Scepticism and Moral Knowledge*.

Let us then turn to the disagreement. To begin with, if we interpret the Dinka's belief literally rather than symbolically, then we must regard it as simply false. Life does not pass from the mouth of a dying person to members of his tribe. If the Dinka case for killing the spear-masters rests on that belief, then it is a bad case. The symbolic interpretation, however, cannot be so easily dismissed. The tribe *is* sustained by their belief that life passes from the spear-master to them. To be sure, they are not sustained by their belief as food sustains them. But—arguably—psychological sustenance may be as important as its physical analog. Yet while it is true that the Dinka derive psychological sustenance from their tradition, their tradition is complex, and the ceremonies connected with the live burial of the spear-masters are only a small, although important, part of it. If they were deprived of that sustenance, they may still receive it in other ways.

We know that this is so because the Dinka tradition has remained strong after Sudanese authorities outlawed live burial. Indeed, Lienhardt's study was written after the desuetude of the custom. The symbolic interpretation of the Dinka case thus also falls short of making it morally acceptable. For the killing of the spear-masters cannot be justified on the grounds that it was required for the survival of the tribe. And since that was the reason why the burial was thought to be a justified violation of the deep convention protecting life, the symbolically interpreted case for live burial also fails. We must conclude that the Sudanese authorities acted reasonably in outlawing live burial.

Two loose ends still remain however. The first is how the Dinka themselves should think about the matter, and the other is about the moral status of the agents who perpetuated the morally unjustifiable custom. We have no information about how the Dinka actually think about it, but it is not hard to reconstruct how they are likely to think. No doubt, some will perceive in the disappearance of live burial a serious threat to their tradition; others will say that one must move with the times; yet others will attend to their cattle and let the local pundits worry about the matter; and perhaps a small number will celebrate it as a step in the march of progress. The reason why this reconstruction is so plausible is that we can readily put ourselves in the Dinka's position as we reflect on *our* range of attitudes to such changes in our tradition as are occurring about homosexuality or the waning of religious belief, or as a result of the availability of life-prolonging medical technology.

The second loose end is not of the Dinka's actions but of the Dinka agents who took part in what we now see as the morally unjustifiable live burial of the spear-masters. Their moral situation was that they believed themselves to have good reasons for acting as they did, but they were mistaken. Our moral evaluation of them must depend on how we answer the question of whether their mistake was culpable. Given that the custom has persisted in their tradition since time immemorial, that critical reflection on prevailing practices is not part of the Dinka tradition, and that both the victims and their authorities agreed about the value of the custom, it would be wrong to hold the Dinka culpable for perpetuating their morally objectionable custom. The appropriate concrete reaction to the whole situation is to do just what the Sudanese did. Outlaw it, enforce the prohibition, and let that be the end of the matter.

Reflection on the custom of live burial permits us to conclude that conventionalism is mistaken. The strength of conventionalism is its insistence on the richness and variety of human possibilities and its reluctance to condemn moral possibilities from a point of view alien to them. These are useful and needed correctives of moral dogmatism. But conventionalists go too far. There *are* human differences, but they are *human* differences. Traditions allow different possibilities, but there is a limit to the differences among them because they are allowing moral possibilities for human beings. The Dinka and we, Eskimos and New Guinea headhunters, Benedictine monks and green berets, radical feminists and ayatollahs, Tibetan lamas and futures traders are all human beings, and therefore they are—we are—united at a deep level of our being. The minimum requirements of good lives for us are the same. These requirements create a case for meeting them. And this case will be found persuasive by all reasonable human beings who pause to reflect on it. For the case is simply that if we can, we should want the human enterprise to go on as well as possible. This is what morality is about. Beyond this elementary yet deep level, significant differences emerge about what different traditions regard as the human enterprise's going well. But these differences all occur on that third level, which is so close to the surface— the level on which we disagree with the Dinka about live burial.

What conventionalists miss is that moral disagreements are possible only if there are moral agreements in the background. For *moral* disagreements presuppose that the parties to it are committed to morality—which on any view of the matter involves commitment to good lives—and they are also committed to the shared procedure of settling some moral disagreements by evaluating some of the conflicting possibilities on the basis of their contribution to good lives. Disagreements need not be moral, and many moral disagreements are not open to being settled by following this procedure. The procedure makes some conflicts tractable, while it leaves unresolved conflicts about other matters. But the commitment to morality and to the procedure is sufficient to establish that conventionalism is mistaken. For it is not the case, as conventionalists claim, that moral disagreements may affect *all* judgments made within the contexts of differing traditions. If a tradition is healthy, then there must be *some* agreement in the judgments that can reasonably be made within it. And it is this layer of agreement, made possible and inevitable by our common humanity, that constitutes the context-independent basis for some moral judgments. Pluralism allows for it, conventionalism does not, indeed cannot, and that is one reason for preferring pluralism to conventionalism.

Monism Redux?

We have seen throughout our discussion that a logical peculiarity informs the argument between relativism, monism, and pluralism. The stronger the pluralistic case is against one of its opponents, the closer pluralism appears to move toward the other. This is true also in the present case. For monists may endorse everything pluralists adduce against relativism, and so they may justifiably wonder whether there is anything distinctive left of pluralism. If there is a context-independent standard by which we can evaluate the reasons offered in reaching various moral decisions, then have we not subscribed to just the sort of claim that monists wish to defend? In particular, since the context-independent standard on which the pluralistic argument relied was the minimum requirements of good lives, how, it may be asked, is pluralism different from one kind of monistic theory, namely, utilitarianism? We must now face and respond to this question.

The answer to it will be twofold: it will be argued first that even if pluralism were committed to some version of consequentialism, there would still be a difference between pluralism and monism; and then it will be argued that pluralism is committed neither to utilitarianism nor to any other form of consequentialism. For the purposes of our discussion, we shall understand by consequentialism the claim that the moral evaluation of actions, character traits, or conventions (the last is used broadly to include rules, principles, customs, practices, and so on) depends ultimately and exclusively on the consequences they are likely to produce. Ultimate dependence allows that an action or a character trait may be evaluated with reference to the convention to which it conforms or violates, but then it is the convention that is evaluated on the basis of the consequences of adopting it. Exclusive dependence on consequences means that moral evaluation depends only on the likely consequences. In so far as other considerations are adduced, their moral credentials must also depend on the consequences they are likely to produce. Utilitarianism, then, is the version of consequentialism that interprets the consequences that provide the ultimate and exclusive standard of moral evaluation to be good lives. This interpretation of consequentialism and utilitarianism does not distinguish among the different forms these theories may take, since those details are irrelevant to our present purposes.

Following the first approach, then, let us grant, if only temporarily and for the sake of argument, that pluralism is committed to utilitarianism. The claim to be established is that even so, pluralism is distinct from monism. The reason why it may appear that by being committed to utilitarianism pluralism is also committed to monism is that the appeal to good lives looks very much like the appeal to an overriding value. What else, it may be asked, is good life but the overriding value? And has the pluralistic case not rested on the claim that deep conventions can be reasonably violated only if good lives are thereby more likely to be achieved? Good lives thus may seem to function both as the overriding value and as the canonical scheme of conflict-resolution. And since the central claim of monists is that one or the other exists, have pluralists not subscribed to monism in the course of their criticism of relativism?

The negative answer can be conveniently framed by borrowing a distinction from the context of trying to interpret Aristotle's notion of *eudaimonia*.[19] The distinction is between dominant and inclusive ends. From our present point of view, it does not matter whether the interpretation of Aristotle's view that is based on this distinction is accurate. It is the distinction itself that is important.

A dominant end is a goal in life that the person whose life it is values so highly as to subordinate all other considerations to it. For example, one of wealth, fame, happiness, artistic or intellectual creativity, social justice, family ties, or passionate love of some one person may be the dominant end of a life. The dominant end is thus a specific value, which others may also recognize as valuable, but it is one that has achieved dominance in a life, although it need not dominate other lives. One interpretation of utilitarianism may then be that it is the moral theory according to which living a good life ought to be the dominant end of all lives.

By contrast, an inclusive end is not a specific value but a way of ordering the various specific values that we should like to realize in our lives. In normal lives, comfort, security, self-respect, freedom, recognition, loving relationships, satisfying work, a profession, or engagement in some project are among the recognized values. If living a good life is regarded as an inclusive end, then being committed to it does not imply commitment to any specific value as dominant. In being committed to living a good life, we are committed to so ordering primary and secondary values as to maximize our chances of realizing them. According to this view,

---

[19] The distinction is in Hardie, "The Final Good in Aristotle's Ethics." It is discussed by Ackrill, "Aristotle on Eudaimonia," and John Cooper, *Reason and Human Good in Aristotle.*

living a good life cannot be the specific value that ought to dominate over other specific values because it is not a specific value at all. If specific values are first-order values, then living a good life is a second-order value whose value consists in balancing the conflicting claims of first-order values. Another interpretation of utilitarianism, then, is that it is a moral theory that advocates commitment to living a good life as an inclusive end.

Dominant-end utilitarianism is committed to monism because it identifies living a good life with a specific value that has achieved overriding status. Inclusive-end utilitarianism, however, is not so committed because it takes commitment to living a good life to allow for commitment to a plurality of values.[20] It is true that specific primary values will be part of this commitment, but these values are recognized only as necessary for good lives, and they are not supposed to dominate a life. According to inclusive-end utilitarianism, living a good life is achieving whatever values are required by our conceptions of a good life. On this interpretation, by being committed to a good life different people need not be committed to the same thing. Pluralists could therefore accept inclusive-end utilitarianism without thereby accepting monism, were it not that there are other reasons for rejecting all versions of utilitarianism as well as of consequentialism.

Let us turn, then, to the second answer and consider why it is that pluralism implies neither inclusive-end utilitarianism nor any other form of consequentialism. There are two reasons for considering the relation between consequentialism and pluralism. One is that consequentialism has very serious difficulties as a moral theory.[21] If pluralism could not be separated from it, their connection would saddle pluralism with the same difficulties. The other reason is that by being clear about how pluralism differs from consequentialism, we can deepen our understanding of the kind of moral theory that pluralism is.

The first thing to note is that the separation of pluralism from consequentialism does not mean that pluralists must regard consequences as irrelevant to moral evaluation. There are deontological moral theories that do take this view, but we need not embrace deontology as we divorce ourselves from consequentialism. One difficulty with consequentialism is that it supposes that moral evaluation depends ultimately and exclusively on consequences. Pluralists can admit the moral relevance of consequences and still reject consequentialism by insisting that moral evaluation depends, in addition to consequences, on other considerations as

---

[20] An example of inclusive-end utilitarianism is Brandt's *A Theory of the Good and the Right*.

[21] The literature on which this claim is based is immense. A representative sample of some of the important critical essays is in Sen and Williams, *Utilitarianism and Beyond*.

well. Accordingly, pluralists are committed only to rejecting the ultimacy and exclusiveness of consequences as the standard of moral evaluation.

It is easy to see why pluralists must hold this commitment. If consequences were the ultimate and exclusive standard of moral evaluation, then they would constitute that very canonical scheme of conflict-resolution whose existence pluralists deny. Pluralists can allow that consequences matter, but they cannot allow that only consequences matter. If pluralism is correct, then there is no one thing that matters ultimately and exclusively. Moral evaluations, then, are based on a plurality of considerations, and if they conflict, there is a plurality of ways in which their conflicts may reasonably be resolved.

To show why consequences fail as the ultimate and exclusive standard of moral evaluation consider the interpretation of good lives that is favored by inclusive-end utilitarianism. Why is living a good life, interpreted as the balanced realization of a plurality of values, not acceptable as *the* consequence that establishes the overriding value of moral evaluation?

We shall discuss three reasons why it is not acceptable. The first has to do with how we conceive of the relation between whatever brings about the consequences and the consequences themselves. One way of thinking about their relation is that actions, character traits, or conventions are *means* that contribute to producing the consequence of living a good life. Whatever moral value attaches to these means is thus instrumental, for it derives from their propensity to maximize the chances of living a good life. To the extent they fail to contribute optimally to bringing about good lives, they would lose their value. And how much value they have depends, ultimately and exclusively, on how much they contribute to living a good life.

But it is clear that this is not a defensible way of thinking about the moral value of actions, character traits, or conventions. For we often continue to value them even though they obviously failed to contribute to living a good life. A well-intentioned action that fails to achieve its goal due to unforeseeable circumstances still has some moral value. Honesty in a corrupt society may produce only pain for the agent and contempt in others, but it does not, on that account, cease to be a virtue. The conventions of a disintegrating tradition do not lose their moral credentials just because times are changing, as chivalry or respect for one's father have not lost theirs just because the traditions sustaining the ideals of knighthood and that of a Confucian gentleman are no longer with us. What is wrong with this way of thinking about contributions to living a good life is that while many actions, character traits, and conventions have instrumental value, they may also have intrinsic value. And thinking of them only as means to living a good life does not allow us to recognize their intrinsic value.

There is, however, another way of thinking, and that is to regard some actions, character traits, and conventions as *constituents* of good lives, rather than as means to them. The relation between them and good lives is that of a part to a whole and not that of a means to an end. If we adopted this way of thinking, it would be readily apparent why some things have both instrumental and intrinsic value. They have the first because they are means to good lives, but they also have the second because they are not merely means that could be dispensed with if a more efficient one were found. Achieving the end *by these means* has become part of the end. Romeo's conception of a good life required the love of Juliet, and it was not obtainable by means of the love of someone else whose family was less unsuitable than hers. Playing the violin is not just the means for a concert violinist, so that if she got arthritis in her fingers, then changing to combo drums would be just as good; for it is by playing the violin that she hopes to live a good life.

If we think about living a good life as being a whole composed of constituents, then inclusive-end utilitarianism fails, because the moral evaluation of an action, character trait, or convention must include more than just ascertaining that it does indeed have the propensity for contributing to a good life. For whatever it is that leads us to value intrinsically some constituent of a good life goes beyond this propensity. We value it partly for what it is, and that is why some other means with the same propensity cannot adequately replace it. Since the ground of this evaluation is something in addition to its being a constituent of a good life, contribution to living a good life cannot be the ultimate and exclusive standard of moral evaluation.

This conclusion can be generalized to hold for all versions of consequentialism, not just for inclusive-end utilitarianism. For all theories that regard consequences of whatever kind as the ultimate and exclusive standard of moral valuation face the same dilemma. If they recognize only instrumental value, they cannot account for many reasonable moral evaluations. If they recognize both instrumental and intrinsic values, then they cannot account for intrinsic value merely in terms of consequences.

The second reason why living a good life cannot be the ultimate and exclusive standard of moral evaluation emerges if we consider the question of just whose life it is that determines the moral value of an action, character trait, or convention. It may be the agent's own; those of some group of people, such as the agent's family, society, tradition, or religious or political cause; or everyone's. It is clear that consequentialists must answer the question, since different interpretations of whose life is to be considered yield different and often-incompatible moral evaluations.

In endeavoring to provide an answer, consequentialists must give reasons why being conducive to the good life of whatever person or group is favored should be the overriding standard of moral evaluation. These reasons are necessary because individual agents may reasonably ask why they should be judged by the contribution they make to the good lives of total strangers or to those of the adherents of a different tradition. Or defenders of a religious or a political cause may wonder what reasons there are for the claim that they should concern themselves with people who are unaffected by, or hostile to, their cause.

There are various answers that could reasonably be given to these questions. It could be said that justice, benevolence, impartiality, decency, self-interest, prudence, or some combination of these and other values should lead reasonable people to adopt one rather than another interpretation of whose good lives they and others should care about. There is one answer, however, that can be given only on the pain of arbitrariness. The reasonable reply cannot be that good lives themselves require the adoption of a particular interpretation. For the question arose in the first place because it was necessary to choose one among the many possible interpretations of a good life. Once we have that interpretation, as well as reasons supporting it, then we can appeal to it. But we cannot do so without arbitrariness until both the interpretation and the reasons for it have been provided.

The significance of this is that it demonstrates that living a good life cannot be the ultimate and exclusive standard of moral evaluation. For in the course of formulating a reasonable interpretation of it, appeals to other standards of moral evaluation are inevitably made. Such appeals are inevitable because in their absence either we would not know which of several different moral evaluations were acceptable, or the adoption of a particular interpretation of what counts as a good life would be arbitrary, in the sense of being unsupported by reasons. And from this it follows that the central consequentialist claim that living a good life is the ultimate and exclusive standard of moral evaluation cannot be correct.

Pluralists can consistently appeal to a conception of a good life as a context-independent standard of moral evaluation without thereby committing themselves to any form of consequentialism. But it lends further support to pluralism to realize that the defect of consequentialism is its commitment to precisely that mistaken moral theory, namely monism, to which pluralism is intended to serve as an alternative. By understanding the reason why pluralism is not committed to consequentialism, we come to a deeper understanding of why pluralists insist on the plurality of standards for conflict-resolution.

This brings us to the third reason for denying that a particular conception of a good life is the overriding standard of moral evaluation. We shall merely introduce this reason here; it will be discussed more fully in chapter 9. Let us assume for the sake of argument that the first two reasons just given fail and that consequentialism is the most reasonable moral theory available. It follows, then, that a particular conception of a good life is the ultimate and exclusive standard of moral evaluation. But this still does not show that pluralism is mistaken. For moral evaluation is not the only kind of evaluation that there is. Self-interest, aesthetics, politics, religion, love, patriotism, personal loyalty, and so on, may also suggest evaluations, and these evaluations also appeal to some standards. Even if a particular conception of a good life were the overriding moral standard, there would still be a plurality of evaluative standards. And, of course, evaluations based on these standards may conflict with each other. It may be that there is a way of resolving possible conflicts between moral and nonmoral evaluations, but whether or not this is so, the resolution of these conflicts cannot be based on appealing to a particular conception of a good life for that standard is a party to the conflict. Thus the dilemma for consequentialists: either there is a further standard or there is not. If there is, then a particular conception of a good life cannot be the ultimate and exclusive standard. If there is not, then the appeal to a particular conception of a good life for resolving conflicts between it and other standards is bound to be arbitrary. We can thus see in yet another way that living a good life cannot be the overriding standard of evaluation, not even if we suppose it to be the overriding standard of moral evaluation.

CHAPTER EIGHT

The Prospects of Moral Progress

> Moral philosophy is the examination of the most important of all human activities, and I think that two things are required of it. The examination should be realistic. Human nature has certain discoverable attributes, and these should be suitably considered in any discussion of morality. Secondly, since an ethical system cannot but commend an ideal, it should commend a worthy ideal. Ethics . . . should be a hypothesis about good conduct and about how this can be achieved.
>
> —Iris Murdoch, *The Sovereignty of Good*

IN THE LAST two chapters we were concerned with the possibilities and limits of pluralism. The belief that there are limits beyond which conceptions of a good life cannot reasonably go distinguishes pluralism from relativism. The belief that these limits are not overriding but conditional is part of what separates pluralism from monism. Another part is that the conceptions of a good life that pluralists recognize as morally permissible are far more numerous than those that monists allow. Pluralists and monists agree that morality allows only those conceptions of a good life that conform to the minimum requirements set by deep conventions. But monists go beyond these minimum requirements and endeavor to impose further limits on permissible conceptions of a good life by appealing to an overriding value. Pluralists reject this attempt to impose further limits, on the ground that the appeal on which they rest is indefensible. But this leaves open the question of whether there may not be some other kinds of reasonable limits beyond those set by deep conventions. The argument of this chapter will be that there are such limits. The reason for this view will emerge from a consideration of moral progress in general and shame in particular.

MORAL PROGRESS IN GENERAL

The moral theory in which the idea of moral progress is most at home is monism. It is not that monists are committed to an optimistic view about the gradual improvement of humanity. Some monists (e.g., Mill) are so committed, but others (e.g., Kant) are not. The point is rather that monists could readily say what moral progress would be, were there any. According to them, moral progress would be toward the realization of whatever the overriding value was. The closer people or traditions came to the realization of the overriding value, the more advanced they would be, from the moral point of view. By contrast, it is a logical consequence of relativism that the contexts to which values are said to be relative cannot be compared on any context-independent ground. According to relativists, the idea of moral progress can make sense only within a context, and the comparative assessment of the moral progress of various contexts themselves is impossible. It is a major difficulty for relativism that some contexts are dominated by vicious, destructive, irrational, tyrannical, and life-diminishing values, and yet they cannot be condemned on independent grounds. The strongest claim relativists can consistently make is that such contexts are deplorable from the point of view of the relativists' own context. But then those who are deplored can with equal justice deplore the relativists' deploring them. The result is that moral criticism deteriorates into cross-cultural name-calling.

The difficulty we need to consider now is that if pluralists reject the monistic claim about the existence of overriding values, how then can they retain the idea of moral progress. Or, to formulate it from the relativistic direction, if values are plural, conditional, conflicting, incompatible, and incommensurable, then what sense can we give to a conception of a good life or a tradition being better than another. After all, traditions and conceptions of a good life differ partly because they have opted for different ways of resolving conflicts among values, so what value is there left to which we could appeal in deciding that one approach to conflict-resolution represents greater moral progress than another?

The central idea underlying the pluralistic answer to this question is that moral progress consists in enlarging the area within which individuals can endeavor to make a good life for themselves. This enlargement involves increasing the number of possibilities individuals have available to them and imposing limits that protect them in their endeavors to choose among the possibilities and to live in the way they have chosen. Moral progress thus consists in removing impediments to people's acting as full-fledged agents. And these impediments, of course, are not merely external obstacles created by repressive conventions, scarce resources, and unjustified coercion but also internal ones due to ignorance, stupidity, and impoverished imagination, which prevent people from making use of their possibilities.

According to pluralists, therefore, moral progress does not consist in the gradual approximation to some ideal, such as the imitation of Christ or living according to the laws of history, psychology, or sociology. It does not require the subordination of passion to reason, or the reverse. Moral progress involves neither getting closer to a preestablished pattern nor removing obstacles to conformity to it, because there is no such pattern. For individuals, moral progress is toward recognizing richer possibilities, growing in their imaginative appreciation of them, and increasing their freedom. For traditions, moral progress is toward creating a context in which individuals are encouraged rather than hindered in their aspirations to make a good life for themselves. And the way traditions can do that is by protecting the conditions individuals need for realizing their aspirations.

The comparison of the moral progress of individuals or traditions, however, can rarely be made in general terms. There are some blatant cases where the respective moral standing of two individuals or two traditions is obvious to any reasonable person. But the usual cases do not lend themselves to obvious answers. The traditions and the conceptions of a good life we are endeavoring to compare incorporate many values, some of which lead us to prefer one conception or tradition, while some others incline us in the other direction. The question of moral progress thus must be settled by concentrating on particular values. And the one we shall consider is shame.

There is no reason to think that shame violates any deep convention. In fact, it is often thought that shame is the best, or at least a good way, of safeguarding deep conventions. Yet, it will be argued, shame is a destructive feeling, and both traditions and conceptions of a good life are better if they provide some alternative motivational source for conforming to deep conventions. If this is so, then a tradition or a conception of a good life with an appropriate alternative to shame is better than one with shame. And that shows that in comparison with that alternative possibility, shame represents a defective possibility, even though it does not violate deep conventions.

But there is more: shame has different forms, and some are less defective than others. This makes it possible to speak of moral progress. Moral progress consists in cultivating a less defective form of shame in preference to a more defective one and in cultivating some alternative to shame rather than shame itself. This allows pluralists to argue for the possibility of moral progress from one conception of a good life and one tradition to another. And it allows as well the possibility of reasonable criticisms of some conceptions of a good life and some traditions on grounds that go beyond the violation of deep conventions. Pluralists are thus provided with yet another argument against two versions of relativism—conventionalism and perspectivism, which concede the context-independence of deep conventions but deny that context-independent grounds exist beyond them.

THE NATURE OF SHAME

The most illuminating contemporary accounts of shame are Gabrielle Taylor's[1] and Arnold Isenberg's.[2] They agree on many points, but they offer conspicuously different assessments. Taylor thinks that "genuine shame is always justified,"[3] while Isenberg concludes that "it is as unreasonable to tolerate the sear of shame upon the spirit as it is to permit a wound to fester in the body."[4] Their dispute is not new. Plato regards shame as one of the important safeguards of morality,[5] but Aristotle thinks that "if shamelessness . . . is bad, that does not make it good to be ashamed."[6]

We can sympathize with both lines of thought leading to these incompatible attitudes to shame. Shame is a response to the realization that we have fallen short of some value we regard as important. Shame is thus morally significant, because it indicates that we have made a commitment and because it is an impetus for honoring that commitment. But it also involves painfully lowering our opinion of ourselves. Shame does not merely alert us to our shortcomings; it makes us feel deficient on account of them. This feeling of deficiency, coming from such an unimpeachable source, is likely to be self-destructive. It tends to undermine our confidence, verve, and courage to navigate life's treacherous waters. Shame threatens to diminish our most important resource, and it jeopardizes the possibility of improvement by weakening the only agency capable of effecting it.

The reasons against shame outweigh the reasons for it. But this is not because it is mistaken to regard shame as an index of the seriousness we feel about our values. Shame is such an index. It is rather that whatever shame accomplishes can be had in less self-destructive ways. The movement away from shame toward other responses to the realization of our deficiencies constitutes a form of moral progress. Understanding how moral progress may occur contributes to the enlargement of our moral possibilities and shows how perspectivism is mistaken on the individual level and conventionalism is similarly mistaken on the level of traditions.

It is futile to seek a precise definition of "shame," for the feeling it denotes shades into embarrassment, humiliation, chagrin, guilt, dis-

---

[1] Gabrielle Taylor, *Pride, Shame and Guilt*, especially chapter 3.

[2] Isenberg, "Natural Pride and Natural Shame," 355–83.

[3] Gabrielle Taylor, *Pride, Shame and Guilt*, 3.

[4] Isenberg, "Natural Pride and Natural Shame," 369.

[5] Plato, *Republic*, 465a, and *Laws*, 671c.

[6] Aristotle, *Nicomachean Ethics*, 1128b31–34. For a comparison of Plato and Aristotle on this point, see Nussbaum, "Shame, Separateness, and Political Unity: Aristotle's Criticism of Plato."

honor, regret, remorse, prudishness, disgrace, and so on. The very search for necessary and sufficient conditions for shame is bound to simplify a naturally complex experience.[7] Another indication of the complex meaning of "shame" is that it has many antonyms referring to feelings incompatible with it: pride, honor, self-respect, propriety, modesty, and self-esteem are some. These feelings are incompatible with different aspects of shame, and it is the presence of these aspects that is responsible for the complexity of shame. The discussion requires a way of identifying cases of shame, but it will be sufficient to have at our disposal many generally recognized instances of shame, rather than a precise definition.

One fundamental characteristic of shame is that it is a self-directed feeling: the subject who has it and the object toward which it is directed are one and the same. It is a bad, unpleasant, painful, disturbing feeling, for it involves regarding ourselves in an unfavorable light. When we feel ashamed, we recognize that there is some value of which we have fallen short. It is essential that we should have committed ourselves to the value, otherwise we would not feel bad about falling short of it. For just because something is regarded as shameful by others, it does not follow that we should feel ashamed on account of it, since we may be indifferent or hostile to the value to which others appeal. Nevertheless, few people are so totally at odds with their tradition as to be utterly indifferent to its values. We usually feel shame about something others also regard as shameful.

Shame is a self-conscious feeling. We are not merely the subjects and objects of it, we are also aware of ourselves *as* objects when we feel ashamed. For the feeling involves seeing ourselves as having failed in some important respect. But to recognize such a failure requires us to compare some aspect of our present self to a better self that would have approximated the value more closely than we have done. One requirement of this self-conscious comparison is detachment. We see a characteristic or action of ours as others would see it—or often as others do see it—and we accept this detached assessment. But we accept it because we are committed to the value by which our action or characteristic is adversely judged. It is true that we have probably acquired the value from our tradition; what matters, however, is not its origin but that the value is now ours.

The failure to recognize this unfortunately permeates the literature on shame. Rawls, for instance, holds that "shame implies an especially intimate connection . . . with those upon whom we depend to confirm

---

[7] An example of this misguided venture is the title essay in Agnes Heller, *The Power of Shame.*

the sense of our own worth,"[8] and part of the explanation of shame is that a person "has been found unworthy of his associates upon whom he depends to confirm his sense of his own worth."[9] The general mistake this view exemplifies is the supposition that feeling ashamed requires an audience.[10] It is supposed that in shame the adverse judgment is largely external and is imposed by witnesses to one's dereliction, while in guilt the adverse judgment is mainly internal, imposed by individuals on themselves.

But this view cannot account for all experiences of shame. We often feel shame when no one is present to observe us. So audience cannot be necessary. It would be pointless to postulate an imagined audience in whose hypothetical eyes our unobserved selves would feel shame, for we often feel shame on account of failures that others would not regard as shameful, such as not achieving our personal best when we want to or falling short of some supererogatory commitment we have made. Furthermore, although we may acquire many of our values by internalizing conventional ones, not all of our values are like this. For if they were, we could not come to reject conventional values in the name of values we regard as higher. And, of course, we can feel ashamed for having fallen short of these higher values, although there may be no one who shares them with us.

Taylor's observation about this is absolutely right: "There is, then, this point to the metaphors of an audience and being seen: they reflect the structural features of the agent's becoming aware of the discrepancy between her assumptions about her state or action and a possible detached observer-description of this state or action, and of her further being aware that she ought not to be in a position where she could be so seen. . . . For in particular cases of shame an actual or imagined observer may or may not be required . . . whether or not there is, or is imagined to be, such an observer is a contingent matter."[11]

What is essential to shame is detaching ourselves from a deficient aspect of what we are, have, or do and coming to view it as violating some value. This value, however, need not be shared by anyone. It may be that it often is shared, that purely private shame is a rare experience, and that there are not many reformers of conventional values who come to feel shame for having violated yet-to-be-accepted values. What needs to be

---

[8] Rawls, *A Theory of Justice*, 443.

[9] Ibid., 445.

[10] See, for example, Sartre, *Being and Nothingness*, part 3, chapter 1, section 4; Danto, *Jean-Paul Sartre*, chapter 4; and Morris, *Guilt and Innocence*.

[11] Gabrielle Taylor, *Pride, Shame and Guilt*, 66. See also O'Hear, "Guilt and Shame as Moral Concepts."

stressed is only the possibility of private shame because, as we shall see, moral progress is connected with it.

Shame is felt, then, when we make a detached comparison between some aspect of ourselves and a value we want to live up to, and the result is that we find ourselves wanting. It often happens that reflection on ourselves yields a conclusion only gradually. If we wonder whether we are oversensitive, stupid, rigid, or tactless, we may need to gather evidence, think through putative confirming or disconfirming instances, compare ourselves to others who clearly lack or exemplify the trait, and ponder what we find. It is otherwise with shame. Shame assails us; it is a sudden realization, a shock, a discovery. This dramatic aspect of shame, as Taylor aptly calls it, occurs because shame disrupts our previous equanimity. Calm prevails up to the occurrence of shame either because we have not engaged in self-conscious examination or because the result of the examination has been to subsume the relevant characteristic or action under a neutral or complimentary description. If we assess ourselves at all, we may say privately that we are cautious, or just, or clever, and then something happens; the veil is lifted, and we realize that, in fact, we have been cowardly, cruel, or dishonest. Self-deception, lethargy, and stupidity have great scope here. But the salient point is that when shame occurs, we suddenly see some aspect of ourselves in a new and unfavorable light. We see what has been there, but we see it for the first time or differently from the way we used to. Shame involves interpretation, which is often reinterpretation, and what produces it is some episode, criticism, or comparison we encounter and whose significance forces itself on us. Like Adam and Eve discovering that they were naked.

Since the interpretation involved in shame is evaluative, shame often has a moral aspect. But if we acknowledge this aspect, we must reject a sharp distinction, drawn by Rawls for instance,[12] between natural and moral shame. According to it, we may feel natural but not moral shame because we are ugly, stupid, deformed, or have the wrong accent. These defects may detract from our self-respect, but they do not violate moral values. They are unfortunate but not blameworthy. Or people may invade our privacy, observe our intimate frolics or rituals, and make us feel ashamed by violating our dignity, even though we had done nothing morally censurable. Moral shame, by contrast, is supposedly caused by the realization that we are in some respect morally deficient. Acting in a cowardly way, betraying a friend, being caught in a lie, carelessly hurting someone we love are such morally blameworthy experiences. Both natu-

---

[12] See, for example, Rawls, *A Theory of Justice*, 444–46.

ral and moral shame depend on injury to our self-respect, but one is and the other is not supposed to be a moral injury.

If, however, we take a sufficiently broad view of morality to accommodate a wide enough range of moral experiences, we must rule out a sharp interpretation of this distinction. This interpretation rests on the assumption that morality and the domain of choice coincide. Since the objects of natural shame are not chosen, natural shame is placed outside of morality. But morality is wider than the sphere of choice. Morality is concerned with living good lives, and there are many constituents of good lives about which we often have no choice. A secure society that is hospitable to our endeavors, the possession of native endowments that could be developed, the absence of paralyzing personal or social handicaps are as necessary for living good lives as are morally praiseworthy choices. If we commit ourselves to living according to a certain conception of life, and we find that we have failed, our self-respect may suffer and we may come to feel shame regardless of whether we are responsible for our failure. What matters to shame, therefore, is not so much that we have made morally blameworthy choices, but that we suffer loss of self-respect. The two often coincide, but they need not. As Rawls himself recognizes, although inconsistently, "we should say that given our plan of life, we tend to be ashamed of those defects in our person and failures in our actions that indicate a loss or absence of excellences essential to carrying out our more important associative aims."[13] But the defects and failures may exist independently of our choices.

It is essential to living good lives that we should not feel bad about ourselves. Our self-respect depends on the sense that we are living up to our values. Shame may occur when we realize that we have fallen short of them. Shame is thus an experience of failure, but it may or may not be culpable failure. Shame is not guilt; it is not the verdict of a private court, as guilt may be the verdict of a public one.

Furthermore, whether we feel ashamed depends on the fact that we have violated some value of ours and not on whether the violation was due to innate or acquired, voluntary of involuntary, accidental or cultivated causes. There is a kind of harsh judgment associated with shame. It understands only success and failure; the language of motive, intention, and effort, the consideration of causes, obstacles, and odds are foreign to it. If we feel it, appeal to these extenuating factors rarely brings relief. For shame painfully brings home to us the brute fact that we have committed ourselves to be in a certain way and we failed to live up to the commitment. Since our reason for making the commitment was that we regarded being in that way good, having failed, we feel bad about the way

---

[13] Ibid., 444.

we are. Shame is this primitive, inexorable feeling. Like grief or unrequited love, it is contingent on an unarguable fact. The fact in its case is that we find some aspect of our lives deficient. Shame is thus a moral feeling because morality has to do with living good lives.

Shame varies in intensity; it is proportionate to the centrality of the violated value to our conception of a good life. The more important a value is, the more shameful is its violation. But all the values whose violation is shameful are constituents of what we think of as good lives. The occurrence of shame, therefore, is always significant. It is true that we often speak of shame casually, in connection with peccadillos. In these cases, shame indicates mere embarrassment. It does not matter much whether we distinguish between serious and trivial shame, or whether we reserve the word "shame" for the serious feeling and use a cognate expression, like "embarrassment," for the lighter one. We shall follow the latter usage, and so even less intense experiences of shame will count as morally significant.

To sum up: in its affective aspect, shame is a painful self-directed feeling; in its cognitive aspect, it is a self-conscious detached comparison yielding the conclusion that we are in some way deficient because we have fallen short of some value we regard as important; and in its moral aspect, we feel the importance of the value we have violated because our conception of a good life requires that we should have lived up to it. In feeling shame, we feel loss of self-respect.

FORMS OF SHAME

We shall approach the connection between shame and moral progress by reflecting on one of the remarkable stories Herodotus tells.[14] It concerns Candaules, king of Lydia, his wife, the queen, and Gyges, the king's friend and advisor. The king was so besotted by his wife's charms that he could not keep his great good fortune to himself. He bragged to Gyges about his marital bliss and bullied him into hiding in their bedroom so that Gyges could have direct evidence of the queen's superior graces. Gyges was horrified at the king's plan: "[W]hat an improper suggestion!" he said. But the king persisted: "'[O]ff with her skirt, off with her shame'—you know what they say about women." Gyges pleaded: "[D]o not ask me to behave like a criminal." Kings have a way of prevailing however, and Gyges finally did as he was told and hid in the bedroom. "Unluckily, the queen saw him. At once she realized what her husband had done. But she did not betray the shame she felt by screaming, or even let it appear that she had noticed anything. Instead she silently

---

[14] Herodotus, *The Histories*, 16–18.

resolved to have her revenge. For with the Lydians . . . it is thought highly indecent even for a man to be seen naked." Next day, the queen summoned Gyges and said to him, "[T]here are two courses open to you, and you may take your choice between them. Kill Candaules and seize the throne, with me as your wife; or die yourself on the spot, so that never again may your blind obedience to the king tempt you to see what you have no right to see. One of you must die: either my husband, the author of this wicked plot; or you, who have outraged propriety by seeing me naked." Gyges chose to live; next night he hid once again in the bedroom, but this time at the queen's behest, and killed Candaules. He succeeded him, married the queen, and reigned for thirty-eight years.[15]

The story could be told from the point of view of each participant, and in each version shame would figure significantly. King Candaules was shameless; Gyges had a proper sense of shame, but he was not strong enough to act on it; and the queen, whose strength matched her charms, was moved by shame. Let us concentrate on the queen's perspective. Her reaction was like a volcanic eruption: majestic, inexorable, and indifferent to morality. Once her passion cooled, quiet descended and life resumed. But why the eruption? If we understand the emotional context from which her reaction follows, we shall have a better grip on both shame and moral progress.

Our first response to the queen's conduct may be that arranging the murder of her husband was a disproportionately violent reaction to his vulgar sophomoric plot. She was certainly badly used, but not so badly as to call for blood. The inadequacy of this first response comes from too simple a view of shame: Lydians are touchy about being seen naked, she was so seen, she was ashamed, she should be resentful of her husband, but let that be the end of it. Behind this line of thought lies the view that shame is the violation of loose commitments to such values as propriety, decency, seemliness. Call this view of shame "propriety-shame." This is what we usually feel when our privacy is invaded. And it is rightly thought that while propriety matters, it is hardly of serious moral concern. It belongs to a class of minor graces of which cheerfulness, politeness, and tact are other members. Good and evil are considerations too weighty for this context to support. But shame is not always a negligible reaction, and that shows that there is more to it than propriety-shame.

The queen's reaction will seem less excessive if we recognize that she had made a basic commitment to the value Lydians attach to propriety. She was not a superficial person who cared a lot about appearances; rather, how she appeared was for her a question of honor. And given her

---

[15] Erich Heller, in "Man Ashamed," 215–32, traces the many literary and dramatic treatments of this story.

basic commitment to it, being honorable was crucial to her conception of a good life. This conception dictated that how the queen was and how she appeared to others should not be distinguishable. Her honor, dignity, status, and self-respect all demanded that she should ring true all the way through. This does not mean that she conflated the public and private spheres. On the contrary, her honor was inseparably connected with maintaining their distinctness. In her view, there were activities proper to each sphere, and her conception of a good life required that she should play the appropriate role and to perform the appropriate actions in both of these different spheres. The language of play, role, and performance, however, should not lead us to suspect her of hypocrisy or insincerity. She was what it was her role to be. Her husband's plot, therefore, was not a superficial offense against her sense of propriety, but a serious damage to her conception of a good life, resulting in her dishonor. Her husband caused her to see herself diminished in her own eyes. Her experience may be called "honor-shame," a feeling much deeper and morally more significant than propriety-shame.

But this is not all. She did not merely feel ashamed because she was dishonored. She realized that her husband, by causing her dishonor, revealed that he did not respect her, did not see how crucial and important was the value of honor in her conception of a good life. Her shame, honor-shame, and the resulting resentment at her husband for having caused it and for not understanding what he was doing in causing it—remember his "off with her skirt, off with her shame"—conspired therefore to produce her revenge. We may still have objections to the conception of a good life from which her reaction followed, but her reaction no longer seems psychologically perverse. Especially not if we realize that the queen's conception of a good life is cast in a heroic mold familiar to us from the literature of ancient Greece. The conceptions of Achilles, Oedipus, and Medea came from the same mold. Each was dishonored, each felt the burn of honor-shame, and each reacted with rage. Its expression in dramatic action did not remove the dishonor, but it made the shame easier to bear by dissipating their pent-up passions.

But now contrast this with Nietzsche's portrayal of Mirabeau, "who had no memory for insults and vile actions done to him and was unable to forgive simply because he—forgot. Such a man shakes off with a *single* shrug many vermin that eat deep into others. . . . [T]hat is the sign of strong, full natures in whom there is an excess of the power to form, to mold, to recuperate and to forget."[16] The trouble with the queen was that her conception of a good life lacked a morally accredited way of

---

[16] Nietzsche, *On the Genealogy of Morals*, 475. The order of the quoted sentences is rearranged.

purging herself of the vermin in her soul. Her inability, however, was not her fault; it was a consequence of her tradition, which came as close as any to being a shame-culture.[17]

In her tradition, the development of individual conceptions a good life had to take the form of the internalization of public conventions. In such traditions, well-trained moral agents cannot distinguish between conventions guiding public and private conduct, for the two are the same. This does not mean that there is no distinction between private and public spheres. They remain separate; the bedroom is private. What happens, however, is that the conventions by which conduct is judged in these different spheres are neither public nor private but both, because the public is made private. In such a tradition, there is no scope for drawing a distinction between conventional morality, where public conventions prevail, and conceptions of a good life that allow for private commitments. Or, since no tradition is perfectly homogeneous, in theirs, drawing a distinction between public conventions and private commitments was a sign of moral failure. For the extent to which the distinction existed was the same as the extent of the failure to construct one's conception of a good life by internalizing public conventions.

The consequence of such a tradition is an impoverishment of life, for there are important possibilities foreclosed by it. It becomes impossible, or a sign of failure, to mount a moral protest against the prevailing conventions. For if all conventions are or ought to be internalized public ones, then individuals cannot have a moral justification for criticizing the prevailing conventions. Such criticism would have to appeal to some moral values, but there are none to which appeal is possible, because all are public and conventional. Individuals therefore must see their own moral dissatisfaction as moral failure. And shame is symptomatic of the perception of this failure. But there is nowhere for shame to go. Like a vermin, it eats deeper and deeper into the soul. The moral reform that would remove the failure is the very thing that is inexpressible in justifiable terms in that tradition. The self-destructive feeling just sits there and then suddenly explodes in some spectacular action, like the queen's revenge. After which, the feeling spent, she could settle into married life with Gyges.

Another way life was impoverished in this tradition was that no room was left in it for a certain kind of excuse for failure. It made no difference to the queen's feeling of honor-shame that she had not in any way contributed to her dishonor. No matter how modest and honorable was the queen, what really counted was that she failed: she was seen naked. De-

---

[17] For a superb discussion of a shame-culture, see Dodds, *The Greeks and the Irrational*, chapters 1–2.

sert, motive, intention, effort were irrelevant to failure in that tradition. What counted was achievement, and it was measured by living up to the prevailing conventions. When people fell short of them and, being well-trained moral agents, felt ashamed, they could not articulate, could not give moral weight to the fact that they were the victims of circumstances, not the agents who brought about their failure. Once again, therefore, frustration and bitterness pervaded their lives, and there was no morally acceptable way of coping with them.[18]

Nietzsche's Mirabeau, however, had such a way available to him. He could shrug off the insults that would have moved the queen to seek blood, because his tradition allowed the distinction between conventional morality and individual conceptions of a good life. It was possible for Mirabeau to maintain a conception of a good life in which what counted were his hierarchy of values and his judgment of success and failure. He could juxtapose the private sphere of his conception of a good life to some prevailing public conventions and say to himself, or to others if need be, that on some occasions it is the private that matters. He could thus dismiss other people's imputation of failure to him, because he had a reason for violating the prevailing conventions to which his critics appealed. Mirabeau's tradition enabled him to associate his self-respect partly with this private sphere, while the queen's had no scope for this moral possibility.

This moral possibility is that of having a conception of a good life that is different from the conceptions of others. It is a possibility that depends on pluralism that fosters individual differences and encourages experiments in living. What her tradition denied the queen was the possibility of differing from others in respect to her hierarchy of values and, consequently, in her conception of a good life. For in her tradition there were only very few conceptions of a good life, and they all included the internalization of the prevailing conventions, which were public and the same for everyone. It was this monistic straitjacket that made it impossible for her to criticize her own tradition. She did not have available a distinct private and yet moral standpoint in terms of which she could disagree with the prevailing conventional morality. And it was for the same reason that she was locked into honor-shame, although the failure she, and others, attributed to herself was not her fault.

This is not to say that Mirabeau, in his different tradition, was immune to shame. On the contrary, he was just as liable to it as the queen was. It was, however, neither propriety-shame nor honor-shame, but what we shall call "worth-shame" that could befall him, were he to fail. His self-

---

[18] In a series of interesting studies, James White, in *When Words Lose Their Meaning*, describes several traditions thus handicapped.

respect partly depended on living up to the values of his private conception of a good life. These values were his own in the double sense of deeply caring about them and their being definitive of his conception of a good life. This is why his estimate of his own worth was connected with his values, and this is why shame, worth-shame, could follow from his violation of them. In possession of an individual conception of a good life, Mirabeau could reasonably criticize some conventions prevailing in his tradition, because he had an independent point of view. He could reasonably reject the criticisms of others on the ground that they judged him by inappropriate conventions. Moreover, he could reasonably excuse his own failure to live up to his values if he could truthfully claim that he had done all he could to avoid failure. Worth-shame would be appropriate for Mirabeau only if these defenses failed.

The availability of the distinction between conventional morality and a plurality of conceptions of a good life is not an unmixed blessing. An individual conception of a good life could be deficient just as much as a conventional morality could be. For the values that constitute the conception of a good life may lead one to violate not merely superficial variable conventions but also deep ones. Conventional morality is not just a device for legislating seemliness; it is also a safeguard of the values whose realization everyone requires for living a good life. The distinction between conventional morality and individual conceptions of a good life thus not only makes possible the criticism of a tradition by its individual members but also introduces the possibility of conflict between the individual conceptions of a good life and the traditions. And through such conflicts comes alienation. Nevertheless, having the distinction is still morally better than not having it, because without it individuals are at the mercy of their tradition, while with it, they can articulate their moral dissatisfactions and possibly remedy them. Yet we should not suppose that such criticism is always justified, nor that when a conception of a good life conflicts with the conventional morality of a tradition, then the former should always prevail. How to balance their conflicting claims is one great question that comes with distinguishing them. But having to answer the question is not too high a price to pay for freeing us from the rigidity of monism.

THE POSSIBILITY OF MORAL PROGRESS

We are now in a position to discuss a concrete case of moral progress. The movement of individuals from the disposition to feeling propriety-shame, to feeling honor-shame, and from there to feeling worth-shame constitutes one kind of moral progress. It consists in developing a deeper attitude toward moral conventions. In propriety-shame, we allow appearances to set the conventions to which we commit ourselves, and we feel ashamed when the appearances count against us. We are seen naked when nudity is improper. In honor-shame, we take conventions based on appearances so seriously as to make them definitive of our honor. Appearances still matter, but not because of the impression others receive, but because the impressions we create have become for us a matter of honor. If we fail, we are ashamed because we are dishonored. We are dishonored *by* giving the wrong impression, but it is honor, not the impression, that we care about. If honor requires the separation of the private and the public, we feel ashamed when our privacy in invaded not because of what others see, but because of what we feel. Worth-shame is independent of appearances. It is caused by our culpable failure to live up to private commitments. We allow our privacy to be invaded when our sense of worth depends on protecting it, regardless of appearances. In propriety-shame, we care about appearances; in honor-shame, we care about appearing as we are; in worth-shame, we care about being in a certain way and we do not care about appearances. The progress is from caring about how we seem to caring about how we are.

Part of the reason why this constitutes progress is that it gives us greater control over our lives. People whose chief moral concern is with appearances are at the mercy of public opinion and depend on it for their choices and judgments; people moved primarily by honor subordinate their choices and judgments to public opinion, but they have made it their own opinion; while people whose commitments include both public and private considerations can criticize and correct their choices and judgments derived from their conventional morality and conceptions of a good life. Greater control brings decreased dependence on others, greater scope for moral criticism, and, consequently, a better chance of moral progress.

Moreover, the prospects for a good life depend on what moral agents do and what happens to them. In both categories, fortuitous circumstances play a considerable role. The more we concentrate our moral resources and attention on what is in our control, the less scope we leave to chance. And since our control over the private sphere is always greater than our control over the public one, a moral attitude that concentrates on the private is more likely to lead to a good life than others. Since the change from propriety-shame to honor-shame to worth-shame is toward greater emphasis on the private, it constitutes progress toward increasing the area in our lives we can control and thus improving the chances of living a good life. It needs to be emphasized again, however, that the claim that progress is possible through greater control is not meant to suggest that it cannot go wrong. It may happen that we progress toward morally noxious commitments. Good lives depend on many things: one is having sufficient scope for control over our commitments; another is having morally acceptable commitments. Both are necessary; neither is sufficient.

Analogous to the moral progress of individuals is the moral progress of entire traditions. A tradition improves as it becomes more hospitable to the moral progress of its members. And since individuals progress by moving from propriety-shame to honor-shame to worth-shame, so the tradition progresses by encouraging this process. As we have seen, this involves maintaining the distinction between conventional morality and a plurality of conceptions of a good life.

A further claim about moral progress is that the reasons for regarding the change through the three forms of shame as moral improvement are also reasons for moving away from all forms of shame toward other responses to moral failure. And, as before, these reasons are reasons first for individuals and then, by implication, also for traditions.

There was a time when the prevailing wisdom in one dominant school of medicine was to respond to illness by administering to patients various poisons as antidotes. It was thought that judiciously selected poisons would counteract the poisons that caused the illness and thus cure it.[19] There actually were some illnesses that responded well to this treatment, but it was found that on the whole the treatment considerably weakened patients and left a residue of poisons with which the patients, in a weakened state, had to contend. Doubts about shame are analogous: it weakens moral agents, and it leaves a residue that adds a burden to the deficiency with which they already have to contend.

But why does shame weaken moral agents? To begin with the obvious: shame is a bad feeling. It is not just painful; the pain it makes us feel is on account of our own deficiencies. Because shame diminishes our self-respect, it puts us in a moral double jeopardy. It not only makes us focus on our deficiencies but also causes us pain for having them.[20] It may be said against this that while shame may be painful, it is a morally necessary pain: "[I]f someone has self-respect then under certain specifiable conditions he will be feeling shame. A person has no self-respect if he regards no circumstances as shame-producing. Loss of self-respect and loss of the capacity for shame go hand in hand. The close connection between these two makes it clear why shame is often thought to be valuable. It is, firstly, that a sense of value is necessary for self-respect and so for shame, so that whatever else may be wrong about the person feeling shame he will at least have retained a sense of value. And secondly, it is

---

[19] For a fascinating account, see Trevor-Roper, "The Paracelsian Movement."
[20] Isenberg, "Natural Pride and Natural Shame," is excellent on this point.

a sense of value which protects the self from what in the agent's own eyes is corruption and ultimately extinction."[21]

There are several reasons for doubting these claims. First, let us agree that shamelessness is bad and self-respect is good. But shame is not the only possible reaction to our violation of commitments. Anger at ourselves, resolution to improve, the desire to make amends, a quest for understanding why we had done what we regard as wrong are some others. Just because we do not feel shame at our own recognized moral failure does not mean that we are bound to lack self-respect. We may sustain our self-respect in other ways.

Second, the protection against corruption and the extinction of the self that shame allegedly provides may be forward- or backward-looking. If it is forward-looking, it is supposed to protect us from doing wrong in the future. But it cannot be shame that thus protects us, since, *ex hypothesi*, the wrong is in the future, so we have nothing yet to be ashamed about. The best that can be said is that the protection is provided by *fear* of shame, not by shame itself. But why should fear be necessary at all, and if there is fear, why should it be of shame? We can be deterred from future wrongdoing by our self-respect itself, by understanding the consequences of our contemplated wrong actions on others, or by pride, honor, vanity, kindness, and so on. And if we have fear as deterrent, then fear of punishment or fear of loss of love, respect, or status may serve just as well as fear of shame.

On the other hand, if the alleged protection provided by shame is backward-looking, concerning a wrong we had already done, then it is hard to see how it can protect the self from "corruption and ultimately extinction." For such corruption as there is has already set in because of the wrong we had done. We recognize it, but, as we have seen, there is no reason to suppose that unless the recognition takes the form of shame, we shall be incapable of limiting or removing the corruption. Not to recognize our corruption is certainly worse than to recognize it, but this recognition may bring about many morally acceptable reactions other than shame. Remember Aristotle: "[I]f shamelessness is bad . . . that does not make it good to be ashamed."

As to the danger of the extinction of the self, it would seem that shame makes it more, rather than less, likely to happen. Recall how Mirabeau's capacity for shame was an improvement over the queen's. The trouble with honor-shame was that it had no outlet, for there was no way to undo the dishonor, not even if it was undeserved. When a likely target appeared in the form of people who did deserve some enmity, the subjects

---

[21] Gabrielle Taylor, *Pride, Shame and Guilt*, 80–81.

of honor-shame reacted to their hapless targets with excessive rage and thereby purged themselves of the large residue of passion that was poisoning them. Mirabeau would have been in a better position, because his shame would have been worth-shame. It would not have been the result of his having internalized conventional morality but of his having developed his own conception of a good life. He therefore could have handled shame better than the queen because he could have spurned public conventions in the name of private values. He would have had a reason for refusing to accept what others regarded as shameful. Nevertheless, while this would have been an improvement, in other respects he remained as badly off as the subjects of honor-shame.

The shame of the queen and of Mirabeau (assuming he had felt shame on some occasions) involved personal failure. They had been counted and found, in their own eyes, wanting. The causes of their shame were different, but their experiences of personal shortcoming, diminished self-respect, and the weakening and undermining of the self were the same; and it is the same for all the experiences of shame we have discussed. The more ashamed we are, the closer we come to the extinction of ourselves. Taylor says that shame is a bulwark protecting the self from extinction because it shows that the agents have retained a sense of values. But the use to which shame puts the retained values is self-condemnation; shame therefore is not the bulwark but part of the invading force against which a bulwark is needed. If we are to live a good life, there must be a robust self capable of living it. It must be able to make more or less detached choices and judgments, it must be able to withstand adversity, it must have strength, confidence, and integrity. Shame undermines all this and weakens the self, and that is why moral progress consists not merely in developing from propriety-shame through honor-shame to worth-shame, and thereby growing in independence and control, but also in developing from worth-shame to less destructive forms of response to the recognition of our moral failures.

This is missed by many writers on shame. Morris, for instance, thinks that "feeling shame because of what we have done, we actually see ourselves as shameful persons and the steps that are appropriate to relieve shame are becoming a person that is not shameful. Shame leads to creativity."[22] But why should it lead to creativity rather than to self-loathing? How could we take the appropriate steps to relieve shame when it is the nature of the experience to make us doubt, suspect, and denigrate the only agency capable of taking those steps? Where do the energy, the confidence, the moral aspiration come from when it is the likely consequence of shame to sap them? The trend of moral economy is that the

---

[22] Morris, *Guilt and Innocence*, 62.

more intensely we feel shame, the less capable we are likely to be of the moral creativity required for reform.

To sum up, some of the reasons for the claim that moral progress leads us away from shame toward other moral responses are that shame undermines our control, reduces the chances of moral reform, and weakens the self. Correspondingly, a tradition that makes available moral possibilities other than shame is better than one that does not.

We need to say something now about the possibilities whose realization constitutes moral progress over the cultivation of shame. We have already mentioned several such possibilities, but let us concentrate on one. In feeling shame, we respond to our moral failure by dwelling on the deficiency that produced it. One alternative is to respond to moral failure by dwelling instead on the attraction of the goal we have failed to reach. The goal is to live a good life. The moral enterprise is far more likely to be carried on if, instead of flagellating ourselves with shame, we concentrate on the attractions of our conception of a good life. It is better to respond to failure by reminding ourselves of what we want to achieve and why than by concentrating on our faults. What make it better are the attractions of the goal, the fact that our moral energy is limited, and that it is a wiser use of our limited energy to motivate such capacities as we have than to focus on the shortcomings from which we suffer.

It may be objected that this assumes that our feelings of shame are voluntary, and this is not so. Nobody wants to feel shame; we are assailed by it. Shame happens to us; it is an experience we can produce or prevent only in the sense of producing or preventing the state of affairs to which shame is the appropriate response. If we have self-respect and know that we have failed morally, shame will come to us. The objection to the suggestion that another feeling would be better than shame is that we cannot control our feelings of shame.

The reply is that while it is true that we cannot have direct control over shame, we can have indirect control over it. We cannot make feeling shame dependent on a decision to have it or not to have it. But once we have it, we can decide to cultivate it or minimize it, strengthen it or weaken it, attribute greater or lesser importance to it. What makes this possible is that in addition to the affective aspect of shame, which is indeed beyond our control, shame also has a cognitive and a moral aspect, and these we can control.

The cognitive aspect of shame involves a self-conscious detached comparison between the deficiency responsible for our failure and the value of which we have fallen short. The moral aspect of shame is the identification of a violated value as a component of our conception of a good life and thus as one basis for the evaluation of our own character and conduct. It is a necessary condition of the experience of shame that we find a discrepancy between how we are and how we ought to be. But once we have diagnosed and accepted the discrepancy, we can direct our attention away from it toward other objects. We can refuse to concentrate on the feeling, relegate it to the background, and deliberately hold some other object in the focus of our attention. Shame is an insistent feeling, however, so the object on which we focus in preference to it must have sufficient force to counteract the pressure of shame to reclaim center stage. This object should be our conception of a good life. It is bound to have sufficient force to counteract shame, for the intensity of our shame depends on how much we mind having fallen short of the conception. The stronger our shame is, the more attractive we must find the goal of which we are ashamed to have fallen short. And if the goal is not very attractive, then we could not mind all that much the failure to achieve it. We can therefore always derive from shame the clue to a better, less self-destructive, response than it.

The exercise of control by the cognitive and moral aspects of shame over its affective aspect requires effort, often great effort. Whether the effort is made depends on many things, but one of the most important among them is the tradition of the agent. We can be trained to regard shame as *the* feeling of self-respect, as Taylor proposes, and then we shall want to hang on to it as our last moral straw, rather than make an effort to minimize it, as has been advocated here. The reason why it is better to shun shame as the feeling of failure is that it further exacerbates the moral difficulty in which we find ourselves. If we recognize the force of this reason, we shall make an effort to demote it to a lesser rank. A tradition that weakens its adherents' vulnerability to shame while it strengthens their moral resources constitutes moral progress over a tradition that regards receptivity to shame as a crucial moral resource.

If these arguments are sound, they lead to the undesirability of regarding shame as an important moral force. But they have another implication as well. They have illustrated how moral progress is possible in one area that concerns matters less basic to living a good life than conformity to deep conventions. This is a significant possibility because it shows that we can have reasons for or against particular conceptions of a good life that go beyond evaluations based on the minimum requirements of good lives. These reasons will not be context-independent; they will not be reasons that count for or against all conceptions of a good life. For the reasons depend on the comparisons of conceptions of a good life with regard to their respective attitudes to shame. There are good reasons for saying that a conception of a good life that favors worth-shame over honor-shame or honor-shame over propriety-shame is in that respect better than one that does the opposite. And there are also good reasons for preferring a conception of a good life that stresses the motivational force of one's values over one that emphasizes instead the motivational force of any kind of shame. Yet although the reasons are good, they are not universally applicable to all conceptions of a good life. For they presuppose a context of comparison in which at least one of the conflicting conceptions has a positive attitude to shame. And there are, of course, countless possible conceptions of a good life that are indifferent to shame and countless possible comparisons based on features that have nothing to do with shame.

Part of the reason why this possibility is important for pluralism is that it reinforces previous arguments showing that conventionalism and perspectivism are mistaken. Both of these forms of relativism agree with pluralism in recognizing the moral necessity of conforming to deep conventions and in stressing the benefits of there being a plurality of conceptions of a good life. But conventionalists and perspectivists deny, while pluralists assert, that there can be reasons for regarding as better one of two conceptions of a good life that are alike in conforming to deep conventions. If the arguments we have presented about shame are correct, then conventionalism and perspectivism are both mistaken.

CONCLUSION

This chapter was about the sixth thesis of pluralism: the prospects for moral progress. We have found that the discussion of moral progress must be concrete. For if the comparison of traditions and conceptions of a good life is to be reasonable, it must be made in terms of the specific values they incorporate. It is useless, for instance, to ask whether Christian morality constitutes moral progress over Aristotelian morality. But it is illuminating to ask whether the Christian conception of love is an improvement over Aristotle's conception of *philia*. Ultimately, the judgment about the comparative moral progress of traditions and conceptions of a good life depends on such detailed analyses of their individual values as was here attempted for shame. And such analyses may well not yield an unequivocal conclusion. It is perfectly possible that in respect to some values one tradition or a conception of a good life represents an advance over another, while in respect to some other values the reverse is the case. If pluralism is correct, this is only to be expected. Yet, as the case of shame demonstrates, this does not lend support to relativism. For the recognition of the plurality of values is compatible with the reasoned criticism and justification of individual values.

The conclusion this chapter was intended to establish is that moral progress with respect to values is possible and that pluralism has sufficient resources to ascertain whether it has occurred. But the generalization from moral progress with respect to individual values to the moral progress of entire traditions and conceptions of a good life is no easy step. If relativism were confined merely to alerting us to the formidable difficulties standing in the way of the generalization, then it would be a salutary warning against epistemological and moral arrogance. Unfortunately, relativists go beyond this and deny the very possibility of nonarbitrary comparisons. We have seen that there are good reasons for thinking that what they say is impossible is in fact possible. We can reasonably judge that some values, and consequently some traditions and conceptions of a good life, constitute moral progress over particular alternatives. For reason allows us to offer legitimate criticisms and justifications beyond the level of primary values and the deep conventions that protect them. It is possible to find reasonable grounds for holding that some secondary values and variable conventions are better than others not merely from the point of view of a particular tradition or a conception of a good life but from the point of view of human welfare.

. . .

This completes the discussion of the six theses of pluralism. They were first presented in a brief form in chapter 2, where their interdependence was stressed. Then each thesis was discussed more fully in a subsequent chapter. These discussions did not aim at completeness or closure. On the contrary, the intention behind them was to provide a vocabulary and some basic distinctions in terms of which pluralism could be further developed, and to show how pluralism differs from the two main alternatives to it: monism and relativism. If pluralism is to become the major alternative to current moral and political theories that, we have argued, it potentially is, then it must be developed beyond the point we have reached here. The formulation and discussion of the six theses we have offered represent merely a beginning.

CHAPTER NINE

Some Moral Implications of Pluralism: On There Being Some Limits Even to Morality

> There is no consideration of any kind that overrides all other considerations in all conceivable circumstances.
> —Stuart Hampshire, *Innocence and Experience*

THE CENTRAL concern of pluralism is with the nature of good lives and with what we can do to achieve them. Pluralists are committed to the view that lives are made good by the personal satisfaction they provide and the moral merit they possess. But in good lives these two good-making components do not merely co-exist; they are intimately linked with each other. For what makes lives good is precisely that people living them take personal satisfaction in being and acting in ways that also have moral merit. Yet this coincidence cannot be complete; not all personal satisfactions can be derived from morally meritorious conduct, because good lives also involve the enjoyment of nonmoral values. Erotic love, beauty, style, creativity, personal projects, a sense of humor, occasional solitude, equanimity, playfulness, physical well-being, and so forth, are often personally satisfying components of good lives, yet normally they neither have nor lack moral merit, since they are only incidentally concerned with moral values, which depend on producing deserved benefits and not producing undeserved harms. The source of personal satisfaction therefore is not merely life in accordance with moral values but also one that involves the realization of nonmoral values.

The discussion up to now has concentrated on moral values. All the conflicts were among moral values, and similarly all the possibilities and limits were evaluated in terms of moral values. But we must now recognize that there are also nonmoral values, and the evaluations prompted by them may conflict with those prompted by moral values. We shall now consider these conflicts as well as the prospects for their reasonable resolution.

The argument is intended to contest the view that reason requires that the conflicts between moral and nonmoral values always be resolved in favor of moral values. Pluralists must contest this view, for if all values are conditional, then this includes moral values as well. If pluralism is correct, there must be conflicts in which moral values are reasonably overridden by nonmoral values.

In approaching these conflicts, we cannot simply assume that moral values should take precedence over the nonmoral values with which they conflict. For anyone tempted to make this assumption owes an analysis of the force of the "should" that establishes the supposed precedence of a particular moral value over a particular nonmoral one. The "should" cannot be moral because it is question-begging to appeal to the force of morality when it is the force of morality that is in question. And if the "should" is nonmoral, then the case for the precedence of at least one nonmoral value over moral values has already been conceded.

There have been some highly interesting discussions in contemporary moral philosophy about the question of whether moral values should necessarily take precedence in conflicts with nonmoral values. The question is usually discussed in terms posed by Philippa Foot: Are moral considerations overriding?[1] These discussions follow a pattern. They begin with some statement of the Kantian or consequentialist positions, both of which are committed to the overridingness of moral values. Then they present particular situations in which it becomes implausible, or at least questionable, that a particular moral value should override some particular nonmoral value. These situations, then, are interpreted as counterexamples to the Kantian or consequentialist arguments that moral values are overriding.[2]

Responses to these provocative arguments also form a pattern. Defenders of the Kantian or consequentialist claim that moral values are overriding charge their critics with failing to recognize the richness and sensitivity of which these conceptions of morality are capable. Given the full resources of Kantian or consequentialist morality, the supposedly nonmoral values with which moral values are taken by critics to conflict can be seen as being themselves moral values. The conflict is thus said not to be between moral and nonmoral values, but the familiar one between different moral values. This being so, would-be critics of the overridingness of moral values are charged with the failure of having presented any reason for doubting the overridingness of morality.[3]

The view to be defended here is that there are genuine conflicts between moral and nonmoral values, that reason does not always require that these conflicts be resolved in favor of moral values, and that the

---

[1] Foot, "Are Moral Considerations Overriding?"

[2] Perhaps the best-known representatives of this approach are Slote, "Admirable Immorality," Williams, "Moral Luck," and Wolf, "Moral Saints."

[3] Two examples of this approach are Bacon, "On Admirable Immorality," and Louden, "Can We Be Too Moral?" See also Louden's fullest statement, in *Morality and Moral Theory*.

conflicts are not the epiphenomena of an impoverished conception of the resources of morality. If this is right, we must doubt that morality is as important a guide to life as was supposed before pluralism appeared on the scene, and we must also doubt the defensibility of the traditional ideal of the coincidence of morality and reasonability. Pluralism thus leads to the subversive belief that our commitment to living a good life may legitimately involve immorality. The argument in this chapter is intended to establish this possibility.

REASONABLE IMMORALITY

The strategy we shall follow in arguing for this pluralistic view is to present two cases in which agents clearly and unambiguously conduct themselves immorally. Yet, it will be argued, they have weighty nonmoral reasons for acting the way they do. The advantage of appealing to incontestable cases of immorality is that, unlike previous arguments that moral values are not overriding, these cases cannot be reinterpreted as involving conflicting moral values. Nor can they be written off as the products of an impoverished conception of morality, since, on any reasonable view of morality, the cases would have to be regarded as involving immorality. Nonetheless, although the conduct is immoral in each case, there still are strong nonmoral reasons for acting that way. When moral and nonmoral values conflict, therefore, there are at least some cases whose outcome hangs in the balance.

The first case is based on Bruce Chatwin's novel, *Utz*,[4] although its development here departs somewhat from the original, in the interest of making a philosophical point. The case concerns a man whose ruling passion, indeed obsession, in life is a collection of porcelain figurines produced in Bohemia during the eighteenth century. There are straightforward psychological reasons why he became the way he was. He had been a clumsy, insecure, ugly, lonely, and rather stupid child, who happened to be given one of these figurines as a birthday present. He had begun to play with it, fantasize about it, and spin stories involving it. Other children, as well as adults, noticed his growing interest and sensed that there might be something special about the boy, that he was, after all, more than just an unlovable wretch. He was thus rewarded with the recognition he craved, he was spurred on in the same direction, he learned to make distinctions, he acquired the relevant facts, he taught himself to be a connoisseur. And as he was growing in skill and knowledge, so his inner life—his dreams, desires, ambitions, hopes, and fears—concentrated on his growing collection of these rare, delicate,

---

[4] Chatwin, *Utz*.

fragile pieces of porcelain. We encounter him as a middle-aged eccentric, a collector and an expert, with his life centered around the treasures whose fame is rapidly spreading among people knowledgeable about such matters. The collection is the focus of his emotional life; his chief preoccupation is with protecting and adding to it; and such human contacts as he has all focus in some way or another on the collection.

He lives in Prague, and the Allied betrayal of his country, the German occupation, the Second World War, the communist takeover, the various waves of terror, the murder of the Jews, the communist purges, the bombings, the show trials, the disappearance and the rare reappearance of people around him all impinge on his life merely as potential threats to the collection or as opportunities to enlarge it by judicious purchases from those who need money and have the goods. He casually cooperates with whomever happens to be in power, and he is quite willing, indeed eager, to exploit the latest wave of victims. He knows that the Nazis and the communists use him to lend a facade of respectability to their vicious regimes. They exhibit him as a testimony to their sensitivity to the finer things in life and to the freedom and support they provide for connoisseurship, and they even let him travel abroad to make some purchases. He allows himself to be used because he sees it as a bargain. What he has to give in terms of collaboration, the occasional public lies, the infrequent newspaper interviews, the mouthing of words of propaganda seem insignificant to him in comparison with the protection the collection receives in exchange.

From the moral point of view, the collector is despicable. His obsession has made him into a spineless accomplice of great crimes, a supporter of vicious regimes, an exploiter of innocent victims. It is true that he personally has not committed any great crimes, and it is also true that he is not selfishly motivated. He lives a life in service of art. He cares about himself, as he does about others, only in so far as he is instrumental to perpetuating the collection. He would readily continue to suffer and endure great hardship, as he has in the past, in the interest of the treasures. All the same, he knows what he is consenting to, he knows what the regimes whose reputation he is shoring up are guilty of, and he is quite heartless in striking a deal with people who are trying to buy their lives by selling some precious figurine. There is no doubt that the collector is immoral, and what is at the root of it is that he attributes greater importance to the collection than to common decency.

But now let us look at this from a nonmoral point of view. The collector has to weigh the respective importance he attributes to common decency and to the collection. What reason could be given by him or on his behalf for thinking that the collection is more important than decency? To start with, the aesthetic value of the collection is considerable. We may not want to go so far as Faulkner in proclaiming that "the 'Ode on a Grecian Urn' is worth any number of old ladies,"[5] but we should begin by recognizing that the collector is protecting a unique assemblage of irreplaceable works of art, and not, say, canceled streetcar tickets. If they were dispersed, lost, broken, or removed from accessibility, there would be a serious loss. Consider further that although the collector's hands are by no means clean, he has not committed horrendous crimes. He lied, he was not morally fastidious, he lent his insignificant support to vicious regimes, and he drove heartless bargains. There were countless people, however, both in Prague and elsewhere, during those wretched days, who did the same for personal gain or out of cowardice or mean-spiritedness and not to protect valuable works of art. But the most important consideration is the appreciation of what the figurines meant to the collector. It is not a cliché to say that they were his life. His identity, the integrity of his personality, his attitude toward the world, the meaning and purpose of his life were inseparably connected with the collection. As some aborigines carry their souls in a box, so the collector's soul was in the figurines. Their destruction would mean the destruction of the psychological props of his life, and without them he would be lost. To say to the collector that the moral value of common decency should take precedence over the nonmoral value of his collection is to say that he should opt for a life he would find unacceptable rather than be guilty of the same banal moral transgressions as many people around him were busily engaged in. The cost of decency for the collector would have been too great. It is just not reasonable to expect that much of people. The point is not that he could not do what morality required of him. He knew what it was, and he had the power to act on what he knew. But the motivation for exercising his powers, given its cost, his context, and the attractions of the alternative, was simply not there. The collector, therefore, did have good nonmoral reasons for acting immorally.

The second case involves a young Englishman in 1940 who felt that he was at the beginning of a promising career. He was from a working-class family, and he had achieved what he had by hard work, talent, and considerable sacrifice. The times, however, were not kind to his career plans. England stood then alone in the Second World War, and the tide was running against her. It was clear to the Englishman that he would soon be conscripted and that the chances of his survival were poor. And, it seemed to him, that even if he were to beat the odds and survive in a reasonably intact state, his future in an England that was likely to lose the war would not have given him an acceptable life. He would have an up-hill struggle, even in peacetime, to make a life suited to his talents, since

[5] The Paris Review Interviews, *Writers at Work*, 112.

he had the wrong accent and the wrong background, but the prospects of an acceptable life in a defeated country, probably under foreign occupation, he found quite dim. It happened, however, that he was offered passage to America and a promising job. He accepted them and settled in America, where he did indeed succeed in making a distinguished career for himself.

The moral criticism of the Englishman is that he acted disloyally. He took the benefits his country offered—namely, security, health care, education, and a decent standard of living—but when the time for repayment came, he left England in the lurch. He put his welfare before the welfare of his country, and he betrayed his fellow citizens who had a right to count on him, especially in those hard times. Being raised in a country confers rights and obligations on citizens, and our Englishman enjoyed the rights without honoring the obligations.

We may reply to this moral criticism by pointing out that it demands too much in exchange for too little. It is true that the Englishman was born into the country and enjoyed the rights and privileges of citizenship. But we all have to be born somewhere, and he did not choose to be born an Englishman. In fact, shortly after he reached the age when people can make responsible decisions about where their allegiances lie, he did make the decision for which he is now being criticized. Moreover, the rights and benefits he received prior to his decision were not all that great, nor were they fairly distributed. His working-class background deprived him of many privileges that more fortunately situated people enjoyed. He had to work much harder for what he got than people higher up in the social scale. Although there certainly was a tacit contract between him and his country, the contract was neither indissoluble nor particularly fair. The most telling point against the moral criticism is, however, that it places unreasonably high demands on the Englishman. For it requires him to risk his life, limb, and future, and what he finds in the balance for all this is very meager indeed. Why would a reasonable person risk all that under such circumstances? He has only one life to live, his talents must be employed now, his resources and opportunities are all that he has, and he is required by morality to endanger all that. For him, to have a chance for an acceptable life, certain conditions had to be met, and morality required him to put those very conditions into jeopardy.

Like the collector, the Englishman can also appeal to a nonmoral value as a reason for his immoral conduct. The value is that which attaches to having the prospect of a minimally acceptable life. If the circumstances of one's life produce a conflict between this nonmoral value and any particular moral value, there is no reason why the moral value should *necessarily* override the nonmoral one, and there is a powerful reason why the nonmoral value may take precedence. The reason is that that particular nonmoral value normally motivates the future functioning of the individual in question as an agent, and, *simpliciter,* as a moral agent. What is involved in the conflict between this nonmoral value and any other moral value may not be the choice between being a morally good or a morally bad agent but the choice between having and not having the motivation to go on living at all. The reason why for many people the nonmoral value of having a minimally acceptable life may override the moral value that being a good moral agent has is that for many people, not being martyrs or heroes, the first is necessary for the second.

This claim may give rise to two skeptical questions. First, it may be asked whether any *moral* conclusions follow from the facts of psychological motivation. It may be that people often opt for a particular nonmoral value when it conflicts with a moral value, but why should it be supposed that what that shows is that it may be reasonable for the nonmoral value to override the moral value? The alternative is to suppose that the people who opt for the nonmoral value are acting immorally.

But this question overlooks the context in which the conflict between nonmoral and moral values in general is being considered. That they may conflict is clear. The question to which such conflicts give rise is whether reason always requires that the conflicts be resolved in favor of the moral value. To reply by simply asserting the affirmative answer is dogmatism, not argument. Reasons have to be given to support either the affirmative or the negative answer. And surely one central type of reason bearing on the question of which of the conflicting values it is reasonable to choose is the agents' judgment about the respective importance of the two different values in their lives. This judgment will strongly influence their psychological motivation, so it has a clear bearing on the resolution of the conflict. Now the judgment may of course be mistaken, but it does not seem that either the collector or the Englishman was unreasonable in judging in his own case that the importance of having a minimally acceptable life outweighs the importance of acting decently or loyally. At the same time, it must be acknowledged that there are heroic or saintly people who may judge differently in similar situations, and their judgments may also be reasonable. As we shall shortly see, in these conflicts reason allows more than one answer.

The second skeptical question concerns the reasons for regarding a minimally acceptable life as a nonmoral rather than a moral value. Why should we not interpret the conflicts of the collector and the Englishman as occurring between two moral values, and thus as a conflict *within* morality and not *between* morality and something else? The answer is two-fold. First, having a minimally acceptable life carries with it no guarantee regarding the balance of good and evil that the person whose life it is will cause. We need to know a great deal about that balance before we can form any reasonable moral evaluation about whether the life is morally good or evil. It may be Hitler's, Einstein's, or our next door neighbor's. One reason against regarding a minimally acceptable life as a moral good is that while it is certainly a benefit to the agent who has it, it may turn out to be morally evil because it may involve causing a preponderance of undeserved harm to others.

Second, having a minimally acceptable life is one normal, shared, and reasonable goal of all human agency, regardless of whether it is moral, immoral, or nonmoral, because if we were deprived of a minimally acceptable life, most of us would not wish to go on living. The relationship between an individual's having a minimally acceptable life and living a morally good life is like the relationship between a society's having institutions and having just institutions. As societies would disintegrate without institutions, so individuals would disintegrate without having such a life. But this is as true of just and unjust institutions as of moral and immoral lives.

From having a minimally acceptable life being a nonmoral value it does not, of course, follow that the life we go on to live if the minimal conditions are satisfied is immune to moral criticism. It is indeed a legitimate goal of morality to influence people toward being morally good rather than morally bad agents. The point has been that the way in which morality can go about achieving this legitimate goal has a reasonable limit. The limit is that it should not oblige people to subject to serious jeopardy that very capacity of theirs that is normally required for the achievement of the goal of morality. This is the reason why at least one nonmoral value *may*, although it need not, override any particular moral value, even if the consequence of doing so is that immoral conduct, in the context of that conflict, may be reasonable.

PLURALISM BEYOND MORALITY

Let us now reflect on the significance of these cases. The nonmoral reasons given for these instances of immorality should not be taken as attempts to make the collector or the Englishman morally or otherwise attractive. The collector has succeeded in making himself an instrument for the perpetuation of the collection. As a result, he has no life apart from his figurines. He is a boring, empty, unprincipled person, whose contact with others is only for the purpose of using them and whose inner life is pervaded by unwholesome fantasies centering on artifacts. The Englishman prospers, but he is psychologically damaged. The trouble is not that he lives in a society that is not his own; it is rather that he knows it about himself that he is permanently estranged, because, when it counts, he is not willing to pay the price of belonging. That is his secret, and when he gets pushed, he is hypocritical, ashamed, aggressive, self-deceiving, and defensive about it. He does not want to let on that when the chips were down, he was disloyal and let his country down. There is, therefore, a considerable cost to living a life in which the non-moral value attributed to having a minimally acceptable life has overrid-den whatever moral value competes with it. In both cases, the agents found themselves in situations in which it was reasonable to incur that cost not because their lives would have been made good by it but because they would not have found their lives worth living if they had chosen otherwise. Nevertheless, in each case we have an example of a nonmoral value reasonably overriding a moral value.

The description of the cases and the attempt to draw out their signifi-cance have perhaps attributed more articulateness and reflectiveness to the two agents than they are likely to possess. It should be stressed, there-fore, that the cases are intended to illustrate a line of thought that fits the agents' conduct rather than give a psychological account of what actually had gone on in their minds. The question is whether a reasonable de-fense can be offered for their conduct and not whether they themselves could offer such a defense.

In a more or less conscious manner, then, each of the agents has made a choice. The choice was based on imperfect knowledge, but, in each case, it was a reasonable choice to make. The collector calculated well in what he did to protect the collection, and the Englishman was realistic in predicting a dire future for himself in 1940. But the strength of the non-moral reasons for the agents' immoral conduct does not hinge on the truth of their beliefs but on their reasonableness. As a matter of fact, the Englishman's judgment was partly mistaken, because England's fortune had eventually improved; however, given the facts he had and his cir-cumstances, it was reasonable to judge as he had, and that is sufficient for the pluralistic case.

Furthermore, it would be a misunderstanding to try to assimilate the conflicts to conflicts between morality and selfishness. If by "selfishness" we mean the habitual and exclusive pursuit of one's interest, especially when it conflicts with the interests of others, then only the Englishman is a candidate for selfishness. The collector cared about the collection and hardly at all about himself. It is true that the deep reason for the immorality of the collector and the Englishman was that they were pro-tecting the fundamental conditions required for minimally acceptable lives for themselves. But what is at the heart of these cases is not selfish-ness but the protection of one's self. Whether successfully protected selves are or will become selfish depends on the nature of the lives the selves go on to live. The type of conflict these cases intend to document is between living a minimally acceptable life and living as a morally good agent. And since, except for some martyrs and heroes, the first is a condition of the second, there must be possible cases in which the first reasonably overrides the second.

The justification for saying that this particular nonmoral value may override the moral value with which it conflicts is couched in terms of reasonableness. It will be remembered from chapter 5 that to say that something is reasonable may mean either that reason requires it or that reason allows it. If something is required by reason, then the alternative to it is unreasonable because only that which is required accords with reason. If something is allowed by reason, then it is reasonable, although some alternative to it may be equally reasonable. Alternatives to what reason requires are thus forbidden by reason, while alternatives to what reason allows may or may not be forbidden. Both being required and being allowed by reason serve to exclude certain alternatives, but being required by reason excludes all alternatives, while being allowed by reason excludes only some of them.

In the light of this distinction, the argument can be interpreted as having a radical and a moderate version. The radical version is that when the nonmoral value that attaches to a minimally acceptable life conflicts with any moral value, then reason requires that the nonmoral value should override the moral one. According to this version, it would have been unreasonable for the collector and the Englishman to conduct themselves morally rather than immorally. The moderate version is that when this nonmoral value conflicts with any moral value, then reason allows that the nonmoral value should override the moral one, but reason does not require it. Although it was reasonable for the collector and the Englishman to act immorally, there was another reasonable alternative open to them, and that was to act morally by allowing the moral value in question to override the nonmoral one. On this view, both the moral and the immoral courses of action were reasonable in both cases.

The argument advanced here should be understood as a defense of the moderate version. The intention behind it is not to establish that there are situations in which the claims of morality are unreasonable but rather to establish that there are situations in which it is reasonable to override the claims of morality and conduct oneself immorally. The intention is not to replace monistic claims on behalf of moral values with monistic claims on behalf of nonmoral values. It is rather to replace monistic claims on behalf of moral values with pluralistic claims that allow that in a certain type of conflict between nonmoral and moral values, each may reasonably override the other.

We have been arguing for one half of this claim, and it may be thought that if the arguments were acceptable, then the second half of the claim would be mistaken. For the more reasonable it is to allow a nonmoral value to override a moral value, the less reasonable it must be to allow the moral value to override the nonmoral one. But this is not so. The judgment of which should override which is made by different people, and they may reasonably judge differently. There is often no canonical answer to the question of how much risk it is reasonable to take in exposing one's self to disintegration, or just how bad would life have to be for it not to be even minimally acceptable. In many situations, reasonable people may reasonably disagree in their answers. And such disagreements may occur because there is not always an authoritative weighing of the respective importance of being physically secure over belonging to a community, as in the Englishman's case, or of enslaving oneself to an ideal over having a sense of worthlessness, as in the collector's case. The reasonable resolution of these conflicts need not involve an all-or-none choice; it may involve balancing, trade-offs, trial and error, the capacity to tolerate ambiguity, and the like. And there can be reasonable disagreements about these matters even for people who face identical situations. The moderate version of the argument here defended allows for these possibilities, while the radical one, in the company of other monistic theories, does not.

What, then, is the significance of the moderate version of the argument? First, it follows from it that a moral theory is faulty to the extent to which it is committed to the view that reason requires that moral values should override conflicting nonmoral values. And since such well-known and widely accepted moral theories as those of Plato, Aquinas, Kant, and Mill, among others, are so committed, the argument has considerable critical import. Second, a deeper reason for holding that reason requires that moral values be overriding is an assumption that permeates moral philosophy from Socrates on, namely, that the requirements of reason and morality coincide. But if reason allows that in cases of some conflicts a particular nonmoral value may override moral values, then the requirements of reason and morality cannot always coincide. Third, it is often supposed that when reasonable agents ask themselves or others why they should act in a particular way, the answer that morality requires it is as conclusive as we can get. The moderate version of the pluralistic argument implies, however, that this supposition is mistaken. For although moral values may require a particular action, nonmoral values may have conflicting requirements, and the question of which should prevail is open. That morality requires an action is thus *a* reason for performing it, but it is not a conclusive reason. The recognition that this is so should have a cooling effect on a lot of moral rhetoric to which we are currently treated. Fourth, if we take pluralism seriously, then we must face its implication that the incompatible and incommensurable values that conflict may not only be moral but also nonmoral.[6]

AGAINST THE OVERRIDINGNESS OF MORALITY

We shall now consider the most serious reason against the pluralistic position we have been defending. This reason has been expressed in a number of ways, but they are all versions of the idea that moral considerations must be overriding because morality just is that to which we attribute overriding importance. One consequence of this idea is that it can be used to defuse the three best-known counterexamples to morality's being overriding that figure in recent discussions.

The first of these is what Kierkegaard calls "the teleological suspension of the ethical."[7] He considers Abraham's willingness to sacrifice Isaac upon being commanded by God to do so. Morality forbids such an action, so it may be supposed that we have a case here where a religious value overrides a moral value. The second case is what has come to be known as "dirty hands" from the English translation of Sartre's play of the same name. In Walzer's description, a reasonable and decent statesman is forced by circumstances to do what he regards as morally abhorrent: to order the torture of a terrorist to extract information needed to save lives that would otherwise be lost.[8] In this case, we supposedly have an instance where a moral value is overridden by a political value. The third case is constructed by Williams, who selected some facts from the life of Gauguin and embellished them.[9] Williams's Gauguin abandoned his family to dire poverty and departed for the South Sea Islands to paint. By producing the great works of art he had, Gauguin provides a putative example in which an aesthetic value overrides a moral value.

Much has been written about these cases, both in support and in criticism. Cooper advanced a simple argument, however, to show that none of these cases succeeds as a genuine counterexample.[10] The argument rests on the distinction between a narrow and a wide sense of morality. The narrow sense is, roughly, conventional morality or the morality of everyday life in some specific context. It is true that Abraham's religious

---

[6] Stocker, *Plural and Conflicting Values*, 41–44, reaches the same conclusion by means of different arguments.

[7] Kierkegaard, *Fear and Trembling*, 79–101.

[8] Walzer, "Political Action: The Problem of Dirty Hands."

[9] Williams, "Moral Luck."

[10] For a detailed version of this argument, see Neil Cooper, *The Diversity of Moral Thinking*, 97–101.

faith, the statesman's political conviction, and Gauguin's passion for art led them to violate conventional morality. This does not mean, however, that their conduct exemplifies the overriding of morality. For Abraham's morality was the command of his God, the statesman's morality was informed by his conception of the common good, and Gauguin's morality was art. We may disagree with these moral commitments and judge the actions based on them immoral, but there is no question here about overriding moral values for the sake of some nonmoral value. Given the wide sense of morality, the requirements of religion, politics, and art can easily be accommodated as forming part of morality. The appearance of conflict is created only by taking the narrow conception of morality more seriously than we should.

This argument in defense of the overridingness of moral values, however, is too simple. For the identification of the wide sense of morality with whatever particular agents regard as having overriding value allows the trivialization of morality. People can attribute overriding value to silly, self-destructive, perverse, or eccentric concerns, and these are surely inappropriate as moral values.[11] To maintain the reasonable identification of the wide sense of morality with what moral agents regard as having overriding value, it is necessary therefore to explain what makes it reasonable to regard some values as overriding. The claim that one's conception of morality is intrinsically connected with what one regards as having overriding value cannot be merely formal. The notion of overridingness must be given some substantive content to rule out reducing morality to absurdity by putting no restrictions on what may reasonably be regarded as overriding.

Williams's distinction between morality and ethics[12] can be seen as an attempt to supply the missing substantive content of overridingness. Ethics is by and large what has above been called the wide sense of morality, whose central concern is with how one should live. It is this concern that makes overridingness inseparable from ethics and, at the same time, gives some content to the notion of overridingness. For all reflective people will recognize that the question of how one should live is of the first importance and that its answer has, or should have, what Williams calls "deliberative priority."[13] And since silly, self-destructive, perverse, and eccentric answers can be shown to be unacceptable, we have some specific restrictions on what may legitimately be regarded as having deliberative priority and thus on what may be part of ethics. By contrast,

---

[11] See Foot, "Are Moral Considerations Overriding?"

[12] Williams, *Ethics and the Limits of Philosophy*, 174–96. For a recent consequentialist response to Williams's argument, see Brandt, "Morality and Its Critics."

[13] Williams, *Ethics and the Limits of Philosophy*, 183.

morality is a particular kind of ethics. Its central concern is with universalizable and impartial obligations. Consequentialism and Kantianism are paradigmatic representatives of it. Champions of morality wish to identify it with ethics, but this is a mistake, because reasonable answers to the question of how one should live must take account of a much more varied set of facts of life than universalizable and impartial obligations.

Given this distinction, defenders of the overriding claim of moral values can show that the putative counterexamples—the teleological suspension of the ethical (that is, of the moral), dirty hands, and Gauguin—miss their mark. For while these cases show that what Williams means by "morality" can indeed be overridden by nonmoral values, they fail to show that what Williams means by "ethics" can similarly be overridden by nonethical values. The cases demonstrate that there are varied answers to the question of how one should live; and pluralists, like Williams, have known and insisted on that all along. The claims of religion, politics, or art may indeed override the claims of universalizable and impartial moral obligations, but they do so because, and only because, they are candidates for answering the overridingly important ethical question of how one should live.

Although Williams is right in his criticism of consequentialism and Kantianism, the distinction between morality and ethics cannot carry the burden placed on it. Let us grant that the central question of ethics (in Williams's sense) is how one should live, that it is an important question, and that if we had an answer to it, then the answer would have deliberative priority. But not just any answer will do. Reasonable answers must be action-guiding, for otherwise they could not have deliberative priority. For answers to be action-guiding, however, they must be capable of deciding between competing and incompatible courses of action. It is all well and good to insist that religious, political, and aesthetic values may conflict with moral values (in Williams's sense), but we still need an argument that would show how the conflicts among these values could be resolved reasonably. This is especially so since Williams himself insists that conflicts are fundamental to (what he calls) ethics.[14]

The consequence of these unresolved conflicting claims is that no answer has been shown to have deliberative priority. If the distinction borrowed from Williams were correct, what would actually follow from it is that we do not know how we should live. The cost of accepting that ethics is richer than morality is that of having to incorporate into ethics the incoherence produced by conflicts between moral and nonmoral values.

---

[14] "[V]alue-conflict is . . . something necessarily involved in human values, and to be taken as central by any adequate understanding of them" (Williams, "Conflicts of Values," 72).

How does it help to defuse the putative counterexamples to moral values's (in Williams's sense) being overriding to relabel them as conflicts between incompatible and incommensurable values and resituate them in (what Williams calls) ethics? The net result of this use of Williams's distinction is the proposal that instead of having external conflicts between moral and nonmoral values, we have them as conflicts internal to ethics. But the change of label contributes nothing to answering the question of how we should live, of which of our conflicting values should be given deliberative priority.[15]

The failure of these two attempts to establish the overridingness of moral values (to return to the accepted usage, and leave Williams's behind) by identifying morality with what we reasonably regard as most important in life makes attractive what is the strongest version of the same idea. This is Becker's notion of "the all-things-considered point of view."[16] Becker distinguishes between special and general conceptions of morality. Special conceptions interpret morality as one human activity among others. Special conceptions of morality thus may indeed conflict with religion, politics, and art. But the general conception of morality is another matter. For this conception interprets morality as the attempt to answer the question of what reasonable people ought to do from the all-things-considered point of view. That point of view cannot conflict with any other, since any conflict would be a sign that all things had not yet been considered. The general conception of morality allows conflicts between special conceptions of morality and other areas of life, but the general conception is intended to answer the question of what reasonable people ought to do, given those conflicts and given all relevant considerations.

Becker's approach thus avoids the difficulty of Cooper's, because the all-things-considered point of view is substantive and not merely formal; and it also avoids the impotence of the version based on Williams's distinction, because it goes beyond registering the possibility of fundamental conflicts and proposes a way of resolving them. Moreover, it can also defuse the putative counterexamples of Kierkegaard, Walzer, and Williams by interpreting them as illustrations of how the values of special conceptions of morality may indeed be overridden. But Becker can insist that we must still decide how to act, and the decision, if it is reasonable, will be made from the all-things-considered point of view of the general conception of morality. The values of that conception cannot be reasonably overridden, because any reasonable consideration proposed as pos-

---

[15] Lack of guidance on this point is one of the difficulties of Frankfurt's discussion in "The Importance of What We Care About"; see especially the concluding section.

[16] Becker, *Reciprocity*, chapter 1.

sibly overriding them would have to be incorporated into the point of view that that consideration was intended to override.

There remains, however, a fundamental difficulty that Becker's argument for the supremacy of the all-things-considered point of view has not avoided. The consideration of all things may take place from different points of view—such as the agents' own; their lover's, family's, political or religious cause's; their country's or humanity's; and so forth—and these may yield incompatible judgments about what the agents, who are in the process of considering all things, ought to do.

Let us take the agents' point of view as an example of one of these and the point of view of what would be best not just for the agents and their dependents but for everyone as an example of another. These two points of view may consider exactly the same set of facts but evaluate them differently. From the point of view of the common good, it would be better for art collectors not to be so obsessed with works of art as to violate common decency; and it would also be better for people not to make their way in the world at the cost of disloyalty. Saying that these courses of action would be better from the point of view the common good is to say that the lives of those affected by the agents' actions would be better if the agents did not act the way they have done in the examples we have given. But from the agents' own point of view a different conclusion follows. Agents may reasonably judge that when what is at stake is having a minimally acceptable life for themselves, then it would be better to safeguard this most important resource of theirs than to subordinate it to the common good. From the point of view of the common good, it would be better if the agents sacrificed themselves; but from the point of view of the agents, it would not be better. The all-things-considered point of view therefore does not remove the possibility of conflicts between points of view that do consider all things but evaluate the considered things differently.

The basic reason why the counterexamples we have provided succeed, while Kierkegaard's, Walzer's, and Williams's fail, is that the nonmoral value to which agents may appeal when they take their own point of view stands to moral values in quite another relation than do the religious, political, or aesthetic values to which Abraham, the statesman, and Gauguin could appeal. It can be said about the latter that if there is a reason for allowing religious, political, or aesthetic values to override moral ones, then, whatever that reason is, it is a reason for assimilating these nonmoral values to moral ones. For the reason that gives overriding force to these nonmoral values must ultimately be that from the point of view of the common good it is better to live according to them than to live according to the moral values with which they conflict. The conflict is thus defused by the enlargement of our conception of morality through its assimilation to the nonmoral values that conflicted with the moral ones. And the justification for this enlargement is that both the previously nonmoral and the moral values serve the same purpose, namely, to answer the question of how we can act so as to promote the common good. If morality is understood as providing that answer from the all-things-considered point of view, then some religious, political, and aesthetic values may reasonably be assimilated to moral values.

But it is otherwise with the counterexamples we have offered. For there is no conception of morality that may legitimately incorporate immorality, and disloyalty and violation of common decency are immoral. The conception of morality centering on the common good cannot be enlarged to include the point of view from which individual agents may resolve conflicts between moral and nonmoral values, because the morality of the common good forbids immorality, while the point of view of the individual may allow it. And the point of view of individual agents allows immorality, because when a conflict occurs between having a minimally acceptable life and acting as a morally good agent, reason allows the first to override the second, since the first is normally a condition of the second. The cases we have offered are intended to give some flesh and blood to the abstract possibility of such conflicts and to reason's allowing that in some situations a nonmoral value may override moral values.

One deep reason for rejecting Becker's argument is the untenability of the optimistic assumptions that underlie it. These assumptions are that if we were indeed to consider all things with sufficient care, then, first, there would emerge a conclusion about what to do, and, second, this conclusion would be one all reasonable people would arrive at if they too considered all things with the requisite care. But it is one of the most important consequences of pluralism that these assumptions are mistaken.

We can certainly consider all things carefully and decide on a course of action. But other people can do likewise and decide on another course. And this is not because one of us operates under some cognitive or moral handicap. Fully informed, reasonable, and morally committed people can reasonably disagree about the same set of considerations, because although some moral judgments in some contexts are required by reason, there are many other moral judgments that are allowed by reason and yet may conflict with each other. When these conflicts concern the question of how far we should go in sacrificing our interests for the common good, reason allows more than one judgment.

There is yet a deeper consideration that counts against Becker's identification of the moral point of view with the all-things-considered point of view. This consideration is independent of the previous claim that the all-things-considered point of view has not succeeded in eliminating the conflicts it was designed to eliminate. Morality is essentially concerned with making life have as much good and as little evil in it as is possible in our imperfect world. Reasonable people will be committed to morality. But this commitment must not become so imperialistic as to exclude other commitments. We must leave room for the thought that we may care deeply and reasonably about people we love, beauty, various personal projects, intellectual or artistic creativity, traditional ways of life, the challenging of mental or physical limits, and many other nonmoral values. And we care about them not because we believe they are instrumental to the common good but because they are constituents of *our* conceptions of a good life.

These nonmoral values could and often do conflict with moral values. The trouble with the identification of the moral point of view with the all-things-considered point of view is that it does not, because it cannot, leave room for this possibility. All things considered, agents may put love, beauty, creativity, and so on, ahead of the common good in many contexts. When they do that, they might act immorally, and yet they might also act reasonably. If the all-things-considered point of view were the same as the moral one, we could not express this thought, and we would thus deprive ourselves of an important possibility in life. This would be an impoverishment of such resources as we have. For while moral values are important, there are also other important values. Commitment to these nonmoral values may limit our commitment to moral values, just as commitment to moral values may limit our commitment to these nonmoral values. If pluralism is right, all values are subject to this condition.

CHAPTER TEN

Some Personal Implications of Pluralism: Innocence Lost and Regained

> No, it is not only our fate but our business to lose innocence, and once we have lost that it is futile to attempt a picnic in Eden.
> —Elizabeth Bowen, *Collected Impressions*

WE HAVE SEEN in the previous chapter that the moral and nonmoral values required by good lives may conflict with each other. It was argued there that when such conflicts occur, reason does not always require the moral value to override the nonmoral value. Reason allows that in some cases the nonmoral value should take precedence over the moral one. The question we shall consider in this chapter is the reaction that reasonable people should have to the realization that aiming at a good life may involve the subordination of moral to nonmoral values and, consequently, that there may be circumstances in which we can remain faithful to our conception of a good life only by acting immorally. We shall be exploring therefore the personal implications of pluralism.

The most important among these implications is that the conflict among moral and nonmoral values is a conflict internal to moral agents and that it is a profoundly unsettling experience. For what causes such conflicts is the incompatibility and the incommensurability of particular moral and nonmoral values both of which are essential constituents of the agents' conception of a good life. And because the agents are basically committed to both, their conflict calls into question the very possibility of living as they think they should. Their nonmoral commitments may call upon them to violate the deep conventions of their tradition, while their moral commitments to the very same conventions make it impossible to realize some of the nonmoral values that are essential to living what they regard as a good life. Reasonable and morally committed agents may find themselves in situations where the best course of action is one that requires them to violate their basic commitments. If pluralism is right, we must face the fact that such destructive possibilities are among the possibilities of life. We need to consider, therefore, what reaction individual agents should have to them.

The outline of the answer is that the reasonable reaction involves the loss of innocence, the cultivation of a certain kind of knowledge and experience, and, if things go well, the development of an immensely desirable frame of mind that makes it possible to regain innocence. This regained innocence will represent moral progress over the naive kind that was left behind.

Prereflective Innocence

"Innocence" may refer to guiltlessness or to an attitude of wholehearted, spontaneous commitment, accompanied by trusting acceptance and the absence of analysis, doubt, or questioning. Throughout the discussion, "innocence" will be used in the second way. Given this usage, innocence is a character trait whose mere possession leaves open the question of its moral standing. The loss of innocence thus may or may not be morally good.

People may be innocent about the good and evil possibilities of life; the explanation of their innocence may be that they have been sheltered from the harsh realities of human existence; and the extent of their innocence may be so great as to make them acquainted only with their own small corner of the world. Children typically possess this kind of innocence; let us call it "prereflective innocence." It will be discussed in this section. But innocence may be possible also for people whose knowledge and experience of life is as thorough as may be desired. What explains their innocence is that they are so completely committed to the realization of some morally good possibilities as to find departure from them unthinkable; and their innocence is thorough because not even at the deepest level of their being are they split or hesitant about their commitments. Some great artists, scientists, and moral exemplars have this kind of innocence. We shall call it "reflective innocence" and discuss it later.

Prereflective innocence may show itself in childlike simplicity, spontaneity, and naive openness. What underlies this trusting attitude is the absence of awareness of possibilities whose presence would make trust inappropriate. Trust would be appropriate if the possibilities were shown not to be real, but in the case of prereflective innocence this has not been done. This kind of innocence predisposes those who have it to be trusting prior to their knowledge of whether their favorable attitude is merited. The situations to which prereflectively innocent agents respond innocently may be full of complexities, fraught with dangers, and charged with moral difficulties, and yet because of their ignorance or lack of experience, these innocent agents respond to such situations as if they were simple. Sometimes they avoid evil because, like sleepwalkers on a roof, they happen to put their feet consistently right. Sometimes their innocence transforms the situations by disarming untoward possibilities, as when a tourist asks a thief at Grand Central Station to watch his luggage for a moment. Sometimes they doom themselves because they fail to see that their expectation of decency and good will enrage rather than placate some people. And sometimes they are just right because the situation they treat as simple is simple, although someone more knowing would not have thought so. Prereflective innocence thus may be a force for good or for evil; it may cut across cynicism, knowing worldliness, and suspiciousness, or it may simplemindedly encourage evil conduct by failing to recognize it as such.

It would be futile to try to say much more than this about innocence in general. Further discussion needs to focus on prereflective innocence manifested in concrete social contexts. Accordingly, we shall begin by concentrating on prereflective innocence as the attitude of reasonable agents who feel thoroughly at home in a certain kind of tradition. For such agents, writes Michael Oakeshott, "[t]he moral life ... does not spring from the consciousness of possible alternative ways of behaving and a choice, determined by an opinion, a rule or an ideal, from among these alternatives; conduct is as nearly as possible without reflection. And consequently, most of the current situations of life do not appear as occasions calling for judgment, or as problems requiring solutions; there is no weighing up of alternatives or reflection on consequences, no uncertainty, no battle of scruples. There is, on the occasion, nothing more than the unreflective following of a tradition of conduct in which we have been brought up."[1]

To be such a person in such a tradition is fortunate indeed. We may perhaps justifiably wonder whether this idyllic belongingness can actually be found in any past or present tradition, but this is not really the point. For Oakeshott describes an ideal that, if it were realized, would make innocence an appropriate attitude. For us, of course, a superficial glance at how we live in our tradition suffices to show how very far short it falls of this ideal condition. To make this perception less impressionistic, consider how it would have to be for the ideal actually to obtain.

First, there would have to be a sufficient number of deep and variable conventions to guide conduct in moral situations that adherents of a tradition are likely to encounter. Second, the moral education of individual agents would have to be so thorough as to acquaint them with all these conventions and so effective as to produce spontaneous, unreflective conduct in accordance with them. In effect, moral education would have to be successful in inculcating a second nature in the vast majority of moral agents. Third, when people, having acquired this nature, encounter some concrete situation that calls for a moral response, they would naturally, without needing to think, fight contrary impulses or resolve conflicts and act according to the appropriate convention of

---

[1] Oakeshott, "The Tower of Babel," 61.

whose motivating force they need not even be aware. As we console a friend, express love, or do the job we like without having to trace the steps that lead to our both wanting and being obliged to do it, so, in this ideal state, would countless moral agents act likewise in the many various moral situations they encounter in their daily lives. These three levels of morality—composed of the motivating convention, the perception of the situation as falling under its jurisdiction, and the appropriate action—form a seamless whole not just for one agent in one situation but for most agents in most situations. If a tradition were to conform to this ideal, then prereflective innocence would be an appropriate frame of mind for those who live according to it.

Our life is otherwise. We encounter serious difficulties on each of the three moral levels described above. With respect to the first, we must recognize that we live in a period of rapid and deep changes, and we routinely find ourselves in new moral situations to which existing conventions provide inadequate guidance. Advances in medical technology, the economic interdependence of distant societies, the end of the Cold War, the spread of AIDS, rampant drug addiction, and the sexual revolution are among the more recent developments that often present us with unprecedented and morally charged questions. To be sure, we are not without conventional resources in trying to answer them, but no one can reasonably claim that the answers do not require much experience, reflection, and the well-informed adaptation of old conventions to new situations. But it is not merely external changes that affect us; our internal moral attitudes are also changing. We think about religious fundamentalism, the relations between the sexes, ecology, medicine, immigration, welfare, and so forth, quite differently from the way our predecessors did, say, fifty years ago. As a result, our conventions themselves have been changing.

The changes in our conventions, circumstances, and attitudes unavoidably influence our perception of particular situations. When conventions are clear and life is familiar, we can be quite confident in our way of seeing the moral situations we encounter. But, as a result of changes, we routinely experience the second level of morality as inviting alternative descriptions. It makes a serious difference whether we see welfare recipients as victims or as underachievers; homosexuals as sick or as members of a besieged minority; or physicians as trusted advisors or as merchants selling health care. We cannot simplemindedly trust how we perceive these and many other situations, because the situations have become morally ambiguous, and they have become so because our conventions, circumstances, and attitudes have themselves become questionable and widely questioned.

Consequently, as we pass to the third level, in many morally important areas of our life we can no longer act both reasonably and with assured spontaneity. No matter how good our moral education has been and how well we have learned what it had to teach, we can no longer trust the unmediated deliverances of our second nature. If our actions result from "the unreflective following of a tradition of conduct in which we have been brought up," then we shall be both innocent and guilty. Innocent because we are guided by an attitude of unquestioning acceptance, and guilty because the attitude is inappropriate in our circumstances and we are blameworthy if we cultivate it in the face of the obvious need to be otherwise.

This is not to say that in our context prereflective innocence is always inappropriate. Not all areas of our life have become morally ambiguous: primary values have remained what they have always been. Yet even primary values take various forms, and we are often unclear about the moral standing of these forms. Murder and torture are primary evils; but is abortion murder, and is the coerced prolongation of moribund lives torture? Kindness and justice are primary goods; but is supplying clean needles to drug addicts kindness, and is reverse discrimination just? Without trying to answer these difficult questions, let us distinguish between simple and complex moral situations. In the first, the conventions are clear, the description of the cases is unproblematic, and the appropriate actions are straightforwardly indicated. In the second, one or more of these conditions is absent. We can, then, say that prereflective innocence is appropriate in simple moral situations and inappropriate in complex ones.

One characteristic of the ideal state Oakeshott describes is that most moral situations in it appear to reasonable agents as simple. *We* deviate from the ideal because so very many of the moral situations we encounter seem to us to be complex. That is why prereflective innocence is generally good in the ideal state but not in ours. And what is responsible for the simplicity of moral situations under ideal circumstances is the general agreement among reasonable people about the conventions they follow, about their interpretation of particular cases, and about what they ought to do in the light of them. This general agreement is most likely to be achieved if the prevailing tradition is monistic; the more pluralistic a tradition is, the farther away it will fall from the ideal. The likelihood that prereflective innocence will be morally appropriate will increase as a tradition moves toward monism and decrease as it moves toward pluralism. Since our tradition is probably the most pluralistic in human history, prereflective innocence is less appropriate in it than at any other time, place, and context. We must conclude, therefore, that pluralism and prereflective innocence exist in a state of tension and that commitment to pluralism ought to bring with it a willingness to question prereflective innocence.

THE LOSS OF PREREFLECTIVE INNOCENCE

Since pluralism obliges its adherents to question their own prereflective innocence, it is a harsh taskmaster. For prereflective innocence cannot survive such questioning, and its loss involves us in coming to distrust our natural reactions. We have to teach ourselves not to be spontaneous, to examine our impulses, to leave behind the uncomplicated, simple, and therefore safe view of the world in which we felt at home and protected. The loss of prereflective innocence is the loss of security.[2] It is bad enough if it happens, but pluralism demands more—it calls upon us to make it happen. The loss of such innocence is familiar, for it happens to most of us, but it is good to have a vivid reminder of it.

In a short story, J.I.M. Stewart tells of a boy who has a perfect childhood.[3] His parents love him and each other. His father is strong, respected, and manly, and his mother is loving, gentle, and understanding. Or so it seems to him, until he overhears a late-night conversation between his parents. They have just come back from an evening out, and they are preparing to go to bed. The first thing that strikes the boy is the tone of their voices; hers is contemptuous, intending to wound; his is groveling, humiliated, and expiatory. And then he hears the actual words. She accuses him of having once again drunk too much and having offended all the wrong people; he tries to make feeble excuses and promises, once again, to reform.

The boy's world is shattered; its security disintegrates; he sees his parents with new eyes and reexamines the past, and, in the light of the overheard exchange, it seems to be other than he thought it was; what he overheard opens up for him previously unimagined possibilities; and with them his protective cocoon bursts.

A few days later he hears his parents having the same conversation. But this time they are on stage, acting in an amateur theatrical production. The boy realizes that what he overheard the first time was not a genuine conversation but his parents' rehearsing their roles. The fact is, however, that this realization makes little difference. For the possibilities that he has learned to entertain cannot be forgotten. He has realized that life could be like that, and he cannot return to the state in which the

---

[2] For a perceptive analysis of the process, see Morris, "Lost Innocence."
[3] Stewart, "Parlour 4."

possibilities were unthought and unthinkable. The external conditions of his life have not changed, but his attitude toward them has, and since the goodness of his life was partly due to his attitude, the idyll is over, and then, as Elizabeth Bowen says, "it is futile to attempt a picnic in Eden."

Loss of prereflective innocence is the price we have to pay for our moral progress. It involves enlarging our awareness of the possibilities of life in the context created by our tradition, character, and circumstances. Sometimes this enlargement is forced on us, as it was on the boy in Stewart's story. At other times, we can make it happen ourselves by deliberately cultivating our moral imagination in the manner described in chapter 6. But if it is so painful and shattering, why would we be motivated to do it? The short answer is that the goodness of our lives depends on it, but a longer answer is needed to explain why this is so.

Making a good life for ourselves depends on the realization of some of our possibilities. We survey our possibilities, we commit ourselves to some of them, and the hierarchical structure of these commitments constitutes our conception of a good life. The wider is the range of possibilities that we have available, the greater is our freedom in forming our conception of a good life. And the better we have employed our imagination in exploring our possibilities and in correcting our attitudes toward them, that is, the more breadth and depth we have, the more reasonable will be the emerging conception of a good life. The richer a tradition is in providing possibilities for its adherents, however, the less appropriate prereflective innocence will be in it. For prereflective innocence is lack of knowledge and experience about the possibilities of life one's tradition provides. Since monistic traditions provide fewer possibilities than pluralistic ones, we can see in yet another way why prereflective innocence is increasingly less appropriate as traditions become more pluralistic. In a pluralistic tradition, therefore, people will have good reasons to lose their prereflective innocence, even if doing so is painful. What will motivate them is not merely the intellectual understanding of their circumstances but also the joint attractions of increased freedom and a greater scope for making better lives for themselves—attractions that will appeal to their feelings, engage their imagination, and strengthen their will.

It may be thought that this is as true of monistic traditions as it is of pluralistic ones. For all traditions require reasonable adherents to develop an appropriately critical and questioning attitude toward the good and evil possibilities that are recognized in their context. This is no doubt true. But there are two differences that set monistic and pluralistic traditions apart. The first is that since the possibilities are far more numerous in pluralistic traditions than in monistic ones, moral progress from prereflective innocence toward a more appropriate attitude is going to be more demanding and difficult in the former than in the latter.

The second difference finally brings us back to the central topic of this chapter: the connection between innocence and the conflict between moral and nonmoral values. Monism fails to countenance the possibility that it may be reasonable to resolve conflicts between moral and nonmoral values essential to one's conception of a good life in favor of the nonmoral ones, while pluralism encourages its recognition. And since the possibility carries considerable moral dangers with it, prereflective innocence, which fails to face the possibility and its dangers, is a vice rather than a virtue in pluralistic contexts.

The thinking behind the monistic refusal to consider the possibility of resolving the conflict in this way may rest on the denial that such conflicts could occur. If the moral and nonmoral constituents of a good life cannot conflict, then of course we do not have to agonize over how it is reasonable to resolve their conflict. The monistic assumption has been expressed with admirable clarity by Nagel: "The no-conflict view would hold that a moral theory like utilitarianism or Kantianism, in telling us what we ought to do, reveals an essential aspect of the good life that cannot be known independent of morality. Not to do what we have decisive moral reason to do is ipso facto to live badly. And even if morality requires sacrifices of us, the fact that they are required implies that it would be even *worse for us* if in these circumstances we did not make them. On this view . . . the best life *is* the moral life, a morality cannot . . . conflict with the good life."[4]

But this assumption is untenable. The moral life is certainly part of the good life, but it cannot be the whole of it because good lives also involve the realization of nonmoral values. The only way this assumption can be defended is to *define* the good life as the moral life, and that involves a verbal sleight of hand whereby nonmoral values are either arbitrarily refused the name of value or, equally arbitrarily, assimilated to moral values.

Yet the motivation to hold this untenable assumption is extremely powerful. Its strength comes from the optimistic belief that if we conduct ourselves so as to seek what is morally good and avoid what is morally evil, then life will go well for us or, if not well, at least less badly than it would do otherwise. But why should this be so? In the past, this optimistic belief was backed by metaphysical and theological doctrines according to which the scheme of things conforms to a rational and morally good order. The reason why life would go better, or less badly, for us if

---

[4] Nagel, *The View from Nowhere*, 192.

we lived and acted according to moral values was supposed to be that we would then live and act in closer harmony with the scheme of things. As we have seen, however, in chapter 4, there is no good reason to accept these metaphysical and theological doctrines, and there are excellent reasons to reject them.[5] Moreover, neither Kant nor such utilitarians as Bentham or Mill used these doctrines to support their identification of the good life with the moral life. In the absence of these props, however, the monistic assumption must be seen as devoid of reasonable support.

One consequence of this is that each of us may encounter internal conflicts between moral and nonmoral values both of which are essential constituents of our conceptions of a good life. We have seen in the previous chapter that the claim that these conflicts should always be resolved in favor of the moral values is unreasonable. The contrary attitude is advocated by pluralists, namely, that the resolution of such conflicts may reasonably go sometimes one way, sometimes the other. For this to be possible, however, moral agents must be aware of the possibility of such conflicts and must be free to resolve them in favor of either. But since the required awareness and freedom are incompatible with prereflective innocence, moral progress toward developing the awareness and making use of the freedom depends on the loss of prereflective innocence.

It would be a bad misunderstanding to suppose that the recommended loss of prereflective innocence is a joyous Nietzschean romp toward liberation from moral constraints. The agents who are wracked by conflicts between moral and nonmoral values do not see either as an obstacle to living a good life. On the contrary, they are committed to both because they see both as essential to the life they want to live. The conflict thus threatens their very conception of a good life. The conflict and its threat, however, may still be of various degrees of seriousness. To see why this is so, we need to return to the distinction drawn in chapter 5 between the different kinds of commitments that constitute the hierarchical structure of our conceptions of a good life.

Commitments are to moral and nonmoral values. Depending on how important these values are within our conceptions of a good life, the commitments to them may be basic, conditional, or loose. As we have seen, some conflicts, then, are simple, because they have a straightforward resolution, while others are complex, because it is difficult to resolve them. Simple conflicts are relatively easy to handle, because they occur either between a more and a less important value to which the agents' commitments are not equally strong, or between equally important values choice among which is possible by appealing to a stronger

---

[5] The point is only asserted here. Arguments for it may be found in Kekes, *Facing Evil*, chapters 1 and 10, where the transcendental temptation is discussed.

commitment of the agents. Conflicts among values to which the agents have loose or conditional commitments are typically simple, while conflicts among values to which the agents have basic commitments are normally complex. And what makes some commitments basic is that the corresponding values are regarded by the agents as indispensable constituents of their conceptions of a good life. The conflicts between moral and nonmoral values that concern us here are complex, because the agents are supposed to have a basic commitment to both of the conflicting values.

The explanation of why the complex conflicts between basic commitments are so wrenching is not merely that the agents find themselves in a situation in which whatever they do will violate one of their most deeply held values. People can get into such situations by having committed themselves to the wrong values or by being responsible for bringing about the conflict through their own stupidity, negligence, ill will, or other vices. In such cases, the agents themselves are responsible for the seriousness of their conflicts. But there are many other cases in which this is not so. The deepest values that conflict in this manner are often well-chosen because they are genuinely valuable. Moreover, they can normally coexist without any conflict, and yet the agents find them conflicting because, through no fault of their own, external circumstances render the values incompatible.

It is supposed by monists that one of the most important functions of morality is to guide people in such conflicts. Some formulation of the Kantian categorical imperative or of the utilitarian greatest happiness principle is taken to be the overriding moral principle, and, although it is granted that it may be difficult to act according to it in serious conflicts, it is still assumed to provide clear moral guidance.

Even if there were a defensible overriding moral principle, however, and we have argued that there is not, it would still be inadequate for resolving complex conflicts between moral and nonmoral values to which the agent has made a basic commitment. Such a principle may help those who accept it to resolve conflicts between moral values. But the case we are considering is a conflict between moral and nonmoral values. And the overriding principle of morality could help in that case only by assimilating the nonmoral value to the moral one. But we have seen in the previous chapter that this assimilation is arbitrary and indefensible.

Moral agents who encounter the relevant sort of conflict have a reasonable conception of a good life, which involves basic commitments both to a reasonably held moral value and to a like nonmoral value. Then, although they are moved by reason and good will, they can honor only one of their basic commitments and must violate the other. As a result, they must either do something morally so objectionable as to make it unacceptable even to themselves or abandon some nonmoral value without which they would regard their life as having lost even even minimal acceptability. Such nonmoral value may be attached to the sensibility of a novelist, the eyes of a painter, the physique of an athlete, the intellect of a scholar, or to the life of someone the agent passionately loves. Reasonable and well-intentioned people emerge from such complex conflicts between their fundamental moral and nonmoral values with a loss that deeply damages them.

The significance of these conflicts and of their consequences is that they establish and make vivid for us a possibility that, if we take it as seriously as pluralists think we should, forces on us a particular view of what we can reasonably expect from our tradition and from our conception of a good life. The possibility is that although we may be as reasonable and morally committed as we could be, and although our tradition and our conception of a good life may be as sound as possible, we may still fail to achieve the good life for which we strive. And the significance of that is that living according to reason and morality does not guarantee that we shall live well. We can do the utmost in our power to combine our moral commitments to produce deserved benefits and not to produce undeserved harms with our nonmoral commitments to realize whatever personal projects we regard as necessary, and we may still fail. Furthermore, the failure cannot be averted by becoming more reasonable and moral, because it is not due to our being insufficiently reasonable or moral. The failure is a reflection of the fact that the scheme of things is not hospitable to human endeavor, that there is no guarantee that the moral and nonmoral values we legitimately seek and need to realize can be made to cohere with each other. And that means that we cannot reasonably believe one longstanding assumption of our tradition, namely, that life according to reason and morality will be good. Since that assumption permeates the classical, Judeo-Christian, and Enlightenment sensibilities, and since its rejection follows from pluralism, we have reached a watershed in the history of our tradition.

The implications of this consequence of pluralism are, of course, far-reaching, subversive, and incalculable. It is not the purpose of this book to explore them.[6] But three closely connected implications must be mentioned here, since they have an immediate bearing on our topic. The first is that the standard answer to the question of why we should strive to be reasonable and moral must, at the very least, be revised. The answer used to be that the more reasonable and moral we were, the better our lives would be. If, however, the reasonably arrived at moral and non-

---

[6] This is the topic of Kekes, *Facing Evil.*

moral values essential to a good life may conflict and exclude each other, then our lives may actually be better if we violate some of our reasonable and moral commitments.

The second implication is that the assumption pluralism obliges us to doubt has been responsible for much of the optimism and energy that motivate our engagement in life. We have thought, and still think, that we could make things better if we try hard enough in a reasonable and morally accredited manner. But if making things better also depends on considerations beyond our capacity to control, then the optimism is misplaced, and the energy is misdirected.

The third implication brings us back to the topic of this chapter: innocence. Prereflective innocence cannot survive the understanding of this consequence of pluralism, since such innocence is possible only if the agents motivated by it unreflectively respond to the conflicts they encounter as if they were simple. The realization that the conflicts *may be* complex, that our basic commitments *may be* incompatible, and that our moral and nonmoral values *may* exclude each other must lead to the dissolution of prereflective innocence, even if the pluralistic argument turns out to be mistaken. For even if all conflicts were proved to be simple, the mere rejection of the possibility that they may be complex requires the kind of reflection with which prereflective innocence is incompatible. Just as the boy in Stewart's story cannot return to his perfect childhood after having entertained the possibility that it is imperfect, so also reasonable and morally committed agents cannot return to a state of prereflective innocence after having entertained the possibility that their best efforts may not be good enough to achieve the reasonable and morally praiseworthy life they aim at.

Reflective Innocence

Let us assume then that reasonable agents in possession of a sound conception of a good life recognize the possibility that the moral and nonmoral values to which they are basically committed conflict with each other. As a result, they lose their prereflective innocence and abandon the optimistic assumption that underlies it. The question we have to consider now is what attitude it is reasonable to aim to develop in place of prereflective innocence.

One possibility is resignation motivated by the realization that our best efforts may not be good enough. This, in turn, may evoke the defeatist response that in that case trying to do our best is pointless. The result is a considerable weakening of the effort to make a good life for ourselves, since the effort is seen to be unavailing.

But this attitude is based on bad thinking. In the first place, the possibility to which it is a response is not a prediction of what *will* happen to make our efforts futile, but a description of what *may* happen. Our best efforts could be rendered pointless, although they need not be. We are confronting a possibility, not an actuality. In the second place, the success of our attempts to achieve a good life depends both on our efforts and on conditions we cannot control. By weakening our efforts, resignation adds to the conditions over which we have no control and thereby causes the prospects for a good life to recede even further.

Another possible attitude comes from the end of our emotional scale opposite to resignation. It is an attitude Hume recommends as a response to "reflections very refin'd and metaphysical."[7] He says that it "fortunately happens, that since reason is incapable of dispelling these clouds, nature herself suffices to that purpose, and cures me of this philosophical melancholy. . . . I dine, I play a game of back-gammon, I converse, and am merry with my friends; and when after three or four hours' amusement, I wou'd return to these speculations, they appear so cold, and strain'd, and ridiculous, that I cannot find it in my heart to enter into them any farther."[8] Call this the attitude of "common sense." Our prereflective innocence is gone, we know the facts of life, we know what may happen to our best-laid plans, but let us not dwell on all this. It does not do any good to keep the abyss in the forefront of our attention, so let us carry on, and hope for the best.

This is a considerable improvement over the previous attitude, for it does not sabotage our own efforts. Yet it is still defective for two reasons. First, a reasonable conception of a good life must contain more than a hierarchical structure of commitments to various values. Conflicts invariably arise in our efforts to live and act according to our commitments, and we would be less than reasonable if we did not formulate some policies for coping with them. We certainly should not dwell on the misfortune, adversity, injustice, social obstacles, ill health, or bad luck that may cause our conflicts, but we should not be unprepared for them either. If we followed Hume's advice, however, our preparation would consist in making an effort to ignore these possibilities, thus making ourselves less able to cope with them, if and when they occur, than we would be if we prepared ourselves in a better way.

The second defect of Hume's answer is that finding ourselves in situations where untoward events force on us the necessity to choose between our basic commitments is, as we have seen, among all else, an emotion-

---

[7] Hume, *Treatise*, 268.
[8] Ibid., 269.

ally highly charged experience. Our natural feelings of anger, resentment, surprise, helplessness, shock, self-doubt, and so forth, are provoked by the fact that we are blameless and yet forced by circumstances to act in ways that we know are self-destructive. These feelings, of course, make an already bad situation even worse. For they divert our attention, consume our energy, undermine our judgment, and thus make it less likely that we should be able to cope with the conflict as well as possible in the adverse circumstances. But if we had prepared ourselves for the possibility that now confronts us in an actual form, it would be much less likely that our emotions would get out of hand. Forethought would remove the element of unexpectedness that lends its force to our inevitable feelings.

And so we might swing back to an attitude whose chief characteristic is the desire to control our reactions, since we often cannot control the circumstances to which we are reacting. Let us call this the "Stoic attitude." It supposes that our conceptions of a good life are reasonable only to the extent to which we can exercise control over what we want and what we get. And, it supposes further that since we cannot rely on our ability to control the world outside us, we should make the good life we want depend solely on our own resources. The key to living well is thus to be entirely self-reliant, and we can do that by teaching ourselves to want only what we can achieve internally, since all else is contingent, uncertain, and hence risky. If we taught ourselves not to want what we may not have, and if we could learn to want only what was within our capacity to attain, then we would be in complete control of the goodness of our lives.

The Stoic attitude, however, is also misguided, for it combines two mistaken assumptions. The first is that the good things we all naturally want, whose sources are external to us and hence not in our control, are not really good and not really necessary for a good life. It is certainly true that the world beguiles us with many false or ephemeral goods: fame, wealth, reputation, and applause are fickle and may turn to ashes. But not all the good things we seek from outside ourselves are illusory and dispensable. Love, friendship, some security, comfort, freedom, and the absence of unrelieved hostility or injustice as a response to our endeavors are truly necessary for a good life. If we tried to teach ourselves to do without them, we would be unlikely to succeed; and if we did succeed, the cost would be a life that no reasonable person would characterize as good. It may be that such lives would be even-keeled, unruffled, and free from great disappointments, but, at the same time, they would also lack sufficient positive content. Nothing that could come in from the world would be valued, and what would be valued is the self-discipline that assures that nothing would come in that could be valued. It would be a life combining the attitude of sour grapes with the refusal to recognize other forms of nourishment.

The second mistaken assumption behind the Stoic attitude is that the internal goods it values, namely, the appropriate virtuous character traits, are free of the vicissitudes that render external goods uncertain and contingent. For whether we could develop the valued character traits, and thus live a good Stoic life, depends on our genetic inheritance; on the possession of various cognitive, emotive, and conative capacities; on being born into a relatively stable society; on not being brutalized as children; on having some scope and encouragement to develop in certain directions and not in others; and on numerous other political, social, historical, and economic considerations. We have as little control over how these factors shape our characters as we have over the love, friendship, security, comfort, and appreciation we also need for a good life. So even if we lived as the Stoic attitude prescribes, we would still not be able to exercise the control that provides the rationale for living that way.

The reason for concentrating on the defects of these misguided attitudes is to find a better attitude in place of the lost prereflective innocence. By becoming aware of the defects of some possible replacements, we can look for an improved attitude that is free of them. Such an attitude will combine the positive feature of recognizing that the moral and nonmoral values to which we are basically committed may conflict with each other and the negative features of not responding to this recognition by resigning ourselves, attempting to ignore it, or trying to persuade ourselves that the goods we value are not really good. The emerging attitude will be reflective innocence.[9]

Prereflective and reflective innocence are alike in being characterized by simplicity and spontaneity and by the absence of calculation, self-doubt, ulterior motives, and being of a divided mind. But the two forms of innocence also differ, because the explanation of what leads agents to them are different. Prereflective innocence is due to lack of knowledge and experience, while reflective innocence is due to having so thoroughly considered one's commitments as to render superfluous further reflection about them. Both kinds of innocence betoken the absence of hesitation between encountering some situation and responding to it. Prereflective innocence, however, is unhesitant because the agents moved by it are unaware of the complexities that should cause them to hesitate, while reflective innocence is unhesitant because the agents

---

[9] Attitudes similar to reflective innocence have been discussed by Frankfurt, *The Importance of What we Care About*, especially in essays 2, 5, 7, and 12; Kekes, *Facing Evil*, chapters 10 and 11; and Charles Taylor, "The Concept of a Person."

whose attitude it is had reflected extensively, and thus complex situations appear simple to them. The difference is like the difference between an inexperienced reader of a topographical map who has not learned to extrapolate from the map to the difficulties in the terrain and an expert mountaineer who takes it all in but to whom what others would find difficult merely appear as features of the landscape. There is no reflection in prereflective innocence because the need for it is not felt; and there is none in reflective innocence either because the need for it has been so amply met that it is no longer felt.

The specific subject about which prereflectively innocent agents have not reflected and reflectively innocent ones have is their conceptions of a good life. Both kinds of innocence have an ideal state in which the distinction between simple and complex moral situations disappears. For prereflective innocence, the ideal state would be one in which the tradition in the background is thoroughly monistic and the agents' conceptions of a good life are utterly conventional. There would be no moral ambiguity, because the conventions of the tradition would be reflected in the agents' commitments, and the particular cases the agents encounter would readily be seen as coming under the jurisdiction of some specific convention.

For reflective innocence, the ideal state would be achieved by exceptional agents whose conceptions of a good life embody a well-ordered hierarchy of commitments that provides a ready resolution for conflicts even among their basic commitments. They would know right off which of the moral and nonmoral values to which they are basically committed is more important to their conception of a good life, and they would know *that* because they have reflected so deeply and in such breadth in the past as to make reflection in the present unnecessary.

Just because in this ideal state reflectively innocent agents would be able to resolve conflicts that others would agonize over does not mean of course that they would not incur the same loss as others. They, as others, would have to violate either a moral or a nonmoral value that is essential to their conception of a good life. It is just that one of the benefits they would gain from their reflective innocence is that of finding it easier to make the required choice, because their ability to transform complex moral situations into simple ones relieves them of the agony of choice, even if they have to endure the agony of loss.

A further benefit of reflective innocence is the amelioration of the agony of loss, if we come to suffer it. The first step toward it is to have a realistic attitude toward the prospects for succeeding in our attempts at trying to make a good life for ourselves. At the center of this realism, there will be knowledge of the contingency of life and the acceptance that contingency is not merely an abstract feature of life in general but a concrete one that may result in serious harm to oneself. The realism this requires will be an intermediate position between the optimistic belief that the scheme of things is ultimately reasonable and beneficial and the pessimistic one that humanity, or oneself, is doomed. What faces us is neither salvation nor damnation but muddling along as well as we can in circumstances we understand and are able to control only imperfectly. Not even the best conceptions of a good life pursued in as reasonable and morally praiseworthy a manner as possible could or would be free from this condition. After we have done all we could to escape from it, it may still make us its victims. The benefits of reflective innocence do not consist in freeing us from this contingency but in freeing us from responding to our acknowledgment of it in defective ways. The attitudes of resignation, common sense, and Stoicism represent some of these defects, and we need now to see how reflective innocence is an improvement over them.

To begin with, in contrast with resignation, instead of exaggerating the possibility of failure and thereby undermining our motivation to succeed, reflective innocence strengthens our resolve to adhere to our conceptions of a good life in the face of both possible and actual failure. This attitude is backed by two considerations whose combined forces override reasonable doubts. One is that the alternative to trying to make a good life for ourselves is to acquiesce in living a life that falls considerably short of what we want it to be; for if it did not, failure would not be such a disconcerting prospect. In fact, the more seriously we take failure, the stronger we must want to avoid it, and the less prone we shall be to resignation. So even if we actually failed in some disastrous way, we would still be better off if we picked up the pieces, patched up the damaged conception of a good life, and carried on.

The other consideration is the attraction of our conception of a good life. Having such a conception means that we want to live according to some set of commitments because the commitments are to things we value. Our conception of a good life thus is not an abstract ideal but an intrinsically motivating force. And when that force is combined with the force generated by our desire to avoid living in a way that we regard as deficient, then we shall want to develop and maintain our commitments with the wholeheartedness that characterizes reflective innocence. The realism about the contingency of life that is at the core of reflective innocence will, therefore, motivate us positively rather than negatively.

Let us now look at how reflective innocence is an improvement over the unpreparedness for, and emotional overreaction to, failure that the common sense attitude engenders. By acknowledging the possibility of failure, reflective innocence reduces the unexpectedness of it, if it happens to us. The realism of it stands as a reminder of the possibility, so that its occurrence will shock us less because we shall have prepared ourselves for it. But the point is not merely that of saving ourselves from unpleasant surprises. We cannot help reacting to some serious threat to the way we think it is good to live. And the feeling with which we shall have to contend will be very strong indeed. We shall have placed ourselves into a double bind. There will be the failure with which we have to cope and there will also be our powerful emotional reactions to the failure. And the feelings will vie for attention with the failure that elicited them. The more manageable our feelings are, the better able we shall be to cope with the failure. And our feelings will be more manageable if, instead of ignoring the possibility of failure, as the common-sense attitude prompts, we have made ourselves ready for its possibility, as the realism of reflective innocence teaches us to do.

There is finally the comparison between reflective innocence and the Stoic attitude. The fundamental defect of the Stoic attitude is its lack of realism. Unlike the attitudes of resignation and common sense, Stoicism both recognizes and tries to cope with the contingency of life. But the recognition does not go far enough, and there are also other facts of life it should, and yet fails, to recognize. Reflective innocence permits us to see that life is contingent through and through, that there is no aspect of it so thoroughly under our control as to form an inner citadel to which we could retreat when adversity threatens to overwhelm us. For our inner life, where our control is perhaps the best, also depends on a multitude of conditions, past and present, over which we have no, or only very weak, control. Our psychological states are influenced by our physiological states, by our capacity and the development of that capacity to be in psychological states of the appropriate sort, and by the conditions of our environment. It is unrealistic to suppose that if our conceptions of a good life were constituted entirely of valued psychological states, then they would somehow be free of contingency. Reflective innocence allows us to recognize that all of our values are vulnerable and that we depend for the realization of many of them on benefits we can obtain, if at all, only from the world external to us.

Reflective innocence thus combines a realistic appraisal of the world and our place in it with the motivation and the reason not to allow ourselves to be deflected by the hard facts we face from continued adherence to our conception of a good life. It is an attitude of innocence because it involves simple, spontaneous, wholehearted conduct according to our commitments. And it is a reflective attitude because the innocence is the outcome of the understanding that we may fail no matter how reasonable and morally commendable our commitments and conduct may be. It is not the innocence of children, but the innocence of those whose ideals have not ceased to shine on account of being uncertain of attainment.

We have been considering the ideal states of prereflective and reflective innocence. The actual states we are likely to encounter in ourselves or in others will fall (usually) more or (rarely) less short of the ideals. But describing the ideals is important for three reasons, each having to do with moral progress. One is that we can see that the ideal state of prereflective innocence is incompatible with pluralism because it presupposes a monistic tradition in the background. If the criticisms of monism have been correct, and our actual situation includes a plurality of conditional, incompatible, incommensurable, and conflicting values, then the closer we come to the ideal state of prereflective innocence, the less able we shall be to resolve conflicts among these values. Moral progress requires therefore a growing reflection on our conception of a good life. And the more we reflect, the farther away we shall move from the ideal state of prereflective innocence. Second, what moral progress will move us *toward* is the ideal state of reflective innocence. For in that state we shall be as clear as possible about our commitments, about our reasons for making them, and about our reasons for ranking them as we do. If the inhospitability of the world forces conflicts on us, we shall at least know how we could opt for the lesser of two serious evils. Third, by understanding and appreciating the benefits provided by the ideal state of reflective innocence, we shall be motivated to do what we can to come closer to it. Holding the ideal state in the focus of our attention will supply part of the necessary motivation for our own moral progress.

Conclusion

In the last two chapters, we explored some moral and personal implications of pluralism. If no value is overriding and all values are conditional, then this is true of moral values as well. There must be circumstances then in which it would be reasonable to override the claim of any moral value on the ground that some nonmoral value takes precedence over it. In the previous chapter, we discussed two such circumstances: those of the collector who collaborated with vicious regimes for the sake of his collection and the Englishman whose ambition led him to abandon his country in a dire emergency. We have argued that in both cases reason allows the agents to resolve their conflict between moral and nonmoral values in favor of the latter. The nonmoral value in each case was what the agents attributed to a minimally acceptable life. They judged reasonably, it has been argued, that this nonmoral value is more important to their conception of a good life than the moral value they violated when the two conflicted. From this it follows that the requirements of reason and morality do not always coincide. This conclusion is implied by pluralism, for pluralism is the denial that any value is so privileged as to exclude the possibility that some other value, in some situation, overrides it.

The conflict between moral and nonmoral values may be trivial or serious, depending on the importance of the conflicting values. The possibility we have been considering is that of serious conflicts brought about by circumstances in which reasonable agents possessing reasonable conceptions of a good life cannot simultaneously honor two of their basic commitments: one to a moral and the other to a nonmoral value. The agents recognize that both values are essential to their conception of a good life, and they recognize also that however they resolve their conflicts, they will suffer a very serious and self-destructive loss. In the present chapter, we have considered how reasonable agents ought to respond to the possibility that this may happen to them through no fault of their own.

The argument was that the reasonable policy is to do what we can to progress from prereflective to reflective innocence. The progress consists partly in remedying our trusting, unquestioning attitude by bringing ourselves to the realization that reasonable and moral conduct does not guarantee a good life. And the progress consists further in not allowing this realization to affect our commitments to the values that alone could make our lives good. We have thus seen in yet another way how moral progress is possible both for individuals and for traditions. Individual moral progress involves development toward the ideal state of reflective innocence; the moral progress of traditions is toward a system of conventions that would encourage, rather than hinder, the moral progress of individuals. Both result in a movement away from monism and toward pluralism.

CHAPTER ELEVEN

Some Political Implications of Pluralism: The Conflict with Liberalism

> [C]ontemporary debates within modern political systems are almost exclusively between conservative liberals, liberal liberals, and radical liberals. There is little place in such political systems for the criticism of the system itself, that is, for putting liberalism in question.
>
> —Alasdair MacIntyre, *Whose Justice? Which Rationality?*

IN THIS CHAPTER, we shall consider some of the many political consequences of pluralism. Perhaps surprisingly, these consequences lead us in the direction of questioning the supposedly close connection between pluralism and liberalism. Liberals have claimed, and their critics, largely by default, have conceded, that pluralism is most at home in a liberal society. Actually, however, this claim is mistaken; there are good reasons for supposing that pluralism and liberalism are incompatible. As a first approximation of these reasons, we may note that pluralism is committed to the view that there is no particular value that, in conflicts with other values, always takes justifiable precedence over them. By contrast, if liberalism is to avoid the charge of vacuity, it must be committed to holding that in cases of conflict the particular values liberals favor do take justifiable precedence over other values. How, then, could liberalism and pluralism be compatible?

The intention behind examining their supposed incompatibility is to show that the connection between pluralism and liberalism is contingent on historical circumstances, that pluralists need not be liberals, and that pluralism, consistently with its nature, is hospitable to a much wider range of values than those of liberalism.

LIBERALISM AND PLURALISM

The difficulties in the way of giving a general account of liberalism are formidable. These have been noted by liberal thinkers themselves. Raz, for instance, writes, "It is probably true to say that no political cause, no one vision of society nor any political principle has commanded the respect of all liberals in any given generation, let alone through the centuries."[1] Waldron says the same thing: "If we examine the range of views that are classified [as liberal] . . . we are unlikely to find any set of doctrines or principles that are held in common by all of them, any single cluster of theoretical and practical propositions that might be regarded as the *core* or the *essence* of the ideology in question."[2]

In the light of these difficulties, it is better to restrict the discussion to one version of liberalism, namely, the contemporary one as it exists mainly in America and to some extent in the rest of the English-speaking world. To describe this version, we may begin with a list of typically liberal causes: liberals are "for greater economic equality, for internationalism, for freedom of speech and against censorship, for greater equality between the races [and, we may add, the sexes] and against segregation, for a sharp separation of church and state, for greater procedural protection for accused criminals, for decriminalization of 'morals' offenses, particularly drug offenses and consensual sexual offenses involving only adults, and for an aggressive use of central government power to achieve these goals."[3] We may add to these causes affirmative-action programs, the equal rights amendment, unrestricted abortion, decreased funding for defense, and increased funding for welfare. The reason why liberals favor these causes is that they seem to them to be implementations of the most important liberal values of freedom, equality, the protection of human rights, and a particular conception of distributive justice, to which we shall refer as "Rawlsian justice."

As a first approximation of the theoretical position underpinning the most important liberal values, we may turn to what Sandel has called "deontological liberalism": "'Deontological liberalism' is above all a theory about justice, and in particular about the primacy of justice among moral and political ideals. Its core thesis can be stated as follows: society being composed of a plurality of persons, each with his own aims, interests, and conceptions of good, is best arranged when it is governed by principles that do not *themselves* presuppose any particular conception of the good. . . . This is the liberalism of Kant and of much contemporary moral and political philosophy."[4]

It is advisable, however, to adopt a broader conception of liberalism than Sandel's, because there is no good reason for excluding versions of liberalism that give pride of place to freedom or equality or human rights or to some combination of these values, as well as to justice. To put

---

[1] Raz, *The Morality of Freedom*, 1.

[2] Waldron, "Theoretical Foundations of Liberalism," 127.

[3] Dworkin, "Liberalism," 113.

[4] Sandel, *Liberalism and the Limits of Justice*, 1.

the point concretely, Sandel thinks mainly of Rawls's *A Theory of Justice* when he describes deontological liberalism, while we shall allow also for such works as Berlin's *Four Essays on Liberty*, Dworkin's "Liberalism," Gewirth's *Reason and Morality*, Hampshire's *Morality and Conflict* and *Innocence and Experience*, several of Nagel's essays in *Mortal Questions*, and Strawson's "Social Morality and Individual Ideal," to mention a few examples among many. The main historical influences on this version of liberalism (simply "liberalism" from now on) are Locke's *Second Treatise*, Kant's writings on moral philosophy, and John Stuart Mill's *On Liberty*.

Liberals disagree among themselves about what value or combination of values should have the overriding importance that Rawls gives to justice. But central to our present concern is the agreement among them that whatever the overriding values are, liberals should recognize the plurality of values. Pluralism is thus built into liberalism, as it were, on the ground floor. Indeed, this is the significance of the liberal insistence on the priority of the right to the good. The "right" is conformity to the rules that define the framework within which individuals can pursue "the good," that is, pursue those among the plurality of values that they wish to realize in their lives. As Rawls puts the point, "A just system defines the scope within which individuals must develop their aims, and it provides a framework of rights and opportunities and the means of satisfaction within and by which these ends may be equitably pursued. . . . We can express this by saying that the concept of right is prior to that of the good."[5] And Dworkin makes the same point: "[P]olitical decisions must be, so far as possible, independent of any particular conception of the good life, or what gives value to life."[6]

The commitment to the priority of the right to the good and to the state's neutrality regarding the good are thus fundamental to liberalism. But this commitment implies pluralism, since the reason why the state should be neutral and the rules defining the social framework should be accorded a status prior to the values that may be pursued within the framework is that there is a plurality of incompatible and incommensurable values.

Let us now turn to the disagreement among liberals about which value or values are overriding. There is a general agreement among liberals that the strongest candidates for overriding values are freedom, equality, the protection of human rights, and Rawlsian justice. Their disagreement is over the question of which of these values, or which combination of them, should be overriding. Berlin thinks that for "the liberal tradition . . . only rights can be regarded as absolute; . . . and . . . there are

---

[5] Rawls, *A Theory of Justice*, 31. The order of quoted passages is reversed.
[6] Dworkin, "Liberalism," 127.

frontiers, not artificially drawn, within which men should be inviolable";[7] and so he regards rights as the overriding values. Rawls, on the other hand, thinks that the overriding liberal value is justice: "Justice is the first virtue of social institutions . . . [and] an injustice is tolerable only when it is necessary to avoid even greater injustice. Being the first virtue . . . of human activities . . . justice [is] . . . uncompromising."[8] Whereas Dworkin's overriding value is equality: "I want to argue that a certain conception of equality . . . is the nerve of liberalism . . . [and that it] requires that the government treat all those in its charge as equals, that is, as entitled to equal concern and respect."[9] Raz holds that the overriding liberal value is freedom: "The specific contribution of the liberal tradition to political morality has always been its insistence on the respect due to individual liberty. . . . Indeed the argument of this book will demonstrate how far-reaching are the implications of political liberty, how they affect our conception of justice, equality, prosperity and other political ideals."[10]

The reason for pointing at the disagreements among liberals with respect to the question of which value is overriding is to document the claim, central to the present argument, that liberals do regard some values as overriding. And the reason why that matters is that pluralists deny that there are any overriding values. In fact, it is an essential claim of pluralism that all of our values are conditional. Indeed, the unjustifiability of regarding any values as overriding is a straightforward implication of the incommensurability and incompatibility of values, which excludes a highest value, a medium for comparing values, as well as a canonical scheme for ranking values. It seems, therefore, that liberals who regard some values as overriding cannot consistently adopt pluralism as well.

It should be recognized that although this argument for the incompatibility of liberalism and pluralism has been stated in terms of liberals regarding some particular value as overriding, the argument applies with equal force if the overriding value is not taken to be single but some combination of a few single values. For the pluralistic claim is about the unjustifiability of regarding any value or combination of some few values as overriding, quite independently of the identity of the value or values so regarded. Liberalism would be incompatible with pluralism therefore even if liberals recognized a plurality of conflicting values within the combination of values they regard as overriding. For even if they held that the values within the combination were conditional, they would still

---

[7] Berlin, "Two Concepts of Liberty," 165.

[8] Rawls, *A Theory of Justice*, 3–4.

[9] Dworkin, "Liberalism," 115 and 125.

[10] Raz, *The Morality of Freedom*, 2.

maintain that the combination of values taken as a whole was overriding. And what is incompatible with pluralism is overridingness *per se*. Liberals must hold that some particular value or combination of values is overriding, because they must hold that in the last analysis liberal values are better or higher than the other values with which they conflict. They must be committed, that is, to resolving conflicts in favor of liberal values, and that means that they must hold that liberal values should always override other values with which they conflict. And it is just this that pluralists reject.

Yet, this inconsistency notwithstanding, liberals do regard themselves as being committed to pluralism. They say: "At the heart of the liberal position stand two ideas . . . *pluralism* . . . and *toleration*";[11] "the plurality of distinct persons with separate systems of ends is an essential feature of . . . [liberal] societies";[12] "society being composed of a plurality of persons, each with his own aims, interests, and conception of good, is best arranged when it is governed by . . . the liberalism of Kant and of much contemporary moral and political philosophy";[13] "one who experiences sympathy with a variety of conflicting ideals of life . . . will be most at home in a liberal society";[14] and that it is "itself an argument for liberal society that that society expresses more than any other does a true understanding of the plural nature of values."[15]

Should we, then, just conclude that this is a plain inconsistency, that pluralism and liberalism are incompatible, and that liberals must abandon either pluralism or the supposition that the values to which they are committed are overriding? This would be premature, for liberals can appeal to an important distinction for removing the seeming inconsistency.

The Neutrality Thesis

The distinction in question is between substantive and procedural values, which was introduced in chapter 5. Substantive values are derived from various conceptions of a good life; they are the virtues, ideals, and goods intrinsic to particular conceptions of a good life. All such conceptions require some virtues, hold some ideals in high regard, and promise the enjoyment of some goods. But the identity of many of these virtues, ideals, and goods varies with conceptions of a good life. On the other hand, procedural values regulate the pursuit of substantive values by

---

[11] Larmore, *Patterns of Moral Complexity*, 22–23.
[12] Rawls, *A Theory of Justice*, 28–29.
[13] Sandel, *Liberalism and the Limits of Justice*, 1.
[14] Strawson, "Social Morality and Individual Ideal," 44.
[15] Williams, "Introduction" to Berlin's *Concepts and Categories*, xviii.

being rules or principles for settling conflicts, distributing resources, protecting people, and setting priorities among substantive values. Substantive values have an intrinsically valuable component, whereas procedural values are purely instrumental. Liberals regard freedom, equality, the protection of human rights, and Rawlsian justice as the most important procedural values, while the virtues, ideals, and goods constitutive, for instance, of the life of an artist, a theist, an athlete, a scholar, or a social critic are substantive values.

The distinction between substantive and procedural values is complicated by the fact that it does not coincide with the distinction between primary and secondary values. Some substantive values, like human rights, are primary in that they are among the minimum requirements of good lives and consequently must be recognized by all reasonable conceptions of good lives. Similarly, some procedural values are secondary, because some of the ways in which the pursuit of substantive values is regulated vary with social contexts, such as tax rates, divorce proceedings, or criminal law regarding sexual offenses. But regardless of whether they are primary or secondary, if the pursuit of substantive values were not endangered, then there would be no need for procedural values protecting them. For instance, if the substantive values collectively referred to as "human rights" were not often violated, then the procedural values represented by various legal and moral protection of human rights would be dispensable. As things are, we need both the substantive values of human rights and the procedural values protecting them.

Appealing to this distinction, then, liberals can restrict their pluralism to substantive values and claim overridingness only for some procedural values, thereby removing the inconsistency involved in regarding some values as overriding and being a pluralist.

This has been well-expressed by Larmore: "In modern times we have come to recognize a multiplicity of ways in which a fulfilled life can be lived, without any perceptible hierarchy among them. And we have also been forced to acknowledge that even where we do believe that we have discerned the superiority of some ways of life to others, reasonable people may often not share our view. Pluralism and reasonable disagreement have become for modern thought ineliminable features of the idea of the good life. Political liberalism has been the doctrine that consequently the state should be neutral. The state should not seek to promote any particular conception of the good life. . . . [T]he neutrality of the liberal state . . . is not meant to be one of *outcome*, but rather one of *procedure*. That is, political neutrality consists in a constraint on what factors can be invoked to justify a political decision. Such a decision can count as neutral only if it can be justified without appealing to the presumed intrinsic superiority of any particular conception of the good life."[16]

But why should we accept the liberal claim that pluralism should be limited to substantive values? That claim can be contested from two directions. One is to point out that all the reasons liberals give for regarding some procedural values as overriding also apply to some substantive values. After all, the minimum requirements of good lives include not only procedures but also specific values that need to be obtained by these procedures. Health, personal relationships, some security and comfort, and so forth, are substantive values, and they are as essential to good lives, whatever form they may take, as the procedural values liberals favor. And if some procedural values are overriding because they are minimum requirements of good lives, then, for precisely the same reason, some substantive values would also have to be regarded as overriding. In that case, however, the attempt to avoid the incompatibility between liberalism and pluralism would fail, for pluralism is incompatible with regarding any value as overriding, and liberals are committed to regarding as overriding both some procedural and some substantive values. This argument, however, tells against both pluralism and liberalism, so, given our interest in defending pluralism, we shall contest the liberal claim from another direction.

This leads us to ask the following: Why should pluralism not be extended across the whole range of values, including both procedural and substantive ones, and thereby exclude overriding values from all areas of life? Now the answer that regarding some procedural values as overriding is justified because they are required by all conceptions of a good life will not do. For we can recognize that some procedural values are indeed among the minimum requirements of good lives and signal that recognition by regarding them as conditional values, whose claim on us is particularly strong, rather than as overriding values. We may agree with liberals about the importance of freedom, equality, the protection of human rights, and Rawlsian justice, yet disagree that we should regard any of them or any combination of them as overriding.

The disagreement is based on the pluralist argument that these procedural values will inevitably conflict in concrete political and moral situations and how such conflicts should be resolved cannot have an a priori answer. For instance, if freedom and equality conflict, then one consideration relevant to the resolution of their conflict is how much freedom and how much equality actually exist in the context in which the conflict arises. And if the human right to the protection of legitimately acquired property conflicts with Rawlsian justice, then it is crucial to know

---

[16] Larmore, *Patterns of Moral Complexity*, 43–44.

whether the conflict occurs in the context of mass starvation or in that of a socialist policy of redistribution in a context where there is no poverty and there is a high standard of living. Both examples demonstrate the need to take into account the historically, socially, and politically varying circumstances in which procedural values may conflict. As a result, pluralists are surely reasonable in indicating their recognition of the importance of procedural values without making the reasonable resolution of such conflicts impossible by handicapping themselves with regarding as overriding one or another of the procedural values. The rejoinder to the liberal defense of their position against the charge of incompatibility with pluralism is that the distinction between procedural and substantive values does not remove the incompatibility, because procedural values are also plural and conditional rather than overriding.

But liberals still have a reply to this objection. They may point out that what makes the notion of an overriding procedural value suspect is that the procedural values liberals regard as overriding may conflict with each other. In claiming an overriding status for one of these values, however, liberals also offer a supporting argument whose intent is to show that the other procedural values are analyzable in terms of the overriding procedural value. This is just the claim Rawls makes for his conception of distributive justice, Berlin for human rights, Dworkin for equality, and Raz for freedom.

Let us assume, for the sake of argument, that one of these reductive analyses is actually correct. It yields a fundamental procedural value that incorporates the other three; call this "the fundamental liberal procedural value." If there were a fundamental liberal procedural value, then it would make no difference whether it was thought to be overriding or conditional, for there would be no other procedural value whose conflicting claims could defeat its claim. There would be no question then of liberalism being incompatible with pluralism, since on the level of procedural values there would be, as a result of the reductive analysis, only one value to which both liberals and pluralists could commit themselves.

This rejoinder, however, is unsatisfactory, because it rests on the mistaken assumption that the four procedural values from which liberals select one as overriding are all the important procedural values there are. In fact, an acceptable level of law-abidingness, order, prosperity, and social solidarity are as important as the four values liberals favor, and they are important for exactly the same reason: their claims must be recognized by all conceptions of a good life if they are to yield the substantive values they promise. So even if there were a fundamental liberal procedural value, conflicts among procedural values would not disappear, because the fundamental liberal procedural value would conflict with the procedural values named above. Some liberals recognize this. Dworkin, for instance, writes, "Liberalism shares the same constitutive principles with many other political theories, including conservatism, but is distinguished from these by attaching different relative importance to different principles."[17] From this, however, consequences follow that raise the most serious questions about the compatibility of liberalism and pluralism.

First, liberals face a dilemma caused by the possible conflict between the fundamental liberal procedural value and one of the other important procedural values. If liberals resolve the conflict by appealing to the overridingness of the fundamental liberal procedural value, then their position remains incompatible with pluralism, since pluralism excludes the overridingness of any value. On the other hand, if liberals regard the fundamental liberal procedural value as conditional rather than overriding, then their position is compatible with pluralism. But then they must allow for the possibility that other procedural values may defeat the claims of the fundamental liberal procedural value. In that case, however, they have abandoned liberalism, or, at least, that form of it that Berlin, Dworkin, Rawls, and Raz defend, namely, the form that attributes overriding value to freedom, equality, the protection of human rights, or Rawlsian justice. And this point holds even if three of these procedural values are reducible to the fourth. Liberalism and pluralism thus cannot be held together.

It should be noticed that liberals cannot avoid this dilemma by claiming to recognize that law-abidingness, order, prosperity, and social solidarity are important procedural values. For the dilemma is not occasioned by their supposed failure to acknowledge the status of these other values but by their insistence that in conflicts with the fundamental liberal procedural value, these other procedural values are always to be overridden by it. The reason why this insistence occasions a dilemma is that insofar as liberals are pluralists, they must reject overriding values, while insofar as they are committed to the overridingness of the fundamental liberal procedural value, they must reject pluralism. If they proposed to meet this difficulty by rejecting the overridingness of the fundamental liberal procedural value, then their position would lose whatever it was that distinguished it as liberal. As Dworkin says, liberals are distinguished from conservatives "by attaching different relative importance to different principles."

Nor would it help to avoid the dilemma to jettison the notion of a fundamental liberal procedural value and claim instead that there is some combination of procedural values that are jointly fundamental to liberal-

---

[17] Dworkin, "Liberalism," 123.

ism. For the procedural values liberals would include in this combination could not be all the procedural values there are. For in that case, liberalism would be transformed into the vacuous recommendation that we should adopt whatever procedural values would yield the result we want. If, however, liberals included some procedural values and excluded others, then the excluded procedural values could conflict, and are likely to conflict, with the included ones, and liberals must claim that the included ones must then override the excluded ones. If they did not claim it, their position would again be rendered vacuous. Yet by claiming it they would once again commit themselves to regarding some values as overriding, thereby making their position incompatible with pluralism.

Second, assume for the sake of argument that there is some way of avoiding this dilemma. Another problem remains. The procedural values liberals favor often conflict with other procedural values. How these conflicts ought to be resolved is one of the fundamental political and moral questions we face. Liberalism is surely committed to resolving conflicts between the liberal procedural values of freedom, equality, protection of human rights, and Rawlsian justice, on the one hand, and such other procedural values as law-abidingness, order, prosperity, and social solidarity, on the other hand, in favor of the liberal values. By contrast, the sort of conservatism to which Dworkin refers above is committed to the opposite answer. The point here is not that either liberals or conservatives are right but that pluralism could be just as much at home in a conservative society as in a liberal society, were we to have either. Stressing the connection between liberalism and pluralism, as liberals do, misleadingly suggests that liberalism is the political system that is most hospitable to pluralism. Even if liberalism and pluralism were compatible, the connection between them would be contingent on historical accidents, and it is perfectly possible that in concrete political situations pluralists would find conservatism, or even some form of radicalism, like anarchism or libertarianism, more hospitable to their views than liberalism.

Third, consider the liberal claim about the neutrality of the state. The claim is that the state should be neutral in regard to the plurality of substantive values so long as substantive values do not conflict with the relevant procedural values. The reason behind the claim is that some procedural values are necessary for the pursuit of all legitimate substantive values, and that is why the state should be neutral about substantive values but committed to the protection of the appropriate procedural values. Several questions arise however: Which procedural values should the state protect? All of the important ones or only those to which liberals have committed themselves? What if some substantive value conforms to the procedural values of freedom, equality, the protection of human rights, and Rawlsian justice but conflicts with the procedural values of law-abidingness, order, prosperity, or social solidarity? The usual liberal response is that the latter sort of conflict does not require the state to abandon its neutrality. And that of course shows that the liberal interpretation of neutrality is a political commitment to uphold procedural values that liberals regard as important and to neglect procedural values that their opponents favor. This kind of neutrality conservatives could also accept. They could say that the state should not interfere with the substantive values its citizens pursue so long as they do not threaten law-abidingness, order, prosperity, and social solidarity. So, as far as neutrality is concerned, once again there is nothing characteristically liberal about it; conservatives could be just as much in favor of it as liberals.

Lastly, there remains a possibility that ought to be acknowledged. This is that there may be some analysis that would succeed in reducing all important procedural values to some one fundamental procedural value. If this were to happen, then pluralism would indeed be eliminated from the domain of procedural values, and then it may not be incompatible with liberalism. But we should note, first, that this is no more than a logical possibility, since no such analysis has been provided. Second, even if the logical possibility were realized and the reductive analysis succeeded, there is no reason now to suppose that the procedural value that emerged as the fundamental one would be liberal. Third, the briefest glance at some actual contemporary political and moral conflicts between procedural values reveals how very unlikely it is that such conflicts would be open to resolution by reductive arguments. For the deep disagreements are precisely those in which the opponents recognize the value of each others' conflicting procedures but are nevertheless committed to upholding their own evaluation of them on the grounds that they are more important. For instance, when equality and prosperity conflict in debating the merits of the free market, when freedom and social solidarity conflict over the issue of the enforcement of morality, or when the protection of human rights and order conflict in deliberations about how to prevent the spread of AIDS, then the prospects for a successful reductive analysis must appear dim. For such an analysis would have to show that somehow prosperity is reducible to equality, that social solidarity is really a question of freedom, or that order can be fully analyzed in terms of human rights. The chances of actually showing any of this are so negligible as to justify us in not taking them seriously.

We need to consider one last rejoinder that liberals may make to the criticism of their position. This is that in the course of the argument, the pluralism with which we began, and with which liberalism was said to be incompatible, has degenerated into radical relativism. Liberalism is incompatible with radical relativism, it may be said, but the original claim

was, liberals may remind us, that their position is incompatible with pluralism. The reply liberals may make to the criticism as presented here is
that if pluralism is to avoid radical relativism, pluralists must recognize
the objectivity of primary values. But, then, they must also hold that the
primary values override the secondary values with which they conflict,
and so pluralists must also regard some values as overriding. Pluralists
therefore cannot consistently object to liberalism on the ground that
some liberal values are overriding.

The trouble with this objection is that it mistakenly assumes that the
recognition of the objectivity of primary values commits pluralists to regarding them as overriding. Actually, pluralists can combine their recognition of the objectivity of primary values with regarding them as conditional. It will be asked, however, by liberals pressing their case, what
could reasonably defeat the claims of primary values if primary values are
indeed minimum requirements of good lives independently of how such
lives are conceived?

The answer is: secondary values. Individuals may reasonably judge in
some cases that their realization of primary values is worth very little to
them if they cannot combine that with the virtues, ideals, and goods
peculiar to their particular conception of a good life. Life, liberty, and
possessions may turn to ashes if they are protected at the cost of the
destruction of some favored way of life. And, of course, whole societies
may judge in the same way as individuals. Colonization, for instance, may
leave intact or even enhance the realization of the primary values of the
colonized while destroying many of their secondary values. The people
to whom this happens may reasonably value the lost secondary values just
as essential as the protected primary ones. The recognition of the objectivity of primary values thus may go hand in hand with regarding them as
conditional. Consequently pluralists can maintain their rejection of radical relativism—by claiming objectivity for conditional primary values—
without becoming inconsistent, as liberals do, by regarding primary values as overriding.

The fundamental difference between pluralists and liberals need not
be that they are committed to different values; it is rather that pluralists
deny, and liberals assert, that when the values to which they are committed conflict, there are some values or combinations of some few values in
whose favor reasonable people would always decide. If pluralists are
right, such decisions need not always be in favor of liberal values. We
must reject therefore the liberal claim that it is "itself an argument for
liberal society that that society expresses more than any other does a true
understanding of the plural nature of values,"[18] or that "one who experiences sympathy with a variety of conflicting ideals of life . . . will be most

---

[18] Williams, "Introduction" to Berlin's *Concepts and Categories*, xviii.

at home in a liberal society,"[19] or that "society being composed of a plurality of persons, each with his own aims, interests, and conceptions of good, is best arranged when it is governed by . . . the liberalism of Kant and of much contemporary moral and political philosophy."[20]

BEYOND NEUTRALITY: THE POLITICS OF PLURALISM

The inspiration behind the liberal ideal of the neutrality of the state is certainly one with which pluralists find it easy to sympathize. If the plurality of values is good, then it would be bad to allow the state to single out some values and treat them as if they were overriding. And the danger of this becomes especially evident if we bear in mind that the state wields immense political, economic, legislative, judicial, and educational powers. It is thus one thing for individuals or groups to advocate some set of values and to try to persuade others to adopt them, but it is quite another for the state to do so with the backing of its formidable powers. Pluralists and liberals, therefore, see eye-to-eye about the danger of the state's getting into the position of dictating to its citizens what particular values they should hold.

Pluralists object to the liberal ideal of neutrality not because of the diagnosis of the danger that inspires it but because it is a misdirected attempt to avoid the danger. The way to avoid the state's favoring some values over others is not to give power to the state to enforce some procedural values as overriding, for that would merely increase the danger. Rather it is to make sure that the values the state favors will be hospitable to the flourishing of the widest possible plurality of values. And the first step toward achieving that is to make sure that the state has no *overriding* commitment to any particular value, be it procedural or substantive.

As pluralists see it, the fundamental difficulty with liberalism is not that freedom, equality, the protection of human rights, and Rawlsian justice are defective procedural values; the difficulty is that liberals suppose them to override over all other values in all conceivable conflicts. And this fault, if it is that, is not peculiar to liberalism. All political ideologies must regard *some* values as overriding, otherwise they would cease to be ideologies, and it is this very fact that makes them incompatible with pluralism. That our discussion has singled out liberalism is simply a reflection of the fact that in our present context liberalism is the dominant ideology.

What, then, *is* wrong with regarding some particular value as overriding? If a value is overriding, then it defeats the claim of any other value that conflicts with it. If it is a procedural value, as liberals say it is, then it

---

[19] Strawson, "Social Morality and Individual Ideal," 44.
[20] Sandel, *Liberalism and the Limits of Justice*, 1.

must take precedence over all substantive values. If freedom, equality, the protection of human rights, or Rawlsian justice were overriding, then, in cases of conflict, they would have to take precedence over such substantive values as self-respect, deep love of another person, or continued engagement in a personal project that gives meaning to one's life. If the liberal procedural values were indeed overriding, then states that favored policies contrary to them and individuals whose choices had gone in the other direction would have to be unreasonable and morally mistaken. The fact is, however, that if states or individuals were customarily required to resolve conflicts in this manner, they would regularly have to subordinate the values that make life worth living to abstract and impersonal procedures. And in that case, it would be justified to regard not the violation of the requirement but the requirement itself as unreasonable and morally mistaken.

Nor does the thesis fare better if the allegedly overriding procedural value is supposed to conflict with a lower-ranked procedural value. Are there *no* anarchic circumstances in which order should prevail over freedom? Can there *never* be a sufficiently serious challenge to law-abidingness to defeat the claims of equality? Can *no* economic threat to prosperity justify the curbing of Rawlsian justice? Anyone not blinded by ideology would have to admit that there are circumstances in which the decision would have to go against the values liberals regard as overriding. And that means that they cannot reasonably be thought of as overriding.

Furthermore, the case for the overridingness of some values would not be strengthened if the liberal formulation of the case in terms of procedural values were combined with, or abandoned in favor of, the overridingness of some substantive values. For even if we take such rock-bottom substantive values as life, physical security, or some minimum degree of respect, the case for their overridingness could not be maintained. They must certainly be recognized as primary values, but how could it be reasonably supposed that, say, physical security should always take precedence over adventurousness of spirit manifested in rock climbing, skydiving, or engaging in arctic expeditions? Or who could reasonably maintain that life has an overriding value when we refuse to lower the speed limit, ban dangerous occupations, or outlaw smoking and drinking? And is there no torturer, child rapist, wholesale drug dealer, terrorist, or dictator toward whom we could reasonably cease to feel even minimum respect?

The conclusion is unavoidable that although it is reasonable to hold that many procedural and substantive values are primary, and hence required by good lives, it is unreasonable to hold that the claims of any of these primary values could not, in some circumstances, be overridden by the conflicting claim of some other value that is, in that context, even more important than it. But what is it to which we appeal in finding this conclusion so obvious and the overridingness of values so implausible?

The answer is that we appeal to the third thesis of pluralism and recognize that good lives require a *balance* among a plurality of values, and that the balance depends on resolving conflicts among them. The conflicts are occasionally so severe as to exclude altogether from their resolution one or the other of the conflicting values. But this is exceptional. The conflicting values usually allow for degrees, and the conflicts concern the extent to which one or the other of the conflicting values should dominate in the state that replaces the conflicting one. This is why it is more accurate to think of conflict-resolution as aiming at a balance rather than at a decision to allow one value to override another. What motivates the search for balance is the realization that the conflicts matter because the values are required by our conceptions of a good life. Primary values are important because there are some specific substantive and procedural requirements that all good lives must meet, and they jointly constitute the minimum requirements of all good lives.

Good lives require more than this minimum: in addition to primary values, there must also be secondary values. And the claims of secondary values may often be defeated by the claims of primary ones. But what cannot be claimed reasonably is that there are some primary values that should always prevail over any other primary or secondary value that may conflict with it. In so far as ideological claims take this form, they cannot be made reasonably; and this is true regardless of whether the ideology is liberal, Marxist, Catholic, fundamentalist, or whatever.

The reason for laboring this point is that we can derive from it the answer to the question of what, according to pluralists, the state should do, and how and why it should do it, if it should not do as liberals advocate, namely, to maintain neutrality about all substantive values and to enforce the overridingness of some procedural values.

What the state should do is, first, use its power to protect all the procedural and substantive values necessary for all good lives and, second, make it possible for its citizens to pursue, within appropriate limits, such secondary values as they may require, beyond the primary values, to make a good life for themselves. As to how the state should do it, the pluralistic view is that it should take an active role in protecting both primary procedural and primary substantive values, and it should maintain neutrality about secondary values whose worth varies with conceptions of a good life. But taking an active role does not mean that the state should regard as overriding the claim of any particular value. It means that it should do what it can to balance the claims of all the primary values. Finally, the reason why the state should do all this is that it should be guided by a conception of its function, namely, to guarantee the conditions in which its citizens could make a good life for themselves. That conception is at once the motivating force behind, and the ultimate standard for, conflict-resolution. Stated briefly, these are the assumptions underlying the politics of pluralism.

The detailed working out of this conception of politics would take another book, and probably more. But we can make a beginning toward enlarging what has been said by considering its more important implications. Some of these implications are positive, having to do with the possibilities that the politics of pluralism protects and encourages, while others are negative, concerning the limits that it must recognize.

All the limits, as also all the possibilities, are derivable from the pluralistic conception of the state's function, namely, to guarantee the conditions in which its citizens can make for themselves whatever they regard as good lives. The limits concern values that normally may not be legitimate parts of good lives and values whose legitimate violation requires extraordinary circumstances. The first kind of limit prohibits some values, while the second kind prohibits some violations. The prohibited values will be those whose pursuit would be likely to endanger the conditions required for other citizens' attempts to make good lives for themselves. Similarly, the prohibited violations will be of those values that, in the normal course of events, are recognized by all acceptable conceptions of a good life.

This may seem suspiciously like the political program of liberalism. What else, it may be asked, do the two kinds of limits amount to but a rephrasing of Mill's famous principle: "The only purpose for which power can be rightfully exercised over any member of a civilized community, against his will, is to prevent harm to others."[21] But this appearance will alter if we consider further the implications of the pluralistic criticisms of the liberal insistence on the state's neutrality about substantive values and on the overridingness of some procedural values.

To begin with, many of the prohibited values and many of those whose violation is prohibited are substantive. The pluralistic position differs therefore from the liberal one in rejecting the neutrality of the state about substantive values. But how far should this rejection go? How extensive, according to pluralists, should the state's commitment be to substantive values? The answer is that it should be much more extensive than liberals would find acceptable. Some liberals would not balk at the state's advocacy of primary substantive values. After all, primary values are not all that different from human rights, and since liberals are com-

---

[21] Mill, *On Liberty*, 9.

mitted to the procedural value of protecting human rights, the extension of their commitment to include the substantive values thus protected would not require a fundamental change in their position. The pluralistic view is, however, that the state should advocate not only primary values, which are required by all conceptions of a good life, but some secondary values as well. What these secondary values are is also derivable from the pluralistic conception of the state's function.

If the function of the state is to guarantee the conditions in which its citizens can try to make good lives for themselves, and if good lives are constituted of the realization of a plurality of moral and nonmoral values, then the conditions the state is obliged to guarantee must include those that enable its citizens to make good lives for themselves in *a pluralistic society*. These conditions, at a minimum, will concern the citizens' familiarity with a sufficient range of values from which they may select some as constituents of their conception of a good life and the citizens' capacity to be alive to the inevitable conflicts among the available values; the conditions must also include the general availability of conventional means for resolving these conflicts and the fostering of a social environment that is hospitable to the citizens' exercise of the capacities required for making good lives for themselves.

These conditions could be guaranteed only by the state's support of the institutions that the guaranteeing of the conditions presupposes. These institutions would include an educational system that teaches students about the plurality of values; a judicial and legislative system that would make possible the resolution of public conflicts about values; a loose system of some religious, secular, cultural, or moral advice, such as that provided by the clergy or by its secular equivalents, to which citizens could turn if they wanted help with the resolution of their personal conflicts about values; and some further system, which would probably be quite informal, like an ethos or a prevailing sensibility, that would maintain the spirit of tolerance and encouragement of individuality without which the plurality of values would hardly be possible. Maintaining these formal and informal institutions costs money, so there would have to be a system of taxation designed to support it; and violators would have to be apprehended, prosecuted, and punished, so it would also require a criminal justice system.

If a state were indeed committed to pluralism, it would have to support all these institutions, and others too of course, and by supporting them, it would have to take an active role in advocating very many substantive values. These would include not only primary substantive values, which are part of all good lives, but also many of the secondary substantive values, which while they vary with conceptions of a good life are nevertheless required by the institutions peculiar to a particular society. For it is by supporting the particular system of education, justice, legislature, taxation, and so forth, that have emerged in a society that the plurality of values could be fostered and protected. This conception of a pluralistic state, therefore, would not only permit, but actually require, the state to become the champion of quite an extensive range of substantive values.

But if this is so, then how could a pluralistic state avoid the danger of becoming a moral tyrant and impose the substantive values of some segment of its citizenry on the remaining unwilling segments? How else could this be avoided if not by insisting on the state's neutrality, as liberals do? The answer is that pluralism would restrict the state's advocacy of substantive values by the prohibition of any substantive value being given an overriding status and by specifying one decisive consideration that would defeat the claim of any substantive value. The reason for the prohibition and for this decisive consideration is the same: the protection of the plurality of values. No particular value should be overriding, because if it were, it would undermine the plurality of values by diminishing the ones that were subordinated to it; and it is always a conclusive argument against regarding any value as overriding that doing so would threaten the plurality of values taken as a whole.

According to pluralism, therefore, the state's advocacy of particular substantive values is restricted to particular circumstances and specific conflicts. As a result, the state could not become the advocate of any value in general; it could only become an advocate of particular conflict-resolutions. There is, therefore, no reason intrinsic to pluralistic politics that would lead from the abandonment of the liberal neutrality to moral tyranny. The bulwark that prevents the latter is the prohibition of any value's becoming overriding. And this prohibition, of course, also applies to procedural values to which liberals are disposed to accord an overriding status. Hence, although pluralistic politics may at first look quite similar to liberal politics, as we come to understand the implications of accepting the plurality of values as a political ideal and rejecting both the neutrality of the state about substantive values and the overridingness of any value, so the very considerable differences between the two conceptions of politics emerge.

Two reminders will complete the argument. First, the reason for organizing the state so as to protect the plurality of values is the conjunction of the belief this book aims to defend, namely, that the best way in which individuals can make a good life for themselves is to have a plurality of values at their disposal, and the belief central to pluralistic politics that the state's function is to protect the conditions necessary for the general availability of a plurality of values. Second, the brief description of pluralistic politics we have provided is meant merely as an outline of an ideal whose details need extensive working out. Moreover, what has been sketched is an ideal, not a description of the actual state of our state. One function of such an ideal is to enable us to criticize and improve the present polity. But doing so is a subject for another book.

Works Cited

Ackrill, John L. "Aristotle on Eudaimonia." In *Essays on Aristotle's Ethics*, edited by Amelie Rorty. Berkeley: University of California Press, 1980.

Aristotle. *Nicomachean Ethics*. Translated by H. Rackham. London: Loeb Classical Library, 1934.

Austen, Jane. *Sense and Sensibility*. Reprint. Harmondsworth, England: Penguin, 1969.

Bacon, Marcia. "On Admirable Immorality." *Ethics* 96 (1986): 557–66.

Baier, Annette. *Postures of the Mind*. Minneapolis: University of Minnesota Press, 1985.

Baier, Kurt. *The Moral Point of View*. Ithaca, N.Y.: Cornell University Press, 1958.

Bambrough, Renford. *Moral Scepticism and Moral Knowledge*. London: Routledge, 1979.

Becker, Lawrence C. *Reciprocity*. London: Routledge, 1986.

———, ed. "Impartiality and Ethical Theory." *Ethics* 101 (1991), special issue.

Bellah, Robert N., et al. *Habits of the Heart*. Berkeley: University of California Press, 1985.

Benjamin, Martin. *Splitting the Difference*. Lawrence: University of Kansas Press, 1990.

Berger, Peter L., et al. *The Homeless Mind*. New York: Random House, 1973.

Berlin, Isaiah. "John Stuart Mill and the Ends of Life." In *Four Essays on Liberty*. Oxford: Oxford University Press, 1969.

———. "Two Concepts of Liberty." In *Four Essays on Liberty*. Oxford: Oxford University Press, 1969.

———. "'From Hope and Fear Set Free.'" In *Concepts and Categories*, edited by Henry Hardy. London: Hogarth Press, 1978.

———. "The Apotheosis of the Romantic Will." In *The Crooked Timer of Humanity*, edited by Henry Hardy. London: John Murray, 1990.

———. "European Unity and Its Vicissitudes." In *The Crooked Timber of Humanity*, edited by Henry Hardy. London: John Murray, 1990.

Bowen, Elizabeth. *Collected Impressions*. London: Longmans, 1950.

Bradley, Francis Herbert. *Ethical Studies*. Oxford: Clarendon Press, 1927.

Brandt, Richard B. *A Theory of the Good and the Right*. Oxford: Clarendon Press, 1979.

———. "Morality and Its Critics." *American Philosophical Quarterly* 26 (1989): 89–100.

Chatwin, Bruce. *Utz*. New York: Viking, 1989.

Clarke, Stanley G. and Evan Simpson, eds. *Anti-Theory in Ethics and Moral Conservatism*. Albany: State University of New York Press, 1989.

Conee, Earl. "Against Moral Dilemmas." *The Philosophical Review* 91 (1982): 87–97.

Cooper, John M. *Reason and Human Good in Aristotle.* Cambridge: Harvard University Press, 1975.

Cooper, Neil. *The Diversity of Moral Thinking.* Oxford: Clarendon Press, 1981.

Danto, Arthur C. *Jean-Paul Sartre.* New York: Viking, 1975.

Dodds, Eric Robertson. *The Greeks and the Irrational.* Berkeley: University of California Press, 1971.

Donagan, Alan. *The Theory of Morality.* Chicago: University of Chicago Press, 1977.

———. "Consistency in Rationalist Moral Systems." *The Journal of Philosophy* 81 (1984): 291–309.

Dworkin, Ronald. "Liberalism." In *Public and Private Morality,* edited by Stuart Hampshire. Cambridge: Cambridge University Press, 1978.

Edwards, James C. *Ethics without Philosophy.* Tampa: University Presses of Florida, 1982.

Falk, David. "Morality, Self, and Others." In *Ought, Reasons, and Morality.* Ithaca, N.Y.: Cornell University Press, 1986.

Foot, Philippa. "Are Moral Considerations Overriding?" In *Virtues and Vices.* Berkeley: University of California Press, 1978.

Ford, James E., ed. *The Monist: Systematic Pluralism* 73 (1990), no. 3.

Frankfurt, Harry G. "The Importance of What We Care About." in *The Importance of What We Care About.* Cambridge: Cambridge University Press, 1988.

Fuller, Timothy, ed. *The Voice of Liberal Learning: Michael Oakeshott on Education.* New Haven, Conn.: Yale University Press, 1989.

Gauthier, David. *Morals by Agreement.* Oxford: Clarendon Press, 1986.

Geertz, Clifford. *The Interpretation of Culture.* New York: Basic Books, 1973.

———. "Found in Translation: On the Social History of the Moral Imagination." *Local Knowledge.* New York: Basic Books, 1983.

———. "From the Native's Point of View: On the Nature of Anthropological Understanding." In *Local Knowledge.* New York: Basic Books, 1983.

———. "The Uses of Diversity." In *The Tanner Lectures on Human Values* 7 (1986): 253–75, edited by M. McMurrin. Salt Lake City: University of Utah Press, 1986.

———. "Anti Anti-Relativism." In *Relativism: Interpretation and Confrontation,* edited by Michael Krausz. Notre Dame, Ind.: University of Notre Dame Press, 1989.

Gert, Bernard. *The Moral Rules.* New York: Harper & Row, 1970.

———. *Morality.* New York: Oxford University Press, 1988.

Gewirth, Alan. *Reason and Morality.* Chicago: University of Chicago Press, 1978.

Glover, Jonathan. *Causing Death and Saving Lives.* Harmondsworth: Penguin, 1977.

Goffman, Erving. *The Presentation of Self in Everyday Life.* Garden City, N.Y.: Doubleday, 1959.

Gowans, Christopher, ed. *Moral Dilemmas.* New York: Oxford University Press, 1987.

Gunn, Giles. *The Culture of Criticism and the Criticism of Culture.* New York: Oxford University Press, 1987.

Hampshire, Stuart. *Thought and Action.* London: Chatto and Windus, 1959.

———. "Spinoza and the Freedom of Mind." In *Freedom of Mind.* Oxford: Clarendon Press, 1972.

———. "Subjunctive Conditionals." In *Freedom of Mind.* Oxford: Clarendon Press, 1972.

———. "Morality and Conflict." In *Morality and Conflict.* Cambridge: Harvard University Press, 1983.

———. *Innocence and Experience.* Cambridge: Harvard University Press, 1989.

Hardie, William F. R. "The Final Good in Aristotle's Ethics." *Philosophy* 40 (1965): 277–95.

Hare, Richard M. *The Language of Morals.* Oxford: Clarendon Press, 1952.

———. *Freedom and Reason.* Oxford: Clarendon Press, 1963.

———. *Moral Thinking.* Oxford: Clarendon Press, 1981.

Harman, Gilbert. "Moral Relativism Defended." *The Philosophical Review* 84 (1975): 3–22.

Heller, Agnes. *The Power of Shame.* London: Routledge, 1985.

Heller, Erich. "Man Ashamed." In *In the Age of Prose.* Cambridge: Cambridge University Press, 1984.

Herodotus. *The Histories,* translated by A. de Selincourt. Harmondsworth, England: Penguin, 1954.

Hume, David. *A Treatise of Human Nature,* edited by L. A. Selby-Bigge. Oxford: Clarendon Press, 1960.

———. *An Enquiry Concerning the Principles of Morals.* Edited by L. A. Selby-Bigge. Oxford: Clarendon Press, 1961.

Isenberg, Arnold. "Natural Pride and Natural Shame." In *Explaining Emotions,* edited by Amelie Rorty. Berkeley: University of California Press, 1980.

Kant, Immanuel. *Anthropology from a Pragmatic Point of View,* translated by Mary J. Gregor. The Hague: Nijhoff, 1974.

Kekes, John. *The Examined Life.* Cranbury, N.J.: Associated University Presses and Bucknell University Press, 1986.

———. *Moral Tradition and Individuality.* Princeton: Princeton University Press, 1989.

———. *Facing Evil.* Princeton: Princeton University Press, 1990.

Kierkegaard, Søren. *Fear and Trembling,* translated by W. Lowrie. Princeton: Princeton University Press, 1941.

Kluckhohn, Clyde. "Universal Categories of Culture." In *Anthropology Today,* edited by A. L. Kroeber. Chicago: University of Chicago Press, 1965.

Kluge, Eike-Henner W. *The Practice of Death.* New Haven, Conn.: Yale University Press, 1975.

Kohl, Marvin. *The Morality of Killing.* New York: Humanities Press, 1974.

Krausz, Michael and Jack W. Meiland, eds. *Relativism: Cognitive and Moral.* Notre Dame, Ind.: University of Notre Dame Press, 1982.

Krausz, Michael, ed. *Relativism: Interpretation and Confrontation.* Notre Dame, Ind.: University of Notre Dame Press, 1989.

Labby, Daniel H., ed. *Life or Death.* Seattle: University of Washington Press, 1968.

Larmore, Charles E. *Patterns of Moral Complexity.* Cambridge: Cambridge University Press, 1987.

Lasch, Christopher. *The Culture of Narcissism.* New York: Norton, 1978.

Lienhardt, Godfrey. *Divinity and Experience: The Religion of the Dinka.* Oxford: Clarendon Press, 1961.

Louden, Robert B. "Can We Be Too Moral?" *Ethics* 99 (1988): 361–78.

———. "Virtue Ethics and Anti-Theory," *Philosophia* 20 (1990): 93–114.

———. *Morality and Moral Theory.* New York: Oxford University Press, 1992.

Lovejoy, Arthur O. *The Great Chain of Being.* New York: Harper & Row, 1960.

MacIntyre, Alasdair. ed., *Revisions.* Notre Dame, Ind.: University of Notre Dame Press, 1983.

———. *After Virtue.* Notre Dame, Ind.: University of Notre Dame Press, 1984.

———. *Whose Justice? Which Rationality?* Notre Dame, Ind.: University of Notre Dame Press, 1988.

Mackie, John L. *Ethics: Inventing Right and Wrong.* Harmondsworth: Penguin, 1977.

Mill, John Stuart. *On Liberty.* Indianapolis: Hackett, 1978.

Mitchell, Basil. *Law, Morality, and Religion in a Secular Society.* London: Oxford University Press, 1970.

Morris, Herbert. "Lost Innocence." In *Guilt and Innocence.* Berkeley: University of California Press, 1976.

Murdoch, George R. "The Common Denominators of Culture." In *The Science of Man*, edited by Ralph Linton. New York: Columbia University Press, 1945.

Murdoch, Iris. *The Sovereignty of Good.* London: Routledge, 1970.

Nagel, Thomas. "The Fragmentation of Values." In *Mortal Questions.* Cambridge: Cambridge University Press, 1979.

———. *Mortal Questions.* Cambridge: Cambridge University Press, 1979.

———. *The View From Nowhere.* New York: Oxford University Press, 1986.

Nietzsche, Friedrich. *On the Genealogy of Morals*, translated by Walter Kaufmann. New York: Modern Library, 1966.

Norton, David L. *Personal Destinies.* Princeton: Princeton University Press, 1976.

Novitz, David. *Knowledge, Fiction and Imagination.* Philadelphia: Temple University Press, 1987.

Nozick, Robert. *Anarchy, State, and Utopia.* New York: Basic Books, 1974.

Nussbaum, Martha C. "Shame, Separateness, and Political Unity: Aristotle's Criticism of Plato." In *Essays on Aristotle's Ethics*, edited by Amelie Rorty. Berkeley: University of California Press, 1980.

———. *The Fragility of Goodness.* Cambridge: Cambridge University Press, 1986.

———. "'Finely Aware and Richly Responsible': Literature and the Moral Imagination." In *Love's Knowledge.* New York: Oxford University Press, 1990.

Oakeshott, Michael. "The Authority of the State." *Modern Churchman* 19 (1929–30): 313–27.

———. "The Political Economy of Freedom." In *Rationalism in Politics.* London: Methuen, 1962.

———. "Political Education." In *Rationalism in Politics.* London: Methuen, 1962.

———. "The Tower of Babel." In *Rationalism in Politics.* London: Methuen, 1962.

———. *Rationalism in Politics.* London: Methuen, 1962.

———. *On Human Conduct.* Oxford: Clarendon Press, 1975.

———. *The Voice of Liberal Learning*, edited by Timothy Fuller. New Haven, Conn.: Yale University Press, 1989.

O'Hear, Anthony. "Guilt and Shame as Moral Concepts." *Proceedings of the Aristotelian Society* 77 (1976–77): 73–86.

Olafson, Frederick. "Moral Relationships in the Fiction of Henry James." *Ethics* 98 (1988): 294–312.

The Paris Review Interviews. *Writers at Work*. London: Secker & Warburg, 1958.

Paul, Ellen Frankel, ed. *Gauthier's New Social Contract*. Oxford: Blackwell, 1989. Reprint of *Social Philosophy and Policy* 5 (1988), no. 2.

Pincoffs, Edmund L. *Quandaries and Virtues*. Lawrence: Kansas University Press, 1986.

Plato. *Republic*. In *The Dialogues of Plato*, translated by Benjamin Jowett. New York: Random House, 1937.

Rawls, John. *A Theory of Justice*. Cambridge: Harvard University Press, 1971.

———. "Kantian Constructivism in Moral Theory." *The Journal of Philosophy* 77 (1980): 515–72.

———. "Justice as Fairness: Political Not Metaphysical." *Philosophy and Public Affairs* 14 (1985): 223–51.

Raz, Joseph. *The Morality of Freedom*. Oxford: Clarendon Press, 1986.

Reichly, A. James. *Religion in American Public Life*. Washington: The Brookings Institute, 1985.

Rieff, Philip. *The Triumph of the Therapeutic*. New York: Harper & Row, 1968.

Rorty, Amelie. "Varieties of Pluralism in a Polyphonic Society." *The Review of Metaphysics* 44 (1990): 3–20.

Rorty, Richard. *Contingency, Irony, and Solidarity*. Cambridge: Cambridge University Press, 1981.

———. *Consequences of Pragmatism*. Minneapolis: University of Minnesota Press, 1982.

Ross, William David. *Plato's Theory of Ideas*. Oxford: Clarendon Press, 1935.

Russell, Bertrand. *A History of Western Philosophy*. New York: Simon and Schuster, 1945.

Sandel, Michael. *Liberalism and the Limits of Justice*. Cambridge: Cambridge University Press, 1982.

———, ed. *Liberalism and Its Critics*. Oxford: Blackwell, 1984.

Santayana, George. *Interpretations of Poetry and Religion*. New York: Harper, 1957.

Sartre, Jean-Paul. *Being and Nothingness*, translated by Hazel E. Barnes. New York: Philosophical Library, 1956.

Schweitzer, Albert. *The Teaching of Reverence for Life*, translated by Richard and Clara Winston. New York: Holt, Rinehart and Winston, 1965.

Sen, Amartya and Bernard Williams, eds. *Utilitarianism and Beyond*. Cambridge: Cambridge University Press, 1982.

Singer, Marcus G. *Generalization in Ethics*. New York: Knopf, 1961.

Sinnott-Armstrong, Walter. *Moral Dilemmas*. Oxford: Blackwell, 1988.

Slote, Michael. "Admirable Immorality." In *Goods and Virtues*. Oxford: Clarendon Press, 1983.

Smart, John J. C. and Bernard Williams. *Utilitarianism: For and Against*. Cambridge: Cambridge University Press, 1973.

Sousa, Ronald de. *The Rationality of Emotion*. Cambridge: MIT Press, 1987.

Steinbock, Bonnie, ed. *Killing and Letting Die*. Englewood Cliffs, N.J.: Prentice-Hall, 1980.

Stewart, John I. M. *Parlour 4 and Other Stories*. New York: Norton, 1986.

Stocker, Michael. *Plural and Conflicting Values.* Oxford: Clarendon Press, 1990.

Strawson, Peter F. "Social Morality and Individual Ideal." In *Freedom and Resentment.* London: Methuen, 1974.

Taylor, Charles. "The Concept of a Person." In *Human Agency and Language.* Cambridge: Cambridge University Press, 1985.

––––––. *Sources of the Self.* Cambridge: Harvard University Press, 1989.

Taylor, Gabrielle. *Pride, Shame and Guilt.* Oxford: Clarendon Press, 1985.

Trevor-Roper, Hugh. "The Paracelsian Movement." In *Renaissance Essays.* London: Secker & Warburg, 1985.

Trilling, Lionel. *The Liberal Imagination.* New York: Scribner's, 1976.

––––––. "Why We Read Jane Austen." In *The Last Decade.* New York: Harcourt, Brace, 1979.

Urmson, John O. "A Defence of Intuitionism." *Proceedings of the Aristotelian Society* 75 (1974–75): 111–19.

Velleman, J. David. *Practical Reflection.* Princeton: Princeton University Press, 1989.

Waldron, Jeremy. "Theoretical Foundations of Liberalism." *Philosophical Quarterly* 37 (1987): 127–34.

Walzer, Michael. "Political Action: the Problem of Dirty Hands." *Philosophy and Public Affairs* 2 (1973): 160–80.

––––––. *Spheres of Justice.* New York: Basic Books, 1983.

Warnock, Mary. *Imagination.* London: Faber & Faber, 1976.

White, James Boyd. *When Words Lose Their Meaning.* Chicago: University of Chicago Press, 1984.

White, Nicholas. *Plato's Republic.* Indianapolis: Hackett, 1979.

Wiggins, David. "Truth, Invention, and the Meaning of Life." In *Needs, Values, Truth.* Oxford: Blackwell, 1987.

Williams, Bernard. *Problems of the Self.* Cambridge: Cambridge University Press, 1973.

––––––. "Introduction" to Isaiah Berlin, *Concepts and Categories.* London: Hogarth Press, 1978.

––––––. "Conflicts of Values." In *Moral Luck.* Cambridge: Cambridge University Press, 1981.

––––––. "Moral Luck." In *Moral Luck.* Cambridge: Cambridge University Press, 1981.

––––––. "The Truth in Relativism." In *Moral Luck.* Cambridge: Cambridge University Press, 1981.

––––––. *Moral Luck.* Cambridge: Cambridge University Press, 1981.

––––––. *Ethics and the Limits of Philosophy.* London: Collins, 1985.

Wolf, Susan. "Moral Saints." *The Journal of Philosophy* 79 (1982): 419–39.

Wollheim, Richard. *On Art and the Mind.* Cambridge: Harvard University Press, 1974.

––––––. *The Thread of Life.* Cambridge: Harvard University Press, 1984.

Index